YONDER COMES THE TRAIN

YONDER COMES

Galahad Books · New York

THE TRAIN

BY LANCE PHILLIPS

Copyright © 1965 by Lance Phillips

All rights reserved. No part of this work may be reproduced or
transmitted in any form or by any means, electronic or mechanical,
including photocopying, recording, or any information storage and
retrieval system, without permission in writing from the publisher.

Published in 1993 by

Galahad Books
a division of Budget Book Service, Inc.
386 Park Avenue South
New York, New York 10016

Galahad Books is a registered trademark of Budget Book Service, Inc.

By arrangement with A.S. Barnes,
a division of Oak Tree Publications, Inc.

Library of Congress Catalog Card Number: 86-81168
ISBN: 0-88365-715-5

Printed in Hong Kong

Dedicated to the memory
of my beloved father

Lewis Franklin Phillips
1866   1922

Who between and on runs pulling crack
trains over the Richmond Division of the
Atlantic Coast Line inspired me with his
love for the steam locomotive.

With combined engine and tender weight of 474,735 pounds gracefully spread over 80 feet 9½ inches, this ALCO built 4-6-2 locomotive represented the acme of motive power in passenger service on Atlantic Coast Line in 1920.

The 1566 was the pride of the author's father, and the author was privileged to be in the cab on her maiden run, pulling train No. 80 northbound out of Rocky Mount, North Carolina, on September 29, 1920.

Acknowledgment

I shall ever be grateful to those, many whose names are unknown, who so graciously assisted with hours of research into company files for old records and pictures.

My especial thanks to the members of that great fraternity of railroaders:

Norman Beasley of LOUISVILLE & NASHVILLE

Bill Burk of SANTA FE

Arthur Carlson of ILLINOIS CENTRAL

Stephen Dewhurst of ASSOCIATION OF AMERICAN RAILROADS

Ben Dulaney of NORFOLK & WESTERN

R. B. Eaton of WABASH

George Frank of ERIE–LACKAWANNA

J. W. Hansen of UNION SWITCH & SIGNAL

George Hill of BOSTON & MAINE

J. P. Hiltz, Jr., of DELAWARE & HUDSON

Bob Kirk of RICHMOND, FREDERICKSBURG & POTOMAC

F. V. Koval of CHICAGO & NORTH WESTERN

George Kraus of SOUTHERN PACIFIC

Ann Kuss of NEW YORK CENTRAL

Edwin Long of CHESAPEAKE & OHIO

Don Martin of ATLANTIC COAST LINE

Bob McKernan of NEW YORK, NEW HAVEN & HARTFORD

H. R. Matlack of PENNSYLVANIA

Charlie Mervine, Jr., of RICHMOND, FREDERICKSBURG & POTOMAC

NATIONAL CASTINGS COMPANY

PULLMAN COMPANY

William E. Pyne of BALTIMORE & OHIO

W. E. Rachels of SEABOARD AIR LINE

Edwin Schafer of UNION PACIFIC

John Stover of SOUTHERN RAILWAY SYSTEM

Mrs. Thomason of SEABOARD AIR LINE

Mrs. Esther Throckmorton of ROCK ISLAND

Elizabeth Dance of VALENTINE MUSEUM, Richmond

T. A. Reeve, Superintendent THE SCIENCE MUSEUM, London

The Archives Staff of VIRGINIA STATE LIBRARY

Gary Boyles and "Rich" Richardson of GALESKI PHOTO CENTER

F. L. Worcester, Master Photographer

Richard J. Cook, Master Railroad Photographer

Thomas W. Thomas, SEABOARD AIR LINE RAILROAD and to Bill Alley (whom I accused of being a railroad wreck chaser).

Finally, I am most grateful to my beloved wife, Hazel and to our sweet daughter, Hazel Franklin, for their interest and encouragement in this work.

Lance Phillips

Contents

Preface

As far into the past as my memory goes, steam locomotives, trains, and railroads have held my interest. My father was a locomotive engineer and I grew up in the railroad atmosphere of the little town of Manchester, Virginia. As I look back now, over half a century, the old scenes are still vivid and the personalities alive, in and about the roundhouse. I still remember the tall tales told about "my engine," such as how bridging the nozzle (a piece of wire run through the exhaust pipe, paralleling the flues, to create a vacuum) would "make her pull a forty-car train in half," and so on, ad infinitum.

As a boy herding neighbors' milk cows on Spring Hill in the still of a summer day, I would pass away the hours listening to and committing to memory the whistle calls of those artists with the cord. And across the long years of silence comes back Jim O'Brien's impatient call at a red board; Mr. Ellington's "Old Oaken Bucket" as he headed for Danville around the bluffs of the James River; and the wail of my father's chime whistle as he approached the yard limits at Clopton with the Coast Line's Florida Special.

It was perhaps this background and an unflagging interest in steam railroading that whetted my desire to look back; and in looking back over the years of the steam engine to Thomas Newcomen, and to Richard Trevithick's first steam locomotive, I have truly been impressed to see how splendid was the day of the steam locomotive.

Since the locomotive was the heart that brought life, making the composite whole, a railroad, possible, it would be difficult, if not impossible, to separate one from the other. In this essay it has not been possible to do more than briefly sketch the geneses of a few of the great railroad systems of America; the fact that some have not even been mentioned in no way reflects upon their importance but was necessitated by lack of allotted space.

Since many excellent works of accomplished historians on practically all individual railroads are available, and treatises on the steam locomotive, this contribution is not intended as a comprehensive history on either, but rather to bring in condensed form the story of the steam locomotive from its birth and of some of the American roads over which it pulled its train.

In a lurching cab, the hand of an engineer reached for a plaited cord and the blast from the whistle on a steam locomotive split the air. If in mountainous country, the reverberations kicked and bounced over the terrain; if in level, they followed a more direct path through the ether waves. It might have been two longs and two shorts for a crossing; the long wail that heralded the approach to some lonely station in the night; or some engineer just quilling for the hell of it. Next came a subdued roar, with intensity increasing as the steel-ribbed monster's approach continued its onward rush. Then the exhausts from her stack, heavy and cadenced if on a grade, subdued if on a level stretch. If to stop at a station, only the hiss of escaping steam from her valve chambers when the throttle closed and a rumbling roll as she drifted in.

When these sounds came late in the darkness, whether from some all-steel Pullman limited bustin' into tomorrow or a rattling consist of empty freights, the reaction of the listener was the same, for the sounds brought with them "Blues in the Night." In some instances women cried into their pillows and strong men had the urge to hop a train and ride. In any event the same exclamation came to mind, whether the words were spoken or the thought just fathered—"Yonder Comes The Train." This familiar phrase immediately poses questions—where was yonder? Where did this busy, alive, and romantic steam locomotive originate? What transpired through the years from the birth of the locomotive, its train, and the railroads to bring about the great impact it had on our American way of life?

To endeavor to answer these questions is the purport of what follows.

Yonder Comes the Train

Portrait of James Watt, after Sir T. Lawrence, 1815.
(Courtesy of Science Museum, London)

1
In the Beginning

Ironical as it may seem now, the locomotive, train, and railroad which were to revolutionize America had their origins in Great Britain, a small country by geographical comparison with the United States, and within which no point is further than one hundred miles from the seas which surround it. Then, too, canals, natural waterways, and roads within the country would seem to have adequately furnished means of transportation at the time.

What had been well termed "The Industrial Revolution" had gotten under way in the British Isles soon after the turn of the eighteenth century. Man's search for metals and minerals, having passed the stage of surface mining, had carried him into the ground, where subterraneous operations faced many problems, chief among them being the water encountered. Removal of the water by both animal- and water-powered pumps had proved inadequate, and further advancement in mining operations was at a standstill.

Necessity, often the mother of invention, was perhaps responsible for bringing to the brilliant and inventive mind of Thomas Newcomen, of Dartmouth, serious thoughts relative to solving the dilemma, and in 1712 he invented the first steam engine. Primitive though his invention was, Newcomen had successfully harnessed the power of steam and without question should be recognized as the father of the steam engine. Although used solely for lifting water during its first fifty years of existence, Newcomen's engine was destined to play a most important part in man's industrial progress for many generations to come.

It was 57 years after Newcomen's invention before any radical improvement was made in his engine, and this perhaps through happenstance. James Watt, a Scot instrument maker, had set up shop at the College in Glasgow, and during the session 1763–64 a model of Newcomen's atmospheric steam engine had been brought to him for repairs. This accomplished craftsman not only repaired the engine, but during the process his scientific mind was attracted to the power of steam. So fascinated had he become that Watt began his own experiments. He observed that much steam was being lost through condensation as it entered the cold body of the cylinder at the beginning of the stroke, and he reasoned that the loss might be avoided if the cylinder was at boiling temperature of 212°F. when the steam entered. He likewise reasoned that a vacuum must be produced so that at the end of the piston stroke the cylinder might be brought back to ordinary temperature of 60°F.; with these two knotty and opposing problems Watt's scientific mind came to grips.

After much experimentation Watt solved the problem, and in 1769 he patented his separate condenser. This condenser allowed the cylinder of the engine to remain as hot as the entering steam, thus greatly increasing efficiency by keeping the steam pressure constant.

Apparently giving his full attention to further perfection, Watt came out the same year with what he described as "a new invented method of lessening the consumption of Steam in Fire Engines." Actually this was the double-acting rotative steam engine which translated reciprocal to rotary movement, thereby enabling the engine to drive rotating machinery by means of belts and pulleys.

At this stage a restlessness akin to steam itself had

Watt's original experimental model with separate condenser, 1765. (British Crown Copyright. Science Museum, London)

imbued the minds of many, and in 1769 Nicholas Cugot, a French engineer, built a steam-driven vehicle which would propel itself; but it proved unsuccessful and crashed on its trial run.

William Murdock, a Scot inventor of considerable capacity (incidentally, an associate of James Watt), built what he termed a "steam carriage" in 1785; however, it developed very low steam pressure, insufficient for the required tractive effort, and was also unsuccessful.

The steam locomotive was now just around the corner. But before we attend this birth which was to have the greatest impact and far reaching effects upon man's social and economic life since the advent of gunpowder, we should mention the "railways and trains" which preceded it by at least a century or more.

Railways, a line of rails or track providing a runway for wheels, had existed in and around collieries in England and Wales since approximately the beginning of the seventeenth century. Cars—or, more aptly, wagons—on these ways were at first operated by hand, later by horse power over the wooden rails which at an early date were pegged to sleepers (cross ties). Later, narrow strips of wrought iron were added to the surface of the hardwood rails to lessen

abrasion. Due to the scarcity of timber in 1767, solid rails of cast iron were introduced; at first flat, by 1789 these rails were cast with a flange on the outer edge; a short time later the flange was changed to the inner edge. Brigades—cars coupled together by chains and pulled by horses walking in a towpath between the rails—came on the scene. The actual date of origination is a matter of conjecture, but it is known that these primitive trains on railways antedated the steam locomotive by more than a century.

THE FIRST STEAM LOCOMOTIVE

The stage was now set for the crowning event— the birth of the steam locomotive. Doubtless this "machine" had been contemplated by many engineering minds of the day, and although it can hardly be considered the invention of any one man, it remained for the genius of one man to put it together.

Richard Trevithick, a Cornish mining engineer, had apparently toyed with the idea of a locomotive for we know not how long. He had reasoned that Watt's engine, successful as it had proven for stationary use, was too heavy and cumbersome, and that high-pressure steam was essential for his purpose. Accordingly, this father-to-be put his mind to

16

A section of stone rail on Haytor Tramway, 1820. (Courtesy Science Museum, London)

Newcastle, end of the line for Parkmoor Waggonway, as it looked in 1783. (Courtesy Science Museum, London)

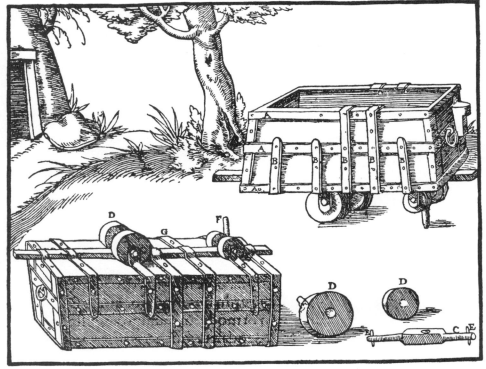

Detail of mine truck from Agricola, 1556. (Courtesy of Science Museum, London)

A—RECTANGULAR IRON BANDS ON TRUCK.   B—ITS IRON STRAPS.   C—IRON AXLE.
D—WOODEN ROLLERS.   E—SMALL IRON KEYS.   F—LARGE BLUNT IRON PIN.
G—SAME TRUCK UPSIDE DOWN.

Model of Ralph Allen's Quarry truck and wooden railway, 1734. Note flanged wheels at this early date. (British Crown Copyright. Science Museum, London)

Model cast-iron rail on wood stringers, 1757. (British Crown Copyright. Science Museum, London)

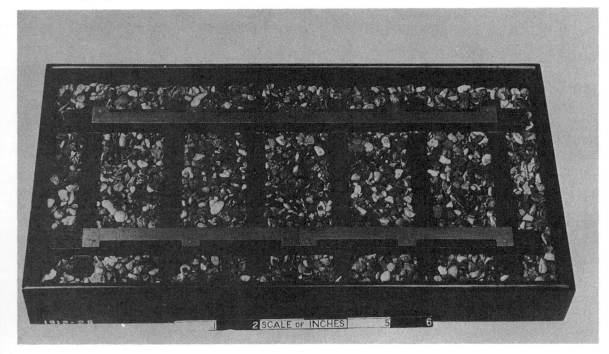

Newcastle coal wagon, 1773. From *Arts et Metiers,* French
Academy of Science. "Train crew" sits on brake-lever as
car rolls down incline, and motive power at the end of the
halter rope will drag the empty back to the pits. (Courtesy
Science Museum, London)

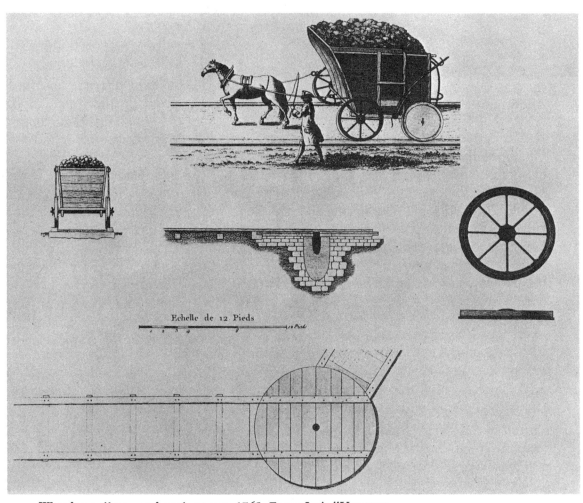

Echelle de 12 Pieds

Wooden railway and coal wagon, 1765. From Jar's "Voyages
Metallurgiques." (Courtesy Science Museum, London)

19

The big Cornishman who started it all. Copy of an oil portrait of Richard Trevithick, by Linnell, 1816. (Courtesy Science Museum, London)

the problem and on March 26, 1802, set forth in his patent specification, the application of his high-pressure steam engine to road and rail vehicle.

Anthony Hill, an ironmaster of the day, had wagered that ten tons of iron could not be hauled over the 9½-mile Pen-y-Daren cast-iron plate tramway by steam power. Encouraged and goaded by his patron, Samuel Homfray, master of the Pen-y-Daren Ironworks, Trevithick built his locomotive, and on Monday, February 13, 1804, had it in place on the cast-iron plate rails of the tramway. It coupled up to the carriages, which contained not ten but twenty-five tons of bar-iron, and we must presume that someone gave the first highball signal as the first steam locomotive in existence started its train. To the accompaniment of great cheers, Trevithick's locomotive pulled its freight over the 9½-mile right-of-way from Pen-y-Daren to Abercynon Wharf at

an approximate speed of 5 mph. Trevithick's own description of the engine's performance on this epochal run stated, "It worked very well, and ran up hill and down with great ease and very manageable." Thus was the beginning of steam locomotive history.

Since Trevithick's Pen-y-Daren engine has the honor and distinction of being the world's first steam locomotive, a few remarks about it here may be in order. The engine had four driving wheels, each 4½ ft. in diameter, and its 6-ft. horizontal boiler carried a single horizontal cylinder recessed above the fire-door. A single U-shaped fire tube extended from the fire-box at one end to the smoke-stack at the other; the fire-box door was directly beside the smoke-stack. In that part of the firetube which was just above the fire-box, Trevithick had placed a lead plug that would melt should the water in the boiler become dangerously low; a simple device but a great safety factor and similarly used in steam locomotives right up to the last. The single piston drove the wheels by means of a crosshead, from which twin connecting rods coupled with a crankshaft on a large flywheel mounted on the opposite end of the boiler. The smooth-tread wheels were flangeless, since at this early stage the cast-iron rails were flanged.

It is apparent that Trevithick had reasoned that smooth wheels on a smooth rail would provide sufficient adhesion for the locomotive to pull a train, provided the weight upon its wheels was sufficient. Although this first run of a steam locomotive on rails was successful, it must be realized that the exhibition was made upon a way built for horse power; understandably, there was a wholesale breakage of the cast-iron templates from one end of the line to the other. Since the railway was not heavy enough for the operation of a train powered by steam, the locomotive was converted to stationary use.

As the fame of this first locomotive spread, Trevithick received an order to build another, from the Wylam colliery in South Wales. This locomotive was built at Gateshead in 1805 and successfully operated on a temporary way at the foundry before a large group of interested spectators. However, it was not destined to go into rail service; its owner-to-be refused acceptance for the reason that the engine was much heavier than expected and would therefore be useless on the Wylam Wagonway. It, too, was taken off its wheels and converted to stationary use in the foundry of the builder. Trevithick

20

Conjectural model of Thevithick's Pen-y-Daren locomotive, the world's first, 1804. (British Crown Copyright. Science Museum, London)

Copy of original drawing of Trevithick's Newcastle locomotive built in 1804. (Courtesy Science Museum, London)

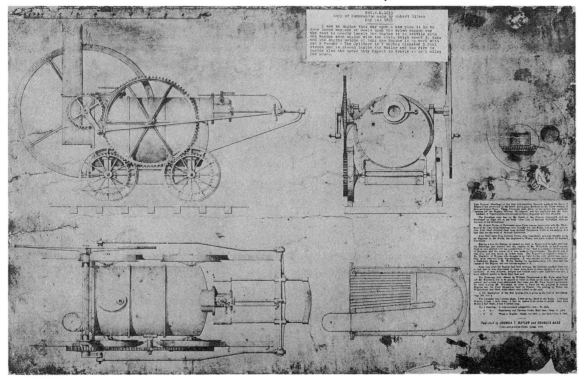

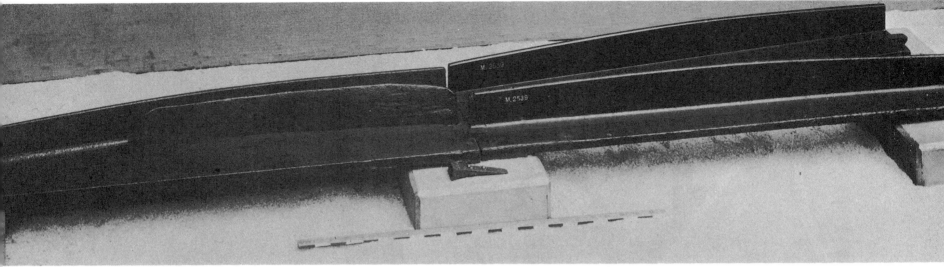

Outram's cast-iron plate rails from Ticknall Tramway, 1799. (British Crown Copyright. Science Museum, London)

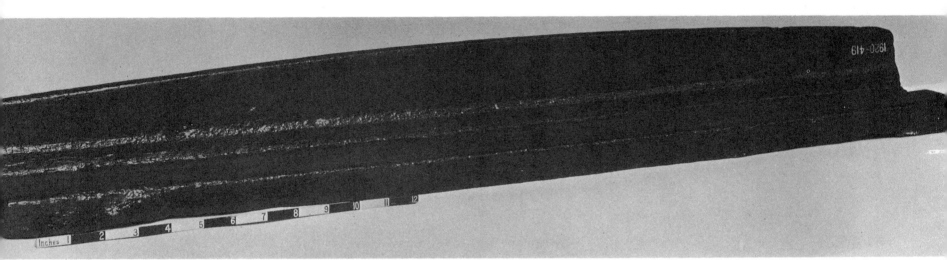

Plate rail from Pen-y-Daren Tramway, 1800. This is a section of rail over which Trevithick's and the world's first locomotive puffed that auspicious Monday, February 13, 1804. (British Crown Copyright. Science Museum, London)

Wrought-iron fish-bellied rail, 1825. Note plates for securing rail to tie. Drilled holes in stone were pegged with wood to receive spike. (British Crown Copyright, Science Museum, London)

First wrought-iron rail, 1808. From Tindale Fell Railway.
Note stone sleepers on which rail rests. (British Crown
Copyright. Science Museum, London)

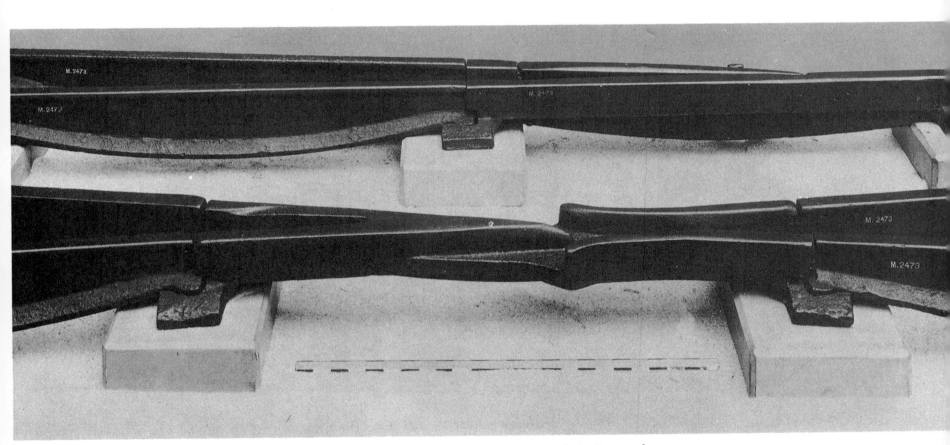

Jessop's cast-iron edge rail, 1815. Note "chairs," or sockets,
where rail lengths join. (British Crown Copyright. Science
Museum, London)

Model of Blenkinsop-Murray locomotive *Prince Regent*,
1812. (British Crown Copyright. Science Museum, London)

came to the conclusion that the advantage of his steam locomotive over horse power was not sufficient to induce the colliery owners to spend the large sums necessary to reconstruct their wagonways to accommodate the weight of his engines, and he went about other applications of his high-pressure engine.

The steam bug was biting freely now and others kept right on experimenting, with the locomotive foremost in their minds. On June 24, 1812, John locomotive to appear with two cylinders, making the large flywheel unnecessary. Given the name of *Prince Regent,* it was the first locomotive bearing a name. *Prince Regent's* success immediately brought an order for a sister, *Salamanca,* and on August 12, 1812, both locomotives were put in regular service on the Middleton Tramway, where they served reliably for a number of years.

Nine years after Trevithick had his second loco-

Hedley's *Wylam Dilly,* built in 1813. Originally wheels were flangeless, but later flanged wheels were substituted. (Courtesy Science Museum, London)

Blenkinsop and Matthew Murray of the Round Foundry at Holbeck made a test run of their rack-wheel locomotive. This innovation had two vertical cylinders recessed in the top of the boiler; long connecting rods from the crossheads drove twin crankshafts mounted under the frame, which in turn were coupled by gears to a central shaft upon which a single rack wheel was mounted. This was the first motive refused by Wylam colliery, the proprietors had a change of mind, and in 1813 their wagonway had been rebuilt as a cast-iron-plate tramway. That same year, William Hedley, associated with the colliery, built his first locomotive, *Wylam Dilly.* This engine also had two vertical cylinders, but they were mounted on each side of the boiler rather than recessed. The connecting rods fastened to a single crankshaft which in turn drove the wheels by means of spur gears. Four flangeless wheels were set to run over the 5-ft. gauge Wylam Tramway, where *Wylam*

25

Side view of boiler of *Puffing Billy*. (British Crown Copyright. Science Museum, London)

Hedley's *Puffing Billy* at work at Wylam Colliery. Hedley's second locomotive, 1813. (Courtesy Science Museum, London)

Dilly and successive sisters gave good service. It was found, however, that as four-wheelers the engines were too heavy for the plateway. But when they were converted to eight-wheelers, for better weight distribution, they gave a good account of themselves for many years.

The steam locomotive was at last catching on, and the foregoing pioneers certainly deserve their share of credit for its development. All that was needed now for the fruition of its promise was the right man, at the right place, at the right time; and like an actor poised in the wings, awaiting his entry upon the

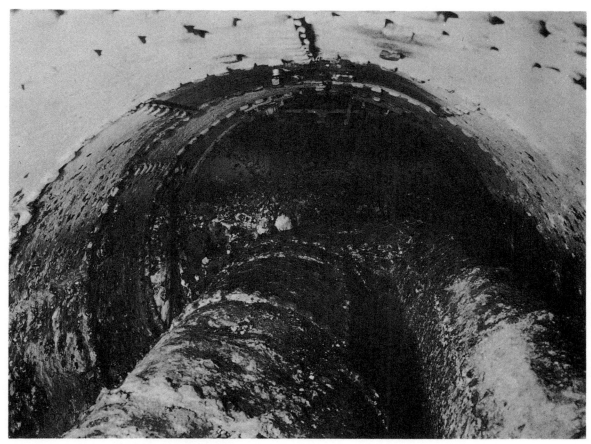

Interior view of boiler of *Puffing Billy*. (British Crown Copyright. Science Museum, London)

stage, the right man for the locomotive was in place and ready to play his destined role.

What his forerunners had, as well as what they lacked, was now embodied in this one man who had been endowed naturally with all the talents necessary for such an occasion. Born at Wylam in 1781, the son of a fireman in the colliery there, George Stephenson, the man predestined to get the railway revolution under way, grew up beside the Wylam wagonway; perhaps his first job was keeping his younger brothers and sisters from getting beneath the feet of the horses that pulled the loaded

wagons over the primitive way. When old enough to "hire out" he had quite naturally found work in the colliery, and following in the steps of his father had become a fireman of one of Watt's stationary engines. Although sadly lacking in formal education and unable to read or write at the age of eighteen, young Stephenson was recognized as a sort of mechanical genius around the Blucher pits at Killingworth. At the age of thirty, in 1812, he had progressed sufficiently to become an enginewright and had established quite a reputation in this field. Straying temporarily from steam engines, he had perfected and patented a safety light for use by miners in the pits in 1815—which, incidentally, is credited in preventing many mine explosions from gas in subsequent years.

Greatly interested in the application of Watt's steam engine to locomotives, Stephenson got his first great opportunity in 1813, when he was asked to supervise the building of a locomotive for the Killingworth wagonway. On July 25, 1814, throngs of interested spectators watched the fruition of this man's brilliant mechanical genius. It was on this date that Stephenson's *Blucher* made its initial run from the colliery shops to West Moor. Similar in many respects to locomotives that had gone before, there

George Stephenson (1781–1848). From a portrait by H. P. Briggs, R. A. (Courtesy Science Museum, London)

Model of Stephenson-built locomotive *Blucher* for Killing-worth Waggonway. Note crankshafts geared to the two axles rather than to a central rack wheel shaft as on Hedley's locomotives. (British Crown Copyright. Science Museum, London)

was one notable exception. Killingworth wagonway had been relaid with cast-iron edge rails and *Blucher* carried flanges on her wheels. Stephenson had proved that with much less contact area of the flanged wheel on an edge-rail, there was sufficient adhesive power for traction. As with its predecessors, *Blucher* lacked steam raising ability, due to the type of boiler then in use, and frequently came to a standstill for lack of steam. George Stephenson's elder brother, James, was *Blucher's* first "engineer," and as legend has it, one day the engine died on a crossing right at the engineer's home. Spying his buxom wife through an open window, James hollered, "Come here, Jinny, and put your shoulder to her." Jinny came, and with her assist the train cleared the crossing.

Now having his hand really in the dough, Stephenson continued with locomotive building, adopting improvements as he progressed. *Blucher's* successive sisters coming out with slide valves actuated by eccentrics on each axle, the contribution of Nicholas Wood. Stephenson's fame as an enginewright spread among influential men now interested in the locomotive, and he became associated with William Losh, senior partner in Walker Ironworks at Newcastle. This association brought about Stephenson's "steam spring," whereby the weight of the locomotive was carried by steam pressure in the boiler rather than solely by the wheels and axles, lessening damage done to the makeshift rails. Other Stephenson contributions during this period were improved wheels made of malleable iron and an improved type of cast-iron rail.

Somewhere along the line, this versatile genius had picked up considerable knowledge of civil engineering, and this coupled with his other attainments had given him a wide reputation as an engineer, such a reputation that this one-time fireman was approached to lay out and construct what was to be the first public steam railroad in existence —the Stockton & Darlington. Although the original idea of the promoters had been that horses would furnish the major motive power, George Stephenson, the road builder, harbored different ideas on the subject.

Early in 1821, John Birkinshaw, of Bedlington, had perfected a new method of rolling wrought-iron "I" rails in 15-ft. lengths. When this news reached the ears of Stephenson there was no question in his mind as to the type of motive power to be used over the road he was constructing. When the type of rails

to be used came up for discussion, Stephenson strongly recommended the new "I" rail. This recommendation, made in spite of the fact that Stephenson held a financial interest in the Stephenson & Losh cast-iron rail, terminated his association with the senior member of the foundry firm that up to this time had built the Stephenson locomotives.

Convinced of the wisdom of using steam motive power on their new line, the proprietors of the Stockton & Darlington specified that their locomotive should be of Stephenson design. The rupture with his former locomotive builders was just another obstacle to be surmounted by this man of action, whose talents flowed in so many different directions. Edward Pease, Michael Longridge, proprietor of Bedlington Ironworks, George Stephenson, and his son, Robert, entered into a partnership to establish a locomotive works. This pioneer locomotive building firm, Robert Stephenson & Company, was set up at Newcastle with Robert Stephenson, then a youth of just twenty, designated as general manager. It was with this new firm that the Stockton & Darlington placed its order for the building of motive power for its new road on September 16, 1824. The great capacity of George Stephenson must have been taxed to the utmost in the ensuing twelve months, for the road was to be opened to traffic over its rails in September 1825.

On September 26, 1825, eve of the crowning event, the Stephenson-built engine, *Locomotion 1,* was loaded on a wagon and pulled by horses from Newcastle to Aycliffe Lane where it was placed upon the rails of the new line; there it was coupled to *Experiment,* a cushion-seated car with carpeted floor, built by the Stephenson locomotive works for this great occasion. James Stephenson took his position at the lever and, with William Gowland as fireman, the little train pulled out of Shildon and made a test run to Darlington satisfactorily.

In the pioneering of the locomotive, no event up to this time had attracted so much attention, and as George Stephenson, father of it all, awaited this great day, his anticipation as well as anxiety can well be imagined; his engineering mind well knew how many things might go awry and that only a hairline often divides fame and fortune from scorn and failure.

Before dawn, on September 27, 1825, thousands from the surrounding countryside had converged upon the scene. Ten loaded coal wagons had been

Robert Stephenson (1803–1859), from an engraving by   of a worthy father. (Courtesy Science Museum, London)
Hall from a portrait by George Richmond. A worthy son

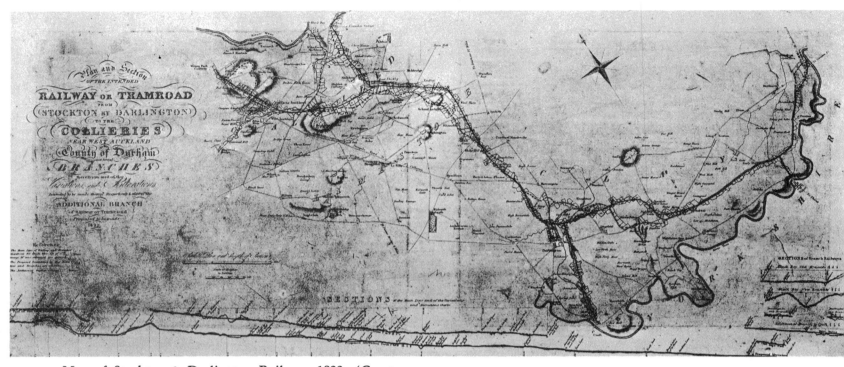

Map of Stockton & Darlington Railway, 1822. (Courtesy Science Museum, London)

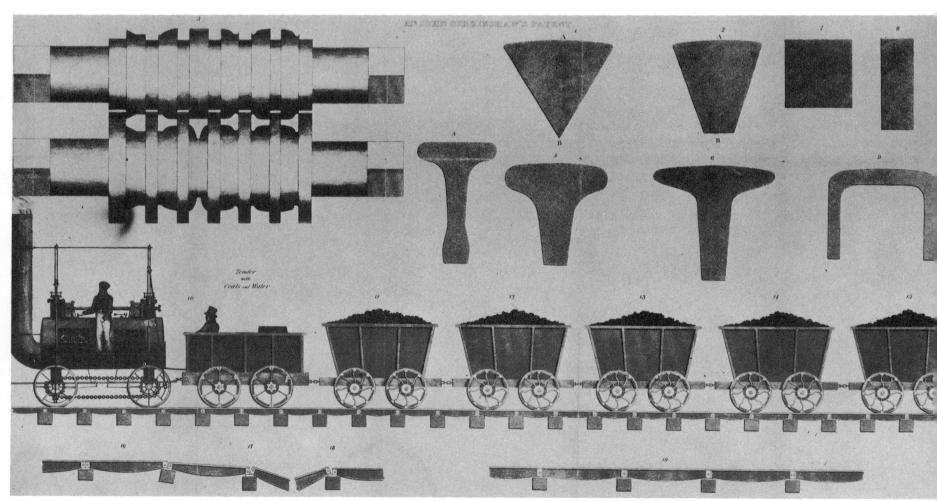

John Birkenshaw's wrought-iron "I" rails, patented 1820. (Courtesy Science Museum, London)

pulled by horses from Witton Park Colliery to Auckland, where a wagonload of flour had been coupled on; thence to Shildon, where *Locomotion 1,* with steam up, stood coupled to *Experiment* and 21 new coal wagons fitted with seats. Just as the horse-drawn train pulled up to be coupled on, the weight on *Locomotion's* safety valve lifted and as the roaring steam shot skyward the great mass of humanity gathered to witness the goings-on stampeded in terror. Noting that the engine crew—frock-coated George Stephenson and his brother James—remained undisturbed at this occurrence, and satisfied

by a man on horseback, George Stephenson eased the throttle open and as slack came out of the coupling chains the 33-car train (first mixed train) rolled forward on its historic run. The train had proceeded only a few hundred feet when due to the shifting of an axle one of the wagons derailed, but as *Locomotion* came to a standstill willing hands lifted the car back on the rails.

The 90-ton train had proceeded only a few miles when it came to another standstill; this time it was "engine breakdown," but in short order the engineer and fireman had removed the piece of oakum pack-

Some of the throng gathered to witness the great event on September 27, 1825. (Courtesy Science Museum, London)

that the engine was not going to explode, the crowd moved in again and it was with difficulty that the horsedrawn freight wagons were coupled to the rear of the train.

Tickets had been issued to 300 stockholders, for whom seats had been reserved, but in the wild rush to get aboard, these carefully laid plans had gone awry; according to accounts of the day, the passenger list was nearer 600 than the intended 300. Preceded

ing that had fouled a feedpump valve and the historic train got under way again.

Averaging 8 mph running time, *Locomotion* carried her train into Darlington Junction at high noon (just 55 minutes late for the nine-mile run). Here, the train was met by an awed and cheering crowd estimated at 12,000, and after setting off six coal wagons for distribution to the poor, two new wagons were coupled to the train, one filled with local dignitaries, the other carrying the Yarmtown band. *Locomotion* pulled out of the junction in great style,

33

Scenes at opening of Stockton & Darlington. (Courtesy
Science Museum, London)

Pioneers of First Public Railway. (Courtesy Science
Museum, London)

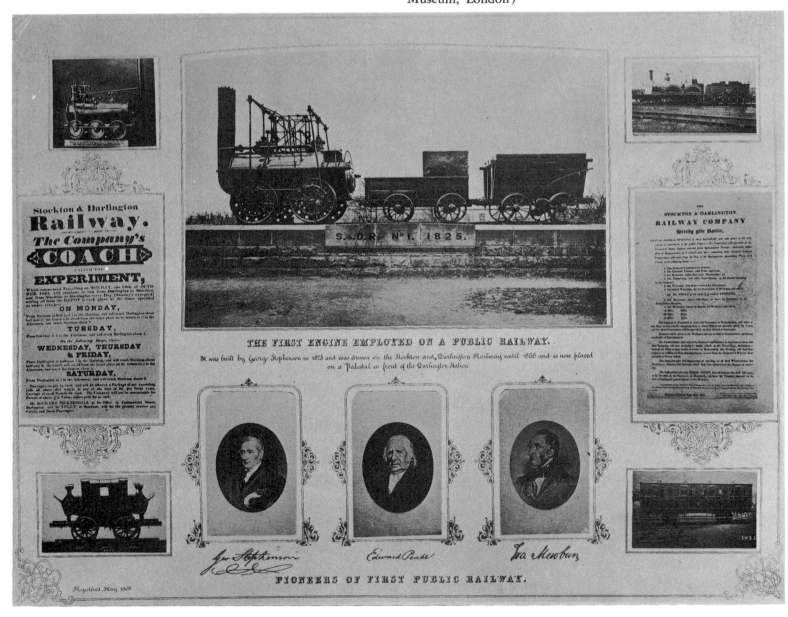

Model of *Locomotion 1*, built 1825. (British Crown Copyright. Science Museum, London)

35

A pencil drawing by J. R. Brown of the historic run
September 27, 1825, showing the train crossing the Skerne,
near Darlington. (Courtesy Science Museum, London)

Model of passenger coach, *Experiment,* built in 1825 by
Robert Stephenson & Company, builders of *Locomotion 1,*
as an added attraction in the consist of the famous train
that made its run over Stockton & Darlington on September
27, 1825. It served for many years thereafter. (British
Crown Copyright. Courtesy Science Museum, London)

Detail of wagon used on Stockton & Darlington, 1825.
(Courtesy Science Museum, London)

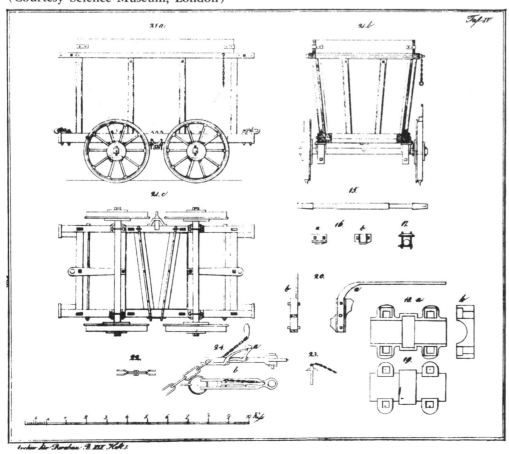

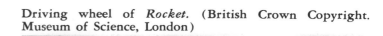

1829 announcement of Rainhill Trials. (Courtesy Science Museum, London)

Driving wheel of *Rocket*. (British Crown Copyright. Museum of Science, London)

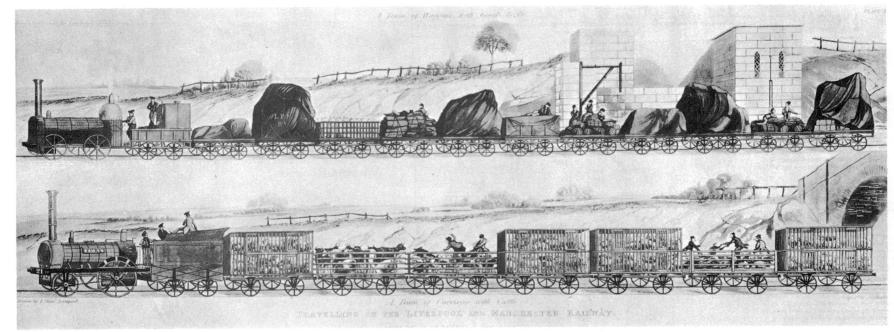

Goods (freight) trains on Liverpool & Manchester, 1831.
(Courtesy Science Museum, London)

Nine years after the passenger coach *Experiment* was built a lot had been learned about coach building, and the Liverpool & Manchester proudly pulled *Experience* (a likely name) over its line. As the cutaway model shows, this was real luxury. (British Crown copyright. Science Museum, London)

to the accompaniment of band music and the cheering crowd.

After making one stop at Goosepool (appropriately named) to take on water, *Locomotion* continued on her way without interruption. When at 3:45 P.M., now only 45 minutes behind schedule (her engineer must have poured it to her on that last lap), the long train clanked over the crossing at St. Johns and onto the quay at Stockton, the crowd of welcomers, estimated at 50,000, went wild. Church bells rang out and a deafening seven-gun salute drowned out "God Save The King," coming from the Yarmtown band aboard and others on the quay.

In the slang of our day, George Stephenson "had it made," but doubtless felt great relief as he closed the throttle and brought *Locomotion* and her historic train to a stop. Thus ended the first run of a steam locomotive and its train over a public rail line.

Model of Stephenson's *Rocket,* built in 1829. In the Rainhill Trials held October 1, 1829, this engine walked away from all competition for the prize of 500 pounds. Averaging 14 miles an hour, she was timed by Nicholas Wood at 29 miles an hour in a burst of speed on the 60-mile run. Her 56-inch cast-iron front wheels were drivers while her 30-inch wrought-iron-tired wooden trailer wheels supported the rear end of the four-and-a-quarter-ton engine.

This locomotive carried some features that set her apart from others up to this time. It had a 40-inch-diameter horizontal boiler, six feet long, in which were 25 copper tubes. Just as in Trevithick's locomotive of 1804, an exhaust steam jet created induced draft. Outside cylinders were connected by rods directly to crank pins on the driving wheels, which did away with cumbersome levers, gears, and cranked driving axles.

On one test in the trials, *Rocket* pulled 38 loaded carriages, with a total weight of 90 tons, at speeds of 12 to 16 miles an hour.

This was the first practical locomotive to be built combining so many advanced features, and it remained a generally accepted model for some years after she was built. (British Crown Copyright. Museum of Science, London)

2
The Steam Locomotive Comes to America

While following the birth and earliest development of the steam locomotive across the Atlantic, Americans had been bitten by the steam bug. Some pioneer American engineers were feverishly dreaming and working, the more farsighted ones predicting that the locomotive would revolutionize transportation in this country.

America was a sleeping giant at the turn of the nineteenth century. Virgin forests stood as they had since the beginning of time; iron deposits had been just barely scratched and for the most part coal fields were yet undiscovered. Perhaps as many as 175,000 pioneering souls were living west of the Alleghenys, and cattle were being driven over Indian and animal trails a distance of some 300 miles from Ohio to eastern markets at Philadelphia and Baltimore.

Virginia and North Carolina pioneers headed west into Kentucky over the old Wilderness Road blazed by Daniel Boone. Travel between Boston, New York, and Philadelphia was by stagecoach. Freight moved from Boston westward through the Mohawk Valley by wagon and pack train; between Philadelphia and Pittsburgh by Conestoga wagon; and from Pittsburgh southwest by flatboat down the Ohio River.

In 1789 George Washington was bounced and thrown about in his carriage as it made its slow way over the narrow, rutted, and winding road from Mount Vernon to New York for his inauguration as first president of the United States. He took along his favorite saddle horse for relief when the lurching coach became too much for him.

Factories were nonexistent and there were only a few steam engines in the country. But even then, 1789, the farsighted John Fitch was working with his experimental steamboat and had run it at a speed approximating five miles an hour on the Delaware River at Philadelphia.

Ohio had come into the Union in 1803 and the government had agreed to connect the new state with the East by a road. Ohioans were sending their farm produce to New Orleans by raft via the Ohio and Mississippi Rivers, thence by ocean to Baltimore and New York.

In 1806 Congress had passed an act creating a "super highway" to be known as "The National Road." The road was to be sixty-eight feet wide with a thirty-foot macademized center strip. On August 1, 1817, the driver cracked his whip over a six-horse hitch and they lunged forward on the new road, pulling the elaborately decorated and silk-upholstered Concord-type stagecoach. Passengers swayed from side to side as the stages rounded curves; occasionally one pitched over some mountainside, carrying passengers, horses and their driver to their deaths.

Conestoga wagons, gaily painted with undercarriage blue, upper woodwork red, and white canvas top, carried household goods, nails, blacksmith iron, and clothing going west toward Ohio, and grain, pork, hides, and whiskey coming east. At night the wagons stopped along the road at their "wagon stands," where the horses were unhitched and tied to each side of the wagon-tongue, to which a long feed box was fastened. As the teams fed, the drivers made merry at the inn with plenty of drink and food and when the frolic was through rolled up in their blankets on the floor to "sleep it off."

Passenger stages from Washington (D.C.) to Wheeling (then Virginia) took two days and eleven

40

hours; traveling night and day from Boston a passenger could make the trip to New York in about forty-one hours. The 126-mile trip from Pittsburgh to Erie could be made in forty-six hours of day and night travel in good seasons; during winter months the road was a bottomless sea of mud in places. Trees were cut and laid across the worst spots, making a "corduroy road," but on those that weren't so bad passengers sometimes had to roll out and put their shoulders to the wheel when the coach stuck in some gooey mudhole.

Although Europe had used canals for over two hundred years, the Santee Canal, from Charleston to the middle of South Carolina, had just been completed in 1800. The Middlesex Canal, connecting Boston with New Hampshire, was completed in 1803; the Erie was started July 4, 1817, the same year the National Road was opened to Wheeling, and seven years later the 363-mile ditch with its 83 locks had been completed from Albany to Buffalo. This smooth, quiet, and serene method of transportation certainly had its charms, but more farsighted

The Wilderness Road, over which Daniel Boone travelled, near Cumberland Ford (Pineville, Kentucky). (Archives Virginia State Library)

"Engineer" astride the near wheel horse as "conductor" holds his perch on side of Conestoga wagon. This was a familiar scene on "The National Road"—until the railroad came. (Archives Virginia State Library)

A stagecoach rolls over "The National Road" in 1817. (Archives Virginia State Library)

men of the day realized that the three to five miles per hour speed, the motive power supplied by horse and mule walking in a towpath beside the canal, was not the answer to the transportation needs of awakening America.

THE EARLY PROPHETS AND PIONEER STEAM LOCOMOTIVES

In Warren, Massachusetts, Nathan Reed had built a steam-driven vehicle in 1790. This machine had a smokestack and moved under its own power along the road, but for lack of financial backing got nowhere and soon vanished from the scene.

One of America's most talented early mechanics, Oliver Evans, had become interested in steam shortly after the American Revolution. His experiments convinced him of steam's practicality to such an extent that he prophesied "the transportation of merchandise and passengers on carriages drawn by steam engines." In 1785 Evans built a steam-driven road wagon; however, this machine developed insufficient steam pressure for the tractive effort needed. In 1804 he built a flat-bottomed steam dredge in his shop at Philadelphia. Faced with the problem of getting his dredge to the river for launching, he mounted the boat on heavy iron wheels and axles to which he connected the engine. He then drove his creation, the *Oructur Amphibolis,* to the launching site, where it was put overboard into the Schuylkill River. Unable to get financial assistance for his schemes, Evans apparently spent his remaining years in prophesying up to his death in 1819.

One of the earliest prophets of what might be termed "the railway revolution in America" was Col. John Stevens. Graduating in law at King's College (later to become Columbia University) in 1768, he practiced his profession until the Revolutionary War, through which he served as a colonel. Having an inventive mind and becoming interested in engineering, Stevens sponsored the patent law in the United States and saw it enacted in 1790. Becoming interested in steam he built and operated the first steam ferryline, operating between Hoboken, New Jersey, and New York City.

In 1811, Col. Stevens endeavored to secure a charter from the New Jersey legislature for the construction of a railroad, and in 1812, when New York State was actively supporting the building of the Erie Canal, he was petitioning that a railroad be built instead. "Let a railway . . . be formed between Lake Erie and Albany," said Stevens. "The angle of elevation in no part to excel one degree. . . . The carriage wheels of cast iron, the rims flat with projecting flanges to fit the surface of the railway. The moving power to be a steam engine, nearly similar to the one on board the Juliana, a ferry boat [operated by Stevens] plying between this city [New York] and Hoboken." Here, Col. Stevens was speaking of tracks, flanged wheels, and a steam locomotive; but this farsighted prophet was ahead of his time by about seventeen years.

So fascinated had the Colonel become with the idea of steam locomotives and railroads that he applied to the state of New Jersey and in 1815 was granted the first charter for a railroad. It was to operate between Trenton and New Brunswick, but for lack of financial support the project died. Undaunted, Stevens continued to push his plans, and in 1823 again obtained a railroad charter, this time from the state of Pennsylvania for a line to operate between Philadelphia and Columbia. This, too, was destined for failure.

A less determined man would have given up, but this intrepid soul was of that breed that dares the unknown and leads the way. To prove that steam locomotives and railroads were practical, the then 76-year-old prophet picked up the crude tools available, built a little circular railway on his estate at Hoboken in 1825, and in 1826 completed the steam locomotive to run on it. His engine had neither crank nor couplings on any of its four wheels but was driven by a connecting rod from a single cylinder to a cogged wheel which in turn engaged a rack rail. A vertical, multitubular boiler furnished steam for this first locomotive to be built in America as it puffed around the circular track.

Although never used on a railroad as such, this little locomotive gave great impetus to the interest in railroads. Now satisfied beyond doubt of the practicality of a steam railroad, Col. Stevens and his sons, Robert and Edwin, concentrated their efforts and in 1830 obtained a charter from New Jersey for the Camden & Amboy Railroad & Transportation Company. In spite of disappointments that would have stopped a less intrepid soul, Col. John Stevens had now realized the fruition of his pioneering dreams. Truly, he was the father of American railroads, as we shall see later in this work.

Col. John Stevens, the prophet. He has justifiably been called the father of American railroads. (Courtesy Pennsylvania Railroad Company)

Another early railroad pioneer in America was Horatio Allen, a young canal engineer whom the Delaware & Hudson Canal Company had sent to England in 1828 to "learn what he could" about railroads in operation there, and to obtain for them rails and a locomotive. Intrigued by the accomplishments of the British pioneers, Allen had Foster, Rastrick & Company, of Stourbridge, build a locomotive, and on May 13, 1829, the *Stourbridge Lion* arrived in New York on the packet, John Jay; whence it was put on a canalboat and sent to its owners at Honesdale, Pennsylvania.

The *Lion* had four wheels, all drivers, made of oak and tired with iron. There were two vertical cylinders operating two overhead beams, variously called "walking beams," "rocking levers," or "grasshopper beams," from which connecting rods,

coupled to the driving wheels, drove the engine. Whereas Allen had specified that the weight of the locomotive should not exceed three tons, the *Lion* weighed in at over twice that—seven tons. It is interesting to note that this locomotive got its name from the fact that a painter in the builder's shop used his artistic talent to paint in vermilion a lion's head on the four-foot-diameter front end of the boiler.

On Saturday, August 8, 1829, the engine was placed on the rails at Honesdale, fired up and made ready for her trial run. Allen's engineering knowledge made him aware of the fact that the locomotive was too heavy for the railway, and when none of the onlookers accepted his invitation to accompany him on this maiden run, he climbed aboard. Waving goodbye, Allen pulled the throttle open and, perhaps to his own surprise, soon found himself highballing over the rails.

In later years, when President of the Erie, Horatio

44

Allen gave his own account of this test run: "When the time came, and the steam was of the right pressure, and all was ready, I took my position on the platform of the locomotive alone, and with my hand on the throttle valve handle, said, 'If there is any danger in this ride it is not necessary that the life and limbs of more than one be subjected to danger.' The locomotive, having no train behind it, answered at once to movement of the hand; soon the straight line was run over, the curve was reached and passed before there was time to think as to its not being passed safely, and soon I was out of sight in the three miles ride alone in the woods of Pennsylvania. I had never run a locomotive nor any other engine before; I have never run one since." The engine proved satisfactory for use on the coal docks· of the Delaware & Hudson Company, but, too heavy for the light railway, it was withdrawn from service and relegated to stationary use.

Allen had ordered three additional locomotives while in England in 1828: the *Delaware* and the *Hudson,* both built by Foster, Rastrick & Company, and the *America,* built by Robert Stephenson & Company. They arrived in America, but as fas as is known were never operated on a railroad track, and their fate is unknown.

The steam locomotive being so much more picturesque than the rails over which it runs, and yet worthless without them, perhaps this is an opportune time to take a quick look at the primitive railways as they existed in this country prior to steam motive power.

The locomotive Col. Stevens built in 1825 and put to use on his own private railroad. (Courtesy Pennsylvania Railroad Company)

Horatio Allen, a man of many talents and one of the greats of all time in American railroad history. Mr. Allen was about thirty-three years of age when this picture was made and serving the "Charleston & Hamburg," which he had built, as Chief Engineer and Superintendent of Transportation. (Courtesy Southern Railway System)

Side view of *Stourbridge Lion*. (Courtesy Delaware & Hudson Railroad)

15997

View from rear of *Stourbridge Lion*. Note the three links
of coupling chain on rear of tender. (Courtesy Delaware
& Hudson Railroad)

With Horatio Allen at the throttle, the *Stourbridge Lion* is just about to pull out on the first run over rails of a real locomotive in America. (Courtesy Delaware & Hudson Railroad)

The first railway to be built in America followed closely those of the British Isles. It had wooden rails and was used to transport crushed stone from quarries nearby to Beacon Hill, in Boston, in 1795. In 1807, Stephen Whitney constructed his inclined-plane railway in the same vicinity and for the same use. Two years later, Thomas Leiper built a three-quarter-mile-long tramway from his stone quarries at Crum Creek to Ridley Creek in Pennsylvania. There was a similar tramway from Falling Creek, Virginia, to move quarried stone a short distance to boat connections on the James River. All of these wooden-rail tramways used horse or mule power and cannot, of course, be considered other than pioneering efforts for the railroads to come.

The first railroad in the United States, the Granite Railway Company of Massachusetts, was chartered by that state March 4, 1826. This three-mile-long road was the first in this country to use iron-faced rails; bar-iron, two and one-half by five-eighths inches, was laid on pine and oak longitudinal sills. The original site of this line (first used to haul granite blocks for the construction of Bunker Hill monument) is now part of the New York, New Haven & Hartford; a granite monument, six miles south of Boston, marks the site of this first American Railroad.

Railroad fever was now spreading over the eastern part of this country like an epidemic; charters were sought from New England to the deep South, and even west of the Alleghenys. To most of the charter seekers, these early railroads were just common roads, to be considered along with macadamized turnpikes, and many railroad charters were patterned after those that were granted turnpikes. In 1828, Kentucky chartered the Lexington & Frankfort Turnpike or Railroad Company, and in 1832 Massachusetts chartered the Hoosac Rail or Macadamized Road Company.

As the fever spread, engineering minds of the day were occupied with the knotty problems brought about by the construction of roads over which the heavy iron horses must travel. The Baltimore & Ohio, which laid its first rail July 4, 1828, had sent their engineers to England to observe the railroads there. Acting upon the reports of these engineers, the company laid granite sills (eight by fifteen inches and six to ten feet long) in two parallel trenches of broken stone ballast. Flat strips of rail, five-eighths of an inch thick and two and one-half inches wide,

were then spiked into wooden plugs inserted into drilled holes in the granite sills. Such construction certainly shows the intention to build a road that would last forever; however, frost split and shifted the granite blocks; rails twisted out of place, spread, and worked loose from their moorings, causing frequent accidents. The best engineering intentions had resulted in utter failure.

Undaunted by the failure of others, engineers for the Philadelphia & Columbia tried three different systems. Six miles were laid with granite sills (as on the B&O), eighteen miles with wood sills and the remainder with stone blocks (eighteen inches square and set three feet apart). Edge-rails, fifteen feet long and imported from England, were then laid over the sills and blocks.

But to return to the locomotives, Peter Cooper, a wealthy New York manufacturer, early became interested in the steam locomotive and, using what was to be found lying around a Baltimore machine shop, built one with his own hands. This little engine, weighing less than a ton and appropriately named *Tom Thumb*, had a twelve-inch vertical boiler in which old musket barrels were used as tubes. With a single cylinder of three-and-one-half-inch diameter and a fourteen-inch piston stroke, *Tom* perhaps put out the equivalent of one horsepower of effort.

Built to convince B&O directors that steam locomotives were entirely practical, *Tom Thumb* was the first American-built locomotive to pull a car full of passengers over a railroad. On August 28, 1830, the pigmy engine made its run from Baltimore to Ellicott's Mills, a distance of thirteen miles and up a grade eighteen feet to the mile, in one hour and twelve minutes. Evidently Mr. Cooper was confident of *Tom's* ability, for the little engine took the grade with a carriage behind it in which some twelve directors of the B&O rode.

It was on the return trip that difficulty was experienced. The double track line could be used by anyone who made the necessary financial arrangements, and Stockton & Stokes, operators of stages, used it regularly. Understandably, the stage lines took a dim view of anything that posed competition and, learning of the trial run, had put a fast horse to their carriage, using the other track. *Tom Thumb* was rolling free when the horse-drawn car pulled up alongside. Engineer Cooper accepted the challenge, pulled the throttle wider and the race was on. *Tom* had left the horse behind when the engine lost

Peter Cooper's *Tom Thumb* (Courtesy Baltimore & Ohio
Railroad Company)

Tom Thumb's engineer waits for the "high green" to start
a run with the replica of the directors' car. (Courtesy Baltimore & Ohio Railroad Company)

Exciting Trial of Speed between Mr. Peter Cooper's Locomotive, "Tom Thumb," and one of Stockton & Stokes' Horse-Cars.

Just before the horse caught up with *Tom* on the return trip. (Courtesy Baltimore & Ohio Railroad Company)

Tom lost her blower belt and head of steam and Dobbin makes a final dash for the "wire." (Courtesy Baltimore & Ohio Railroad Company)

Replica of *Best Friend* as she pulled the first scheduled train over rails in America, Christmas Day, 1830. (Courtesy Southern Railway System)

its blower-belt, also its head of steam, thereby forfeiting the race to old Dobbin; but the directors had been convinced—the little kettle had accomplished its mission.

Sometime after his wild ride at the throttle of the *Stourbridge Lion* over the D&H line in Pennsylvania, Horatio Allen had been invited to fill, and had accepted, the position of Chief Engineer of the Charleston & Hamburg Railroad (officially the South Carolina Canal & Railroad Company, later to become a part of Southern Railway System). Allen had collaborated with E. L. Miller, a director of the road, in designing a locomotive, and drawings and specifications had been sent to the West Point Foundry in New York City for its building.

On October 23, 1830, the ship *Niagara* arrived in Charleston harbor carrying the 4½-ton engine. With a vertical, tubular boiler designed to carry 50 psi steam pressure, two cylinders (each six inches in diameter and sixteen inches long) inside the frame and coupled by two cranks to the driving axles, and four 54-inch driving wheels connected by outside rods, this first locomotive built in America for regular railroad service was appropriately named *Best Friend Of Charleston*. Trial runs were made on November 2nd, December 9th and 14th, and on one of these runs *Best Friend* pulled five cars, loaded with passengers, at speeds up to 21 miles per hour.

December 25, 1830, was not only Christmas day in Charleston. It was an auspicious day for America, for on this day was inaugurated the first run of a scheduled train pulled by a steam locomotive on this continent. Needless to say, the occasion was celebrated in a manner befitting the occasion. Engineer Nicholas Darrell was a proud man as he climbed up, took his stand on the front end, and, getting the word, moved his historic train forward. As the train gained momentum the cheers of the passengers were occasionally drowned out by the U.S. Army gun, mounted on a flat car behind the engine, which was fired "at proper intervals."

On June 17, 1832, after a year and a half of successful operation, *Best Friend* scored another first. As the engine was being turned around on a "revolving platform" her fireman became annoyed by the hiss of escaping steam from the pop-valve and decided to do something about it. There is some disagreement as to whether the fireman tied the valve lever down or just took a seat on it; in any event,

there was a brief period of quiet—just before the boiler blew. Both engineer Darrell and the fireman were carried some distance by the explosion and badly injured. *Best Friend* was demolished in the first explosion of a locomotive boiler in America.

Best Friend was succeeded on the C&H by the *West Point,* named for its and *Best Friend*'s builders. Designed by E. L. Miller, this engine was similar to its predecessor with the exception that it carried a horizontal boiler. Apparently *Best Friend*'s explosion had made prospective passengers a bit leary of the iron horse, for coupled between the *West Point* and first passenger coach was a flatcar, on which had been piled bales of cotton for protection to the passengers "when the locomotive exploded."

West Point Foundry had now earned quite a reputation as a locomotive builder, and in 1831 it delivered to the Mohawk & Hudson (now a part of New York Central) what is generally conceded to be the first American built locomotive for passenger service. Dubbed the *DeWitt Clinton,* this was the first locomotive to be operated in New York State. Designed by John B. Jervis, she and her tender weighed slightly over six tons. Incidentally, the lower part of the tender was a tank for water, probably the first "water bottom tank" on a locomotive.

Apparently Dave Matthews, who had supervised her building at the foundry, had come along with the *DeWitt* upon her delivery to the M&H. Proud of his creation, with her thirty copper tubes inside the horizontal boiler resting on 54-inch drivers, he nervously awaited her maiden trip. Although the firebox had been designed for the use of coal, Dave wanted a hot fire and had seen to it that her tender was piled high with pitchpine.

The "Master of Transportation" (Conductor), John T. Clark, was an important man in Albany on August 9, 1831, as he collected tickets from the excited passengers. After completing the check of his passenger manifest, he stepped gingerly to the little platform on the tender, took his seat beside the woodpile, then pulled a tin horn from his pocket and blew one long, shrill blast.

That was the signal Dave Matthews had so anxiously awaited. Perhaps tense nerves may have caused Dave to yank the throttle too suddenly; whatever the reason, one jolting shock after another followed as the three long links of chain-coupling gave up their slack as the train straightened out.

Many of the passengers were thrown to the floor and those on top of the closed cars and in the open ones, at the rear of the train, were deluged with showers of blazing cinders that flew from *DeWitt's* stack. Passengers in the open cars had been provided with unbrellas, which soon burned to the ribs and were thrown away, and as their clothing caught fire the passengers became cozy neighbors as they beat out fires on each other.

Five miles out of Albany, Dan discovered that his creation needed water and as he pulled the reverse bar back and opened the throttle many

toward Albany, the engineer opened her up and, even with two extra coaches added, *DeWitt* hauled her five-car train at speeds up to forty miles an hour —and made the run in thirty-eight minutes!

Col. John Stevens was not a man to sit idly by and hold his hands while all this was going on. After obtaining charter for the Camden & Amboy he promptly got into action in the construction of his road in New Jersey. His gifted son, Robert, had been made Chief Engineer, and in October 1830 took ship to England for the express purpose

Smoke pours out of the stack from the pitchpine fire under the boiler as *DeWitt Clinton* rolls between Albany and Schenectady. (Courtesy New York Central System)

passengers busily engaged with their personal fire problems were thrown to the floor as the coupling-chains slacked and the cars crashed into each other. Getting under way again, Dan must have let his engine just saunter, for it took an hour and forty-five minutes to make the seventeen-mile run. Arriving at Schenectady, great throngs had assembled to duly honor the arrival of the first steam train, with band music and several salutes from cannon.

Apparently in high spirit as he headed back

of purchasing rail and a locomotive for the new line. Familiar and dissatisfied with the type of rail used on the pioneer railroads, young Stevens was apparently giving serious thought to this problem; perhaps to pass away time, as the little boat plowed through the Atlantic toward England, he picked up some scraps of wood and started to whittle. It is not known what else his knife carved out but he did fashion a small section very similar to what we know today as "T" rail. Liking the looks of what he had made, he then proceeded to carve out a spike with a flanged head.

Arriving in Liverpool, Stevens made contact with John Guest, one of the proprietors of an ironworks in Wales. Assuming full responsibility for any damage suffered by the mill machinery and any extra expense caused the ironworks, Stevens prevailed on Guest to roll rail patterned after the wood model he had carved. The result was twelve- and fifteen-foot lengths, weighing thirty-six pounds to the yard. While the rails were being rolled in Wales, the young engineer proceeded to Newcastle where he met the Stephensons, with whom an order had been placed for building a locomotive for the new line in New Jersey. Doubtless Stevens got his fingers in the pie while visiting the locomotive works, for

Isaac Dripps, a mechanic, had been employed for the job of re-assembly. Figuring out the problems as they arose, Dripps put his heart, mind, and skilled hands to the task. This exceptionally gifted mechanic must have felt justifiably proud when his work was completed and he gazed at the ten-ton *Bull,* with her multitubular horizontal boiler and two-nine-by-twenty-inch cylinders, resting on her four 54-inch driving wheels.

The ingenious mechanic also built a tender, which solved the fuel-carrying problem. Since water was more necessary than fuel, Dripps went to a nearby grocery store and returned with a large whiskey barrel (presumed to be empty) which he made fast

Even the Indians turned out to see the iron horse as the *DeWitt Clinton* and her train rolled along the Mohawk & Hudson. (Courtesy New York Central System)

the engine then under construction had some innovations when completed.

On July 14, 1831, the locomotive *John Bull* was loaded on the packet *Allegheny* at Liverpool. The "engine body" and boiler were battened down on deck, and "two pairs of large wheels and axles, three boxes and 'an iron box' under the deck." This shipment arrived in Philadelphia in due course and was taken to Bordentown, New Jersey, for assembly.

Although he had never seen a locomotive before,

in a corner of the tender nearest the engine. Next going to a shoemaker, the mechanic had a leather hose fashioned, which he mounted between the water-barrel and the engine.

The engine performed well on her test runs. However, Dripps noted that she seemed a bit too rigid for some of the curves on the C&A and decided to do something about it. Removing the coupling rods of the drivers. Dripps gave one-and-a-half-inch sideplay to the leading axle, which remedied the trouble to an appreciable extent.

Now a "ready engine," *John Bull* was put into regular service on November 12, 1831. Although

Robert L. Stevens, son of Col. John, a brilliant engineer and one of the great pioneer railroadmen. (Courtesy Pennsylvania Railroad Company)

his adjustment to the leading axle had improved the flexibility of the engine, Dripps still wasn't satisfied with her performance in taking curves. Experimenting further, he just about solved the problem by putting a two-wheeled "cow catcher" under the front end, thus relieving the leading drivers of some superimposed weight. Delighted with the improved performance from this addition, Dripps gave an encore by putting a bell and headlight on the *Bull*.

This old workhorse served satisfactorily for many years and after retirement was placed in the Washington Museum. In 1893 it was taken from its resting place, placed on the rails, fired up, and coupled to the *John Bull* Train, which it hauled under its own power to the World's Fair at Chicago. Although over sixty years old, the *Bull* wasn't content to stand idly by, and during its stay at the Fair hauled tens of thousands of passengers around the grounds. When the exhibition closed, the old *Bull* growled, bellowed, and snorted its way back to its "roundhouse" in Washington. "The bull goes on forever."

MATTHIAS W. BALDWIN

No matter how brief, any history of American

56

The renowned pioneer locomotive builder, Matthias W. Baldwin. From a portrait made in Mr. Baldwin's later years. (Courtesy Baldwin-Lima-Hamilton Corporation)

locomotives would be incomplete without mention of one of the early builders, Matthias Baldwin. Born at Elizabethtown, New Jersey, on December 10, 1795, Baldwin was not only destined to personally build some of these pioneer locomotives, but to found in the early 1830's the great Baldwin Locomotive Works which has played such an outstanding part in the progress of locomotive building, and therefore railroads, right up to the present day. (It is now Baldwin-Lima-Hamilton Corporation.)

Baldwin, a mechanical-minded genius, first learned to be a watchmaker, then toolmaker and machinist. Needing a small engine in his own little shop, he designed and built one about 1825 which attracted so much attention that many orders for duplicates were received. Hard bitten by the steam bug, Baldwin apparently gave his full attention to building steam engines. As his fame spread, he was asked by Franklin Peale in 1830 to build a working miniature locomotive for exhibition in the Peale

"Old Ironsides," a five-ton locomotive, was built by Matthias W. Baldwin, and made its trial run November 23, 1832, on the Philadelphia, Germantown and Norristown Railroad. The wheels were made with heavy cast-iron hubs, wooden spokes and rims, and wrought-iron tires. The tender was a four-wheeled platform with wooden sides and back, enclosed in a wooden casing, and with a space for fuel in front. (Courtesy Reading Company)

"Old Ironsides," built by Matthias W. Baldwin for the Philadelphia, Germantown, and Norristown Railroad, is shown leaving the old depot at Ninth and Green Streets, Philadelphia. Regular passenger service began on November 26, 1832, when the locomotive with six cars filled with passengers left Philadelphia on its way to Germantown. (Courtesy Reading Company)

Museum at Philadelphia. It has been said, and is probably correct, that Baldwin had never seen a locomotive at this time, but, intrigued with the idea, he got hold of some inadequate sketches of George Stephenson's *Rocket* and from these constructed the miniature engine. On April 25, 1831, Baldwin's "toy" was placed on the rails of a small circular track at the museum and put into regular service hauling two little cars, each seating four passengers.

As the fame of Baldwin's "toy" spread, the Philadelphia, Germantown & Norristown ordered a "full-sized locomotive for regular passenger service" on their railroad, to replace the horses then in use. This was late in 1831, and recalling the *John Bull*, which he had glimpsed as it was being assembled at Bordentown earlier the same year, Baldwin took off to find the *Bull*. Locating the engine, the intrepid locomotive builder made an inspection and a few notes, returned to his shop, and went to work.

In this day it is difficult for us to understand some of the obstacles to be overcome in building a locomotive then. Since there were few mechanics with enough know-how to do any of the work competently, Baldwin was forced to do much of it himself. Suitable tools could not be ordered from some supply house, so this doughty builder had to improvise and make many of those he used. Cylinders were bored by a chisel fixed in a block of wood and turned by hand; the blacksmith who could weld bar-iron thicker than about an inch was practically non-existent But with it all, Matthias Baldwin got his first customer's order completed and on November 23, 1832, *Old Ironsides* was placed on the rails of the PG&N and given its test run.

This forerunner of the 59,000 steam locomotives built under the Baldwin name weighed five and one-half tons. It carried a boiler thirty inches in diameter which contained 72 copper tubes that were seven feet long and one and one-half inches in diameter. The two 54-inch driving wheels, enclosed by a wood frame, were on a crank axle placed in front of the firebox; the two front (carrying) wheels, each 45 inches in diameter, were mounted on an axle just back of the cylinders. Wood spokes and rims, tired with wrought iron, were built around cast-iron hubs. Two horizontal cylinders, each nine and one-half by eighteen inches, were attached to the "D"-shaped smokebox, with their sides receding inwardly to bring the center of each in line with the crank-centers.

The valve motion was unique in that it was produced by a single loose eccentric, placed on the axle between the crank and hub of a wheel for each cylinder. The engine was reversed by changing the position of the eccentrics with a lever operated from the footboard. (This was not a satisfactory operation and was almost immediately changed to a fixed eccentric for each cylinder.)

Another bug that showed up was in the exhaust system. Originally, there was a single straight pipe running across from one cylinder to the other, with an opening in the upper side to which was attached an upright pipe that went into the smokestack. With this arrangement it may be seen that the cylinders were exhausting into each other. However, the defect was remedied by turning each of the cylinder's exhaust pipes upward into the stack, similar to the arrangement of exhaust systems in steam locomotives right up to the last.

In spite of these minor mistakes, if they could be so called, *Old Ironsides* gave a good account of herself on her trial run, averaging about 28 miles an hour. So impressive was her performance, that the *Philadelphia Chronicle* of November 24th stated in part, "From the experiment there is every reason to believe that this engine will draw 30 tons gross, at an average speed of 40 miles per hour. . . . We rejoice in the result of this experiment, as it conclusively shows that Philadelphia always produces steam engines for railroads combining so many superior qualities as to warrant the belief that her mechanics will supply nearly all the public works of this description in the country."

There were similar expressions from other journals. Despite this acclaim Baldwin was discouraged; he had noted the faults of his creation, which were actually minor ones—but he wanted perfection. Then, too, his customer was inclined to haggle about paying the four thousand dollars agreed upon and effected a compromise settlement. Perhaps thinking of the great difficulties experienced in building the engine with unskilled help and poor tools, the pioneer builder stated to a friend, "This is our last locomotive." This statement, however, was just one made upon the spur of the moment by a man who was a bit discouraged.

As the fame of *Old Ironsides* spread, the Charleston & Hamburg Railroad placed an order with Baldwin, which must have cheered his heart. Forgetting his troubles, the locomotive builder immediately went to work on his second creation, and in 1832 delivered the *E.L. Miller* (named for the designer of *Best Friend*). This engine was a distinct improvement over *Old Ironsides* and served for many years as a model for future Baldwin locomotives. *Miller* had but a single pair of driving wheels made of bell-metal brass, and in front of the drivers was a four-wheel leading truck. Another soon followed for the Charleston road, the *Baldwin* (named for its builder), and right on its heels the *Lancaster,* for the Philadelphia & Columbia line.

Orders now came thick and fast and by 1839 the Baldwin Works had turned out 136 steam locomotives. By this time they were not alone, however, for three competitors had come into the field: Rogers in 1835, Locks & Canal Works the same year, and Ross Winans Works in 1837. The locomotive business was booming. None of these pioneer locomotives provided any protection from the elements to the engine crews and, as one historian of those early days of railroading has said, "It was not uncommon to see an engineer covered in ice like a coat of mail."

There were no bells, whistles, headlights, sandboxes, spark arresters, or brakes on the earliest locomotives. Curves posed a real problem in getting the pioneer engines around them and John B. Jervis, Chief Engineer of the Mohawk & Hudson, is given credit for coming up with the idea of a swivelling leading truck. This truck, placed ahead of the drivers, not only provided a flexibility of wheel base but also allowed the weight of the engine to be equalized. These early roadbeds frequently followed old wagon roads, which had naturally taken the lines of least resistance; for this and other reasons the newly laid railroads had many curves in their lines. Apparently no thought was given to banking curves at this time, but as speed was not the factor then, as it would later become, this alone was not accountable for frequent rail climbing by the locomotives.

Warming water in the tank (in the early days a whiskey barrel fixed in a corner of the little flatcar coupled behind the engine) was unknown. A leather hose swinging freely between barrel and engine provided the water supply for the boiler. Frequently water in the hose froze during winter months and on these occasions it became necessary to stop and build a fire under the hose. This "de-icing procedure" had to be watched very closely, else the fire would scorch the hose-leather, causing it to crack or, worse still,

burst. Such delays might last from a few minutes to several hours, and with no means of communication the train's whereabouts was unknown, except to the crew and the disgruntled passengers. On other occasions, in any season, the tender would run out of both water and wood, generally at some lonely spot in open country. On such occasions the disgusted passengers reluctantly joined the crew in cutting and bringing wood from some faraway woodlot, and toting water in buckets (regulation equipment) from some creek possibly a mile or more in the opposite direction from the wood-lot.

As the building of these pioneer locomotives progressed, we find improvements being made. In 1836, Henry R. Campbell, Chief Engineer for the Philadelphia, Germantown & Norristown Railroad, patented a wheel arrangement with four leading wheels (pony truck) and four driving wheels (the firebox being placed between the driving axles). Under the Whyte System of wheel arrangement classification (more about this later) this engine would have been classified as a 4-4-0, commonly known as the American-type locomotive. The wheel arrangement was designed to distribute the weight of the locomotive equally upon the rails.

Campbell had the Philadelphia builder, James Brooks, build the engine to his specifications, and in May, 1837, it was completed. Although this twelve-ton locomotive was theoretically powerful enough to move approximately 450 tons on level track at fifteen miles an hour, its operation was unsatisfactory due to inability to equalize the weight on her drivers and it was withdrawn from service. Recognizing the defect, Campbell had Garrett & Eastwick, of Philadelphia, build another 4-4-0. This engine, the *Hercules,* weighed fifteen tons, had a separate frame arranged with pedestal jaws and equalizers upon which the driving-wheel axles rested, and was delivered to the Beaver Meadow Railroad in 1837.

Pioneer railroading with the motive power available in those early days presented its problems. As far as this writer is able to ascertain, Horatio Allen (of Stourbridge Lion fame and now Chief Engineer for the Charleston & Hamburg) was first to innovate a headlight for night running. In 1834 or 1835, Allen attacked the problem by covering the floor of a small flatcar with iron sheeting, then generously sprinkled the floor with sand. Upon this he built a fire of lightwood knots, placed his headlight car immediately ahead of the engine and proceeded.

A good illustration of the tall smokestack on an early-day locomotive, the *Mississippi.* The Natchez & Hamburg later became a part of Illinois Central. Unfortunately, the engineer and fireman cannot be identified (Courtesy Illinois Central Railroad)

This arrangement, which must have seemed so promising in the planning stage, failed to work out in practice; the flames, encouraged by the increased draft of forward motion, blinded the engineer. To alleviate this little problem, a metal shield was placed behind the fire; however, this failed to improve matters; smoke from the lightwood knots almost suffocated the engine crew as sparks set fire to property along the way, as well as "annoying" the train crew and passengers.

Shortly after this night-running-experiment, Isaac Dripps (the mechanical genius with Col. Steven's Camden & Amboy) fashioned a glass-enclosed oil lamp, which he placed in front of the smokestack of *John Bull*. But with glass on all four sides and no re-flector, its beams went in all directions rather than on the track ahead. Accustomed to failure at first try, Dripps soon came up with a much more effective headlight, and it must be said that these oil headlights served well for many years, until acetylene gas came to be used rather extensively, and it in turn was re-placed by electricity. Credit must also be given Isaac Dripps for use of the first locomotive bell (seen on the earliest pictures of *John Bull*). Incidentally, Baldwin's second locomotive, *E.L. Miller,* was the first to be equipped with a bell by its builder.

The smokestacks, emanating from the smoke-boxes of those early locomotives, were dispropor-tionately tall straight pipes, designed primarily to put the smoke and sparks high enough to keep them out of the eyes of the engine crew and away from the passenger's clothing. Even the towering height failed miserably of its purpose and passengers riding on outside seats suffered many burns and other dis-comforts from the red-hot sparks and cinders. Quite early in their history, wire netting was installed inside and near the top of the stacks; perhaps alleviating it somewhat, this did not remedy the trouble to any appreciable extent; particularly so because wood fires produced most of the sparks, and this fuel was quite generally used in those pioneer days.

Once again, the Camden & Amboy mechanical genius, Isaac Dripps, did something about this prob-lem and in 1833 designed a cone-shaped deflector which was suspended point downward in the stack. Shortly thereafter the so-called balloon stack made its appearance. The sides of these funnel-shaped stacks started to swell soon after leaving the top of the smokebox and in some instances their top

rings were as large or larger than the diameter of the locomotive boiler. However, they were a great improvement in spark abatement and were used generally until George Griggs, first Master Mechanic of the Boston & Providence, designed the "Diamond Stack." This latter type served well over a long period and even though designed primarily for wood-burning locomotives, it had many champions after coal became the generally used fuel. Another stack that came into prominence was the "Rushton," perhaps better known as the "cabbage-head"; this featured spiral baffles that greatly retarded the flight of sparks and cinders toward the sky.

As to schedules in those early days, there were none, other than perhaps a posted time of departure from the starting terminal of the line; at stations along the way, the due time was the arrival time. A few of the early lines did post in their stations sheets called "Arrangement of Trains," which were the forerunners of the timetables to come.

In those long-distant days there was no standard time, as we know it today—that didn't come until 1883. The early railroads operated their trains on "Sun Time," which varied by, and even within, localities. The populace of cities and neighborhoods through which the rails stretched had their own and very pronounced ideas of time. In Boston, for ex-ample, some of the leading jewelers would set up their own standard time, and defend it with religious fanaticism. Philadelphia's time was five minutes slower than New York City's but five minutes faster than Baltimore's. There were in the neighborhood of twenty-five different times in Michigan and about the same variance in Illinois; when it was noon in Chicago it was 12:31 in Pittsburg and 12:13 in Cincinatti.

From these brief references it may be seen what obstacles the railroads faced with the great variance of time in different localities. When Professor Dowd, of Temple Grove Seminary for Young Ladies at Saratoga Springs, New York, urged the adoption of four standard time belts for the nation, the rail-roads put the professor on the bandwagon, so to speak, and pushed hard. In 1872 a number of rail-road officials met in St. Louis and organized "The General Time Convention," which had for its goal a practical solution, or rather a workable system, of Professor Dowd's plans. They named William Allen, Chief Engineer of the Camden & Amboy Railroad, Secretary of the organization. There were

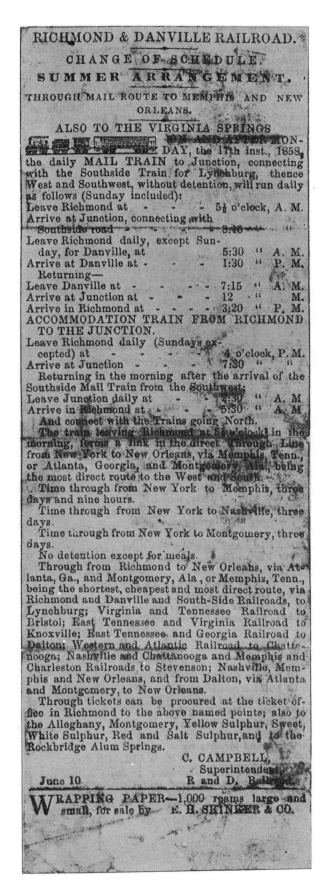

RICHMOND & DANVILLE RAILROAD.

CHANGE OF SCHEDULE.
SUMMER ARRANGEMENT.

THROUGH MAIL ROUTE TO MEMPHIS AND NEW
ORLEANS.

ALSO TO THE VIRGINIA SPRINGS

ON AND AFTER MON-
DAY, the 17th inst., 1858, the daily MAIL TRAIN to Junction, connecting with the Southside Train for Lynchburg, thence West and Southwest, without detention, will run daily as follows (Sunday included):

Leave Richmond at - - - 5¼ o'clock, A. M.
Arrive at Junction, connecting with
Southside road - - - - 8:15 " "
Leave Richmond daily, except Sun-
day, for Danville, at 5:30 " A. M.
Arrive at Danville at - - - 1:30 " P. M.
Returning—
Leave Danville at - - - - 7:15 " A. M.
Arrive at Junction at - - - 12 " M.
Arrive in Richmond at - - - 3:20 " P. M.

ACCOMMODATION TRAIN FROM RICHMOND
TO THE JUNCTION.

Leave Richmond daily (Sundays ex-
cepted) at 4 o'clock, P. M.
Arrive at Junction - - - 7:30 " "
Returning in the morning after the arrival of the Southside Mail Train from the Southwest:
Leave Junction daily at - - 3:30 " A. M.
Arrive in Richmond at - - 5:30 " A. M.
And connect with the Trains going North.

The train leaving Richmond at 5¼ o'clock in the morning, forms a link in the direct Through Line from New York to New Orleans, via Memphis, Tenn., or Atlanta, Georgia, and Montgomery, Ala., being the most direct route to the West and South.

Time through from New York to Memphis, three days and nine hours.

Time through from New York to Nashville, three days.

Time through from New York to Montgomery, three days.

No detention except for meals.

Through from Richmond to New Orleans, via At-lanta, Ga., and Montgomery, Ala., or Memphis, Tenn., being the shortest, cheapest and most direct route, via Richmond and Danville and South-Side Railroads, to Lynchburg; Virginia and Tennessee Railroad to Bristol; East Tennessee and Virginia Railroad to Knoxville; East Tennessee and Georgia Railroad to Dalton; Western and Atlantic Railroad to Chatta-nooga; Nashville and Chattanooga and Memphis and Charleston Railroads to Stevenson; Nashville, Mem-phis and New Orleans, and from Dalton, via Atlanta and Montgomery, to New Orleans.

Through tickets can be procured at the ticket of-fice in Richmond to the above named points; also to the Alleghany, Montgomery, Yellow Sulphur, Sweet, White Sulphur, Red and Salt Sulphur, and to the Rockbridge Alum Springs.

C. CAMPBELL,
Superintendent.
June 10. R and D. Railroad.

WRAPPING PAPER—1,000 reams large and small, for sale by E. H. SKINKER & CO.

An "Arrangement of Trains" which preceded timetables. (Courtesy Southern Railway System)

many obstacles to overcome and it was not until November 18, 1883, that Allen's plan was adopted and put into effect.

Engineers then were not concerned with the comfort of passengers, and when some of them pulled the throttle out, high beaver hats took a backward dive. The car brigades pulled by these pioneer locomotives were coupled by hand with about three feet of chain; in starting, stopping, and even changes of speed while under way, the twenty or more feet in slack would bang the cars together or stretch them out with such force that frequently passengers were thrown about inside like chessmen on an upset board.

There were frequent occasions when brigades broke from the reaction of coupling slack. Then, too, there were accidents originating from other causes. Perhaps one of the first passenger fatalities in rail travel occurred on the Columbia Railroad in Ohio in the early fall of 1836; a mother and her child were killed when a broken axle let the carriage down on the track while the train was under way.

Another fatal accident occurred on June 21, 1837, on the Boston & Providence; for causes never explained, a car loaded with lumber jumped the rails and turner over. The account of this unfortunate occurrence stated in part, "Riding on top of the lumber-laden car were a number of passengers, two of whom, Dennis Conder and William Kervin, Irishmen, were killed." Apparently this was a mixed train, and all available space in passenger cars having been sold, accommodations were offered atop the freight cars.

Frequently the spikes holding down the light bar-iron rail (laid on timbers) would work loose. Sometimes it was a front wheel of the locomotive that ran under the raised rail-end. When this occurred, the entire fifteen-foot section was apt to reach for the sky, derailing the engine with sometimes serious complications. On other occasions the engine and tender might pass over the joint and the "snake-head" raise just in time to head through the wooden floor of a passenger car. When this occurred there were sometimes serious and painful injuries to one or more passengers as they sat braced as best they could on the longitudinal wooden seats. So frequent were these encounters with snakeheads that sledge hammers and spikes on cars were as much a part of standard equipment as the tire-pump and jack would later become with the well-equipped automobile.

63

Captain and engineer compare time before starting the run. (Courtesy Norfolk & Western Railway Company)

In 1842, twelve years after *Best Friend of Charleston* made her auspicious run on the Charleston & Hamburg, Charles Dickens was taking in the sights on this side of the Atlantic. The famous writer was so impressed (although unfavorably) by a memorable trip he made over the Nashua & Lowell line (later to become part of the Boston & Maine) that upon his return home he made some comments relative thereto in his *American Notes*:

There are no first or second class carriages, as with us, but there is a gentleman's car and a ladies car; the main distinction between which is that in the first, everybody smokes; and in the second nobody does. . . . The train calls at stations in the woods, where the wild impossibility of anybody having the smallest reason to get out is only to be equalled by the apparent desperate hopelessness of their being anybody to get in. . . . It rushes across the turnpike road, where there is no gate, no policeman, no signal—nothing but a rough wooden arch, on which is painted, *When the Bell Rings, Look Out for the Locomotive.*

On it whirls headlong, dives through the woods again, emerges in the light, clatters over frail arches, rumbles upon the heavy ground, shoots beneath a wooden bridge which intercepts the light for a second like a wink, suddenly awakens all the slumbering echoes in the main street of a large town, and dashes on haphazard, pell-mell, neck or nothing, down the middle of the road.

On, on, on . . . tears the mad dragon of an engine with its train of cars; scattering in all directions a shower of burning sparks from its wood fire; screeching, hissing, yelling, panting, until at last the thirsty monster stops beneath a covered way to drink. The people cluster round, and you have time to breath again.

In the above article, Mr. Dickens gave his version of what it was like to ride on an American railroad in those early days.

3
Pioneer Railroads

Since the steam locomotive and the train it hauled were so inextricably bound together with the whole, the railroad line, we must briefly discuss some of those early lines.

Colonel John Stevens should without question be considered the father of American railroads. His first interest in the steam engine was its use to power boats, and in 1803 he patented a multitubular boiler as well as screw propellers for driving boats. In 1807, this early-day engineering genius, then sixty years old, built the *Phoenix*, a side-wheel steamer. Prevented from plying the waters of the Hudson by the monopoly of Fulton and Livingston, he put his boat under command of his son, Robert, a brilliant engineer in his own right, and in 1808 sent the ship to Philadelphia. On this voyage the *Phoenix* proved her seaworthiness (and Robert his ability as a skipper) by taking a violent storm before putting into Barnegat; doubtless this was the first steam-driven craft to navigate the open sea. Arriving at Philadelphia, she was put into ferry service between that city and Trenton, New Jersey, where she successfully operated for a number of years.

Colonel John, the prophet, who in 1812 had prepared a pamphlet entitled "Documents tending to prove the superior advantages of Railways and Steam Carriages over Canal Navigation," was even then endeavoring to have the New York legislature see the advantages of a railroad as against the Erie Canal—but as most prophets, he was ahead of his time. Never a man to give up, Stevens applied for and received from his home state of New Jersey in 1815 a charter to build and operate a railroad from New Brunswick to Trenton. For lack of finan-

cial backing this came to naught. Giving up the plan he stated, "The public mind was not sufficiently enlightened to induce moneyed men to embark their funds in a project then considered wild and impracticable."

Col. Stevens then cast his eyes westward and proposed to the Pennsylvania legislature that they give serious consideration "to the expediency of a railroad from Philadelphia to Pittsburg." On March 21, 1823, Col. John, Robert Stevens, Stephen Girard, and Horace Binney, as incorporators, received a charter for the construction of a road from Philadelphia to Columbia. The charter stipulated that the motive power for the road was to be steam and that the name should be Pennsylvania Railroad Company.

Now 76 years of age, the intrepid prophet, leading his fellow incorporators, proceeded with surveys, and upon completion endeavored to raise capital by popular subscription. But these farsighted men were looked upon as impractical dreamers and their efforts were to no avail. Perhaps disgusted but undismayed, Col. John returned to his estate in Hoboken —and not only built himself a locomotive but also a railroad on which to run it.

In 1826 the legislature repealed the Stevens charter; however, it passed an amendatory act that would keep the project alive, also the name Pennsylvania Railroad. In 1828 the legislature enacted a law providing that the Pennsylvania Railroad should be built with state funds, appropriating two million dollars for the construction of forty miles (twenty miles from each terminus—Philadelphia and Columbia). The forty miles of line was completed in

Remains of old roadbed on Portage Railroad (Pennsylvania), a 36-mile line between Holidaysburg and Johnstown which went over the Allegheny Mountains. Rails have been removed but stone sills on which they were laid remains. Picture made near Hollidaysburg, Pennsylvania. (Courtesy Pennsylvania Railroad Company)

ger bound for Pittsburg could leave Philadelphia by rail and travel the 82 miles to Columbia. At Columbia he would leave his railroad car and take passage on a canalboat, which plied the waterway paralleling the Susquehannah to its confluence with the Juanita, thence paralleling this river to Hollidaysburg, a total distance by canalboat of 173 miles. Here, the passenger would disembark and again travel by rail the 26 miles to Johnstown. However, the grades were too steep for a locomotive and stationary engines would haul the cars by cable over ten inclined planes enroute. Perhaps a bit weary and somewhat concerned for his safety, the passenger was happy to reach Johnstown where he could again enjoy the restful canalboat in its peaceful and quiet movement over the 106 miles to Pittsburg.

The Pennsylvania got a lucky break in 1834 when John Edgar Thompson became associated with the road as Chief Engineer. Having served earlier in the same capacity for Col. John Stevens on the C & A, gone to England to make a study of the railroads there, and still later served with the Georgia Railroad, this man had much to offer. Through his foresight, John Thompson, abrupt and difficult though he was, is today recognized as one of the greatest all-around railroad men of all time. He later became president of the road, and the Pennsylvania grew to become one of the greatest railroads of the country.

November 1829, but since all of the appropriation had run out, eighteen months was required to wheedle more wherewithal from the legislature; an additional 800,000 dollars was made available in March, 1831.

By 1834 the road had been completed its entire eightly miles and on April 16th was officially opened with fitting ceremony provided by state dignitaries. The horse was the motive power at first, and any individual wishing to do so could pay the required toll and put his horse and wagon on the line. Frequent altercations occurred when two drivers, coming from opposite directions, met at or near a turnout and a fist-fight usually decided who had the superior rights to the mainline.

The Pennsylvania Railroad had one of the most remarkable systems in existence in 1845. A passen-

The Pennsylvania, as we know it today, is not unlike many other great rail systems in that it is composed of many individual small lines which originated in the early days. It will be recalled that Col. John Stevens had apparently given up this road, of which he was one of the original incorporators, gone back home, and got the 61-mile Camden & Amboy (later a part of the Pennsylvania) under way. Col. John's freight trains were doing a lucrative business hauling vegetables, fruit, and livestock; on one consignment thirty tons of green corn had moved over the line. Passenger business was also brisk, despite the fact that the coaches were more uncomfortable than usual during the winter months when "children of Bordentown made considerable pocket money by selling heated bricks to chilly passengers."

A passenger in those early days has left a typical account of a trip over Col. John's C&A. Having debarked from a New York steamer at South Amboy, our passenger went into the railroad station

Monument to old Portage Railroad, built from stone sleepers that carried the rails of the old railroad. (Courtesy Pennsylvania Railroad Company)

The 26-mile railroad from Hollidaysburg to Johnstown was so steep in some places that inclined planes were necessary. At these locations cables operated by stationary engines pulled the cars up the plane. (Courtesy Pennsylvania Railroad Company)

At the top of the inclined plane. (Courtesy Union Switch
& Signal Company)

Approaching the top of the inclined plane. (Courtesy
Union Switch & Signal Company)

The *George Washington,* a 4-2-0 engine built by William Norris of Philadelphia, with 48-inch drivers and weighing just short of 15,000 pounds, was put into service in 1836. Operating on the 13-mile level between plane 1, at Styple Ben Tunnel, and the foot of plane 2, near Portage, this locomotive showed her tractive power when on July 10th she pulled ten tons up the Belmont Plane. This was a 2800-foot-long grade rising 377 feet to the mile. Previously, traffic over this plane had been handled by stationary engine and cable, but with a steam pressure of only 60 pounds *George* walked the grade at a speed of 15 miles an hour. (Courtesy Pennsylvania Railroad Company)

No. 166, originally built for the Philadelphia and Columbia Railroad in 1853 and named the "Wheatland." This photo shows the old No. 166 as it appeared after being rebuilt at the Altoona shops. (Courtesy Pennsylvania Railroad Company)

The decorative stage for the locomotive had begun about 1850 and when Baldwin turned the *Tiger* over to the Pennsy in late 1856 she was really a dressed-up lady. On the sides of the headlight were painted jungle scenes and following was a stack as black as pitch; next came the bright bronze bell swung on a vermilion hanger. Her domes were black with brass collars, with their fluted tops decorated with brass, and their bases resting on a blue boiler; her leading trucks and four drivers were vermilion red. The cab-panel carried a painting of a Bengal Tiger on a stalk in an emerald green jungle. The tender was done in rose with a fancy ribbon, edged in gold, gaudily carrying the railroad's name. She must have been the pride and joy of her crew, but the wipers in the roundhouse probably cursed the day she was made. (Courtesy Pennsylvania Railroad Company)

and after stating where he was from and where he was going, purchased a ticket and boarded his coach "through the side door." The gentleman was so impressed that he later recorded, "The engine proper had only four wheels. Ahead of it pushed a cow-catcher, which had two wheels under it. The cow-catcher was a wooden arrangement about four feet long, and looked to me like a big stove grate, and was not more than two inches above the rail. It had three very sharp hooks fastened on it, which was bound to hold a cow or anything else that it would run against.

"On the rear end of the tank, setting up high, there was a coop which looked like those old style sulky tops. There is where the guard (conductor) would sit. His duty was to watch the rear end of the train in case it broke. At first I did not know what they were for." Incidentally, the above description clearly fits the Stephenson-built locomotive, *John Bull*, mentioned earlier. The cow-catcher was an innovation of Isaac Dripps, and there is more than one recorded instance of its catching a cow.

Such conditions as cited, however, were not to

No. 325, a neat little 4-4-0 built by Baldwin in July 1864, and her sister, 331 (built the same year), ready to pull out of West Philadelphia with President Lincoln's funeral train. (Courtesy Pennsylvania Railroad Company)

The Pennsylvania Railroad's fleet Congressional Limited as it appeared in 1900, fifteen years after it began to ply between Washington, Baltimore, Philadelphia and New York. The cars were painted olive green with cream color between the windows. In this drawing the train is drawn by engine No. 4 of the Philadelphia, Wilmington & Baltimore Railroad, now an integral part of the Pennsylvania System. The Congressional, now completely refitted with stainless steel cars of ultra-modern design, has carried more famous personages than any other train in the world. (Courtesy Pennsylvania Railroad Company)

remain long, for the well-heeled, farsighted, and progressive citizens of the Quaker State now wanted a real railroad and decided to remove the road from political dominance. Spurred on by the development of "foreign competitors," principally the Baltimore & Ohio and the New York & Erie, a new charter was obtained in 1846. Sixty thousand shares of the new corporation were quickly subscribed, and on February 25, 1847, the Pennsylvania Railroad Company was a reality. This great system has justified its slogan—Standard Railroad of the World.

Like the Pennsylvania (after business men took over), but unlike many of the railroads springing up in every direction in those early days, the Baltimore & Ohio Railroad came about through the vision of far-seeing, financially able, and hard-headed business men.

Baltimore had been one of the leading seaports of young and growing America since the Revolution. To the north, New York had recently opened the Erie Canal (in spite of Col. John Stevens' endeavor to sell the idea of rail lines "stretching from the East to Pittsburgh, even into Ohio and toward the Great Lakes"); then, too, the handwriting on the wall clearly evidenced Philadelphia's intention of really going after the seaboard business.

Prodded by these signals ringing in their ears, leading citizens of Baltimore began holding informal meetings to discuss ways and means of stemming the tide of competitors. At a meeting held in February, 1827, a committee was appointed to "look into the matter of a railroad extending from Baltimore to the Ohio River"; within a very short time this committee reported back that "A double RAIL-road

should be built and that the legislature should immediately be asked to grant a charter for the road . . . its corporate name to be Baltimore & Ohio Railway . . . with a capitalization of 5 million dollars."

Five million dollars was a lot of money in 1827, but those men of action meant business and forthwith contacted attorney J.V.L. McMahon to draw a charter. Mr. Sholes' first typewriter was then nearly fifty years in the future, so realizing the urgency of the matter McMahon went into action with a pen. As soon as the document was completed the attorney called the group together and read it aloud. During the reading one of the interested listeners interrupted, "Stop, man! You are asking for more than the Lord's Prayer!"

Pausing a moment the attorney explained, "All this is necessary. The more we ask for, the more we'll get." (He was a man well versed in politics.)

A good business man, the questioner bawled, "Right, man, go on!"

Evidently the request was favorably received by the legislature, for on February 28, 1827, the charter was granted—with one slight change: the corporate name was to be Baltimore & Ohio Railroad Company.

With the stock offering oversubscribed, Philip E. Thomas became the first president and his banker-associate, George Brown, treasurer. One of the directors was 91-year-old Charles Carroll, a signer of the Declaration of Independence, and, surrounded by a crowd estimated at over ten thousand, Mr. Carroll turned the first dirt as the cornerstone of this great railroad was laid at Gwyn's Run on July 4, 1827. Straightening up, his hand resting on the handle of his spade, the venerable gentleman remarked, "I consider this among the most important acts of my life, second only to my signing the Declaration of Independence, if even it be second to that."

By January 1828, part of the road had been

Pennsylvania Special, forerunner of Broadway Limited,
ng water on the fly in the late '90's (action cameras
e a bit slow then). (Courtesy Pennsylvania Railroad
npany)

The 6495 on the head end of the Broadway Limited in the
late 1920's. This was a beautiful train with de luxe equipment on a twenty-hour schedule between Chicago and New
York. This train and the Central's Twentieth Century
Limited were on identical schedules and were hot competitors. Coming east out of Chicago, the tracks of the
two lines paralleled each other for several miles toward
Gary, Indiana, and as the two trains ran side by side the
race between them afforded real excitement to many of
the passengers. (Courtesy Pennsylvania Railroad Company)

Mr. Carroll stands erect after turning the first spade
at the laying of the first stone at Gwyn's Run, July 4, 1827.
(Courtesy Baltimore & Ohio Railroad Company)

Replica of the "Windwagon" that was tried out on Carrollton Viaduct in January 1828. (Courtesy Baltimore &
Ohio Railroad Company)

Horse-on-treadmill motive power. (Courtesy Southern Railway System)

graded and a few miles of track laid. It had been the intention to use horses as motive power on the new line; however, President Thomas' brother had somewhere heard about a wagon propelled by sails. Accordingly, a wagon was fitted up with canvas and hauled up the grade to Carrollton Viaduct, where it awaited a favorable breeze. The breeze finally came and under full sail the wagon moved off in grand style.

It is evident that all of the viewers were not sufficiently impressed with the demonstration, perhaps feeling that dependence could not be put in the whimsical breezes, and very shortly a horse in a treadmill-car demonstrated his abilities to furnish motive power. Dobbin and the treadmill got along famously for a few days—until a cow wandered on the track ahead, considerably exciting the motive power; in the ensuing smashup several passengers were injured, the horse suffered a broken leg and had to be destroyed, and the treadmill itself was wrecked beyond repair.

After the horse-treadmill incident, the conclusion was reached to resort to "known-to-be reliable motive power," and horses walking in a towpath pulled the wagons and carriages for several months. During this period the horses were changed at a station appropriately named "Relay," seven miles west of Baltimore. Relay is still a station on the B&O.

As mentioned in a preceding chapter, Peter Cooper had built a little miniature steam locomotive of odds and ends with the idea of interesting the B&O in this type of motive power. Convinced by the performance of Cooper's *Tom Thumb* that "steam was the thing," the powers-of-the-road on January 4, 1831, advertised for four locomotives,

Phineas Davis's second creation was the *Atlantic*. The watchmaker, now Master Mechanic for the road, put some improvements into this engine, which went into regular service in 1832 and served well until 1892. On her runs she frequently reached speeds of up to 60 miles an hour. The little grasshopper is to this day a ready engine and frequently is fired up on special occasions. (Courtesy Baltimore & Ohio Railroad Company)

The watchmaker's masterpiece, the locomotive *York*. Phineas Davis's creation was put into regular service in 1831, pulling the York Express over the 13-mile run between Baltimore and Ellicott's Mills. The time card gave the *York* 60 minutes for the run each way. (Courtesy Baltimore & Ohio Railroad Company)

offering a prize of four thousand dollars for the best American-built engine. Trials for the competition were set for June 1, 1831.

Phineas Davis, a watchmaker at York, Pennsylvania, heard about the advertisement and, having become interested in locomotives, set about building an entry for the competitive prize. Although the watchmaker had to work night and day to make the deadline, Phineas had his engine ready in early May. Loading his entry, christened the *York,* on a wagon, Davis and his team of oxen set out over the sixty miles of mountain road toward Baltimore.

The *York* not only laid all competition in the shade at the June 1st trials but was immediately

purchased by the B&O; a condition of the purchase was that the *York's* builder accept a position with the road; agreeing, Phineas Davis became the first Master Mechanic for the B&O. Davis was immediately requested to build a second locomotive, and in the summer of 1832, the *Atlantic* went into regular road use, where it served creditably for the next sixty years, until 1892—when the great little engine, which had done 60 miles an hour on many occasions, was retired.

The B&O was on its way to becoming a real railroad by this time and its progressive management kept up with the times by availing itself of every improvement, notable among which was a car designed and built by Ross Winans. A director of the railroad and publisher of the *Baltimore Gazette,* Winans was an exceptionally versatile man. He had an inventive mind and built models of railroad cars as a hobby; becoming more seriously interested, in

Getting away from the grasshoppers, the *Lafayette* was built by William Norris of Philadelphia. Put in service in 1837, she gave an excellent account of herself. She is still kept in operable condition and has been a "movie star" on several occasions. (Courtesy Baltimore & Ohio Railroad Company)

In 1834 Davis again came up with an improved model, the *Arabian*. This was also a fast engine and served the road well for many years. (Courtesy Baltimore & Ohio Railroad Company)

1832 he built a car sixty feet long which was mounted on four-wheel trucks at each end—the *Columbus*. This was followed by the *Dromedary* and *Sea Serpent*. Later turning to locomotive building, Winans built the *Camel* in June 1848, to be followed by the *Iris, Mars, Phoenix, Apollo, Savage,* and others. By 1858 this man of many interests had built over two hundred engines—over one hundred for the B&O.

When Winans introduced his "new style car of long, enclosed corridor type, with double truck of eight wheels," the B&O was one of his first customers. President Thomas stipulated that a Bible be placed in each car.

All of the pioneer roads really suffered in the great panic of 1837, many not surviving; however, the B&O weathered the storm to go forward and become one of the largest and best run railroads in the country.

No historical sketch of American Railroads would be complete without some reference to "The Work Of The Age," "The Appian Way," "The Bride's Railroad," or some of the other titles that have been given through the years to the Erie Railroad.

Young Henry Pierson and his pretty bride left the wintry blasts around Ramapo, New York, in early December 1830 for a honeymoon in the sunny clime of Charleston, South Carolina. Excitement buzzed around the Charleston Hotel about "The Railroad," and "Most everybody" wanted a ride on this new innovation—a train pulled by a steam locomotive. Anxious to please his wife, Henry busied himself among influential friends until he secured

The top of the stack says the fireboy has his fire right as the 5227 pulls the first Capitol Limited along the Chesapeake & Ohio Canal. This great train was inaugurated May 13, 1923. In 1925, her advertised time was: leave Baltimore 1:52 P.M. Arrive Chicago 9 A.M. (central time) the following day. (Courtesy Baltimore & Ohio Railroad Company)

Nothing was dearer to the heart of an engineer than a hot engine on a fast schedule, and this one is as she hustles the Capitol Limited across Thomas Viaduct, at Relay, Maryland. (Courtesy of Baltimore & Ohio Railroad Company)

82

With the smoke from her stack barely visible, the big 4-6-2 rolls the Limited over a level river stretch of roadbed near Weverton, Maryland. (Courtesy of Baltimore & Ohio Railroad Company)

Still following the water level, the Limited takes a curve
on the Patterson Creek cutoff, not far from Cumberland.
(Courtesy of Baltimore & Ohio Railroad Company)

The 5229 rolling the Capitol Limited west near Cumberland, Maryland. (Courtesy of Baltimore & Ohio Railroad)

With just a wisp of steam spewing from her pop valve and a mere shadow of smoke from her stack, indicating that the fireman has a hot fire and "knows his onions," the Limited takes a grade just west of Cumberland. (Courtesy Baltimore & Ohio Railroad Company)

86

A heavy coal drag up a grade on Salt Lick Curve, near Terra Alta, West Virginia. Both the engine on the head end and the pusher are really working on this grade. (Courtesy Baltimore & Ohio Railroad Company)

reservations, and when engineer Nicholas Darrell pulled the throttle open on *Best Friend of Charleston* that auspicious and historic Christmas morning in 1830, the honeymooners sat in the first coach (probably holding hands).

When the young couple returned north both were confirmed railfans and never missed an opportunity to tell any listener about "the exciting trip over the Charleston & Hamburg line"; one of the most interested listeners was the groom's father, Jeremiah Pierson. Old Jeremiah was a very wealthy man, operating a cotton mill, nail factory, and ironworks. Still fresh in his mind was a pamphlet put out in 1829 by William C. Redfield, President of the American Association for the Advancement of Science, sketching "the geographical route of a great railway . . . to connect the canals and navigable waters of New York, Pennsylvania, Ohio, Indiana, Illinois, Michigan, Missouri and adjacent states and territories. . . . Opening a free communication at all seasons of the year between the Atlantic States and the great valleys of the Mississippi."

It must be admitted that this "Father of the Erie" really had a vision; nevertheless, the route later followed by the Erie Railroad was pretty generally as Redfield predicted. Ever since reading this prediction, the senior Pierson had on numerous occasions discussed with his son-in-law, Eleazor Lord, a New York financier and insurance company executive, the possibilities of such a venture and the great benefits to be derived from such an outlet for their merchandise. Consequently, young Mrs. Pierson did not have to go far to find a most interested listener whenever she spoke of "her exciting trip to Charleston."

Entranced with the possibilities, Jeremiah and Eleazor got busy. In addition to his abilities as a financier, Lord was quite a public relations man in his day and quickly interested influential citizens. John Duer, a New York attorney, drew up a charter and on April 24, 1832, the state legislature authorized the New York & Erie Railroad to "construct a railroad from New York City, through the Southern Tier of Counties and the village of Jamestown to Lake Erie." This also marked the start of misfortunes that would plague the Erie for many years to come.

Politics were in the saddle from the time the charter was granted the Erie, and there was a battle royal in the legislature between those members representing the canal interests and those in favor of a railroad. Subscriptions to stock were slow and payments slower; however, organization was completed on August 9, 1833, with Eleazor Lord the road's first president. A start at actual construction was still two years away; it was not until November 7, 1835, that ground was broken at Deposit, a little town on the Delaware River a few miles east of Binghamton. In the meantime Lord had resigned as president in January 1835 and had been succeeded by James Gore King, another financier.

From early records it appears that Lord had some very pronounced and also revolutionary ideas about building a railroad; he insisted that the guage should be six feet (it was, and later cost nearly a hundred million dollars to change over to standard) and that much expense of grading and maintenance could be saved by laying rails on piles. King disagreed with these ideas and worked up enough support to oust Lord and get himself elected president. King had won the first round but not the fight, for in the coming years Eleazor Lord would be in and out as president like a cat at the door of a fish market. King did not have long to wait for trouble, for on December 16, 1835, a devastating fire laid practically the entire lower side of New York City in ruins, which considerably curtailed the much needed funds from stock subscriptions. Following close behind this setback came the terrific panic of 1837. These two occurrences came close to putting an end to the railroad as it was aborning.

Lord regained his chair in October 1839 and immediately proceeded to put into effect his ideas of how a railroad should be built. Through political pressure the state once more appropriated funds, and with subscriptions and loans from outside, Lord went to work in earnest. One of his first projects was to have piles driven over nearly a hundred miles of proposed roadway through the Susquehannah Valley, at an approximate cost of a million dollars (no rails were ever laid over "Lord's Folly," but the piles remained for nearly fifty years).

By the middle of 1841 rail had been laid from the eastern terminus at Piermont (located in a swamp along the Hudson) to Ramapo (where Jeremiah Pierson had his mansion). In spite of the extremely poor financial condition of the stumbling Erie, it wanted all and sundry to know that operations had begun. Coupling the heaviest of their three engines, the 19-ton *Rockland*, to one of its two

Erie's first President, Eleazor Lord. (Courtesy Erie-Lacka-wanna Railroad Company)

passenger coaches and a couple of platform cars, the management made an excursion on June 30th over the line to Ramapo, where the distinguished guests were royally entertained at Mr. Pierson's mansion.

By late September the struggling road had pushed its rails as far as Goshen, and now for a celebration that would make the June excursion pale into insignificance. Invitations had been sent in all directions and when the steamer *Utica* arrived from New York City at 10:30 on the morning of September 23rd it disgorged Governor Seward and his entire staff (both civil and military), Senator Phelps of Vermont, Congressman King of Georgia, New York's Mayor, its Council, Chamber of Commerce,

and Board of Trade, many prominent judges and attorneys, eminent clergymen, and others conspicuous in society and politics—even Messrs. Chatfield, Graham, and McKay, the legislative committee appointed to investigate the affairs of Erie.

Greeted at dockside by "Father" William C. Redfield, other Erie officials, and Washington Irving, whose home was just across the Hudson, the celebrities made their way to the two waiting trains. All stops had been pulled out for this auspicious occasion, and coupled to the first section was the *Orange* (first engine with a cab owned by the road). Engineer Joseph Meginnis waved and bowed as the distinguished passengers got aboard. After the second section, pulled by the *Ramapo,* was filled, the

Jay's Hotel, beside the Erie tracks at Goshen, N. Y., looked like this in 1862. This was a hostelry for sports and fans as they turned out for the Harness Horse Races held at Goshen. Incidentally, the great Harness Horse Stallion, Rysdyck's Hambletonian (Hambletonian Race is named after him) stood in the stable that can be seen to the left in the picture. (Courtesy Erie-Lackawanna Railroad Company)

trains got under way and three hours later thousands of flag-waving and wonder-struck people from the hills welcomed their arrival at Goshen with cheers and music, interspersed with the boom of cannon.

Disembarking, the celebrants were plied with drink and food, and when the stimulants had taken proper hold a deluge of oratory flowed from the celebrities. Evidently James Bowen, who had just succeeded Eleazor Lord as president of the road, was the chief speaker of the evening and, after impressing the gathering that only three brief hours had been required to come from "the shores of the Hudson, through the counties of Rockland and Orange," predicted "within a few years, when the railroad is completed, the fertile hills and valleys . . . will be covered with a dense population . . . and amid these vast solitudes will soon be heard the hum of cities, the abode of prosperous, intelligent and happy souls."

After more drinking and feasting in the Occidental Hotel, hard by the new railroad depot, the party broke up and the trains departed at sunset for the return trip. There was more food and drink on the *Utica* and when she finally tied up at her pier in New York approaching midnight, all voted "Aye!" This had been a great occasion.

It is perhaps well that the brightness was enjoyed while the sun shone, for within a few months dark clouds had obscured it and the road was bankrupt. It looked as if Goshen might remain the western terminus; it did for two years, as the struggling Erie lived from hand-to-mouth.

Regaining strength, the persevering line feebly pushed westward and by June of 1843 had reached Middletown—but stopped there to "catch its wind" for another three years. By 1849 it appeared that the road was breathing its last; an official report by the company stated, in part: "The condition of the road is such as hardly to permit a train of cars to pass over it safely." It was advertised for sale; however, the state again came to the rescue and the execution date was once again postponed. Meanwhile, the canal and stagelines were exerting every effort for the kill; but in spite of its trials and tribulations the determined railroad snaked its tortuous six-foot-path westward through the rugged country of New York, and in early May, 1851, sixteen years after the first shovel had been turned, the last spike was driven at Dunkirk, on the shore of Lake Erie.

Such an occasion as was about to take place called for more than just the run-of-mine notice. President Millard Fillmore and his Secretary of State, Daniel Webster, and other political bigwigs and hangers on, had arrived on the steamer *Erie* in New York the night before and were in place early the next morning at Piermont.

There were so many celebrities to ride this first train from the Atlantic to the Great Lakes that two

90

The steamboat that brought President Fillmore and other notables up the Hudson to Piermont for the inaugural run May 14-15, 1851. When Erie acquired it in 1845 its name was *Iron Witch*; later the name was changed to *Erie*. (Courtesy Erie-Lackawanna Railroad Company)

Riding in majestic splendour, Daniel Webster and his private flat-car looked like this on that famous Erie inaugural run May 14 and 15, 1851.

sections had been made up. The Presidential party (all save one) and other dignitaries occupied seats on the first section. Daniel Webster, who preferred "to see the sights and beautiful scenery along the way," rode on a special car attached to the rear end of the second section. From his comfortable rocking chair, which had been securely fixed to the floor of an open flatcar, Mr. Webster smiled and waved at the milling crowd around the train. In another car (of Mr. Webster's section) Mrs. Henry Pierson, the bride who had started it all twenty years before, occupied a seat beside her husband, who was now a director of the road.

Gad Lyman, chosen to handle the throttle on the President's Special, had been offered any locomotive he desired. Then, as later, engineers had their preferences for engines and, being a "Rogers Man" through and through, Lyman had asked for the new Rogers-built locomotive #100 and, with some derogatory remarks about Swineburne-built engines, had turned down the #71 of that make.

As his watch split the hair at 8:00 A.M. the morning of May 14, 1851, conductor Henry Ayers (nervously, perhaps) waved Lyman ahead and the proud engineer eased his train out of Piermont. Gad was perhaps in a gleeful mood as the 100 skipped

91

Station at Dunkirk in early 1850's. (Courtesy Erie-Lackawanna Railroad Company)

Old picture of the locomotive *Jay Gould*, built by Brooks about 1870 for Mr. Gould's personal use. The fancy filigree work on the tender carried the state seals of New York and New Jersey. A silver framed portrait of Gould reposed in the filigree work between the drivers (Gould was President of the road at this time). Later the engine's boiler was painted white, when she was known as the "Gray Mare." (Courtesy Erie-Lackawanna Railroad Company)

One of Erie's earliest locomotives, the *Tioga.* (Courtesy Erie-Lackawanna Railroad Company)

over the rails. The train had hardly made twenty-five miles, however, when Gad Lyman's buoyancy departed—steam pressure was dropping. The engineer and fireman tried every trick in the trade, but to no avail. The engine became sluggish, balky, then died on a little grade just east of Middletown. Fortunately a freight had taken a siding just ahead, and with as little delay as possible its engine was coupled to the front end of Gad's pride. Charles Minot, superintendent of the road and a real railroader, was one of the passengers, and stopping at Middletown he went into the office of the little telegraph company and wired ahead to have an engine ready at Port Jervis, to take the place of Lyman's.

Gad Lyman must have been a disappointed and humiliated engineer as the President's Special limped into Port Jervis, over an hour late, and stopped in a nest of fuming Erie officials. Nor were his low spirits boosted when Josh Martin backed the Swinburne 71 up to the train, with orders to put it into Deposit, 88 miles away, on time.

Josh must have been elated over this good break and barely cracked the throttle as he eased out of Port Jervis, but power was soon loosed with a steady hand and the 71 was rolling over the mainline like a scared greyhound. Martin made the 34 miles to Narrowsburg in just 35 minutes and now, really in the mood, kept his engine sifting through the dew over the next 51 miles of his run. When he shut her off and the 71 drifted to a stop at Deposit, Josh Martin probably looked at his watch with a big smile on his face; the 71 had made up the hour and five minutes Gad Lyman's Pride had lost coming into Port Jervis. The Fillmore Special was on time!

The first night was spent at Elmira, 274 miles west of Piermont, and on Tuesday afternoon, May 15th, the two specials rolled into Dunkirk on the shore of Lake Erie. That night a celebration was laid; one that perhaps has never been equalled. Several steers and sheep and hundreds of chickens and ducks had given their lives for this occasion, along with a ton of sausage, tongue, ham, loaves of bread ten feet long, and barrels of cider to satisfy the appetites of the celebrants. Old Daniel Webster ate his fill of beans and clam chowder but complained that "the chowder could be improved with generous dashes of Port and Sherry." (He knew good cooking.)

After twenty years of almost insurmountable hardship, this could and perhaps should have been the beginning of smooth sailing for the Erie, but unhappily this was not the case. Understandably, all of the early roads experienced much difficulty, but like some engines, the Erie seemed to be hoodooed. In 1852 there were snow-drifts up to thirty feet high at Dunkirk and passenger trains were sometimes stalled for a week. In 1855 it took five engines on the head of a train nine days to get over the division east of Dunkirk.

It had taken twenty years for "The Work of The Age" to get to Lake Erie. Another twenty to get into Ohio (by leasing the Atlantic & Great Western) and another decade to operate through trains from New York City to St. Louis. Labor strikes and recurring financial difficulties beset the road, and on Wall Street the Erie was slammed around like a basketball between Jay Gould, Cornelius Vanderbilt, Dan'l Drew, and Jim Fisk. But out of the final receivership of New York & Erie was born the modern Erie Railroad, with its double tracks extending all the way to Chicago.

SOME NEW ENGLAND PIONEERS

With few exceptions, notably the Baltimore & Ohio and the Pennsylvania, none of the great rail systems of the East came into being with their later names, which were generally acquired through consolidations and mergers of many small pioneer lines.

We have previously referred to America's first railroad line, the Granite Railway Company of Massachusetts, chartered March 4, 1826, first used to haul granite to the erection site of Bunker Hill Monument.

Although the Middlesex Canal and stagelines were doing a flourishing business in Massachusetts, farsighted New Englanders envisioned the railroad as the ultimate means of transportation for themselves and their goods. In 1829 textile manufacturers had petitioned the state for a railroad from Lowell to Boston, and with Daniel Webster as their advocate secured a charter on June 5, 1830, for the 26-mile Boston & Lowell line. Following close came the Andover & Haverhill and the Boston & Portland; then the Eastern Railroad, joining East Boston to Salem. These are only a few of the more than one hundred small lines that eventually went into the makeup of the Boston & Maine System.

As the fever spread through New England, the Boston & Worcester was chartered in June 1831. Its incorporators must have been really tight-fisted

Erie Superintendent Silas Seymour designed and built Portage Bridge in 1850-52. In all, 1,600,000 feet of pine timber and 50 tons of iron went into this 900-foot span rising 250 feet above the Genesee Falls. Erie's famous little locomotive *Orange* pulled the first train over the structure on August 9, 1852. It was destroyed by fire in 1875. (Courtesy Erie-Lackawanna Railroad Company)

H. J. Saunders, early-day signal man, ready to pull down the line from Middletown. This type handcar was a three-wheeled affair and after getting started required little hand power. (Courtesy Erie-Lackawanna Railroad Company)

Erie's first big shops on the bend of the river at Susquehannah, Pa. For many years this was mechanical headquarters for the road and in 1868 about 20 locomotives rolled off the assembly line. (Courtesy Erie-Lackawanna Railroad Company)

Although built in 1919 by Baldwin, Erie's class K-5 engine
2937 was a far cry from the little woodburners that hauled
the celebrants to Dunkirk in 1851. A beautiful big Pacific.
(Courtesy Erie-Lackawanna Railroad Company)

With a good head of steam on the 3685, the fireman takes his ease in April 1946 as the crack Flying Yankee pulls out of Portland, Maine, for Boston. (Courtesy Boston & Maine System)

The *Highland Light,* built by William Mason in 1867 for the Cape Cod Central Railroad (later part of New Haven System). Mason was noted for the artistic beauty (as well as quality) he built into his locomotives. This dressed-up lady carried some beautiful artwork on her headlight as well as other decorations of the age. Between the drivers was the name of her builder around the border of the circle, highlighted within by a big M. (Courtesy New York, New Haven and Hartford Railroad Company)

A clean-cut little 4-4-0 built by ALCO in 1896 stopped at Merwinsville on a warm fall day in 1897. With steam spewing from the pop-valve, the fireman keeps his eye peeled for the highball signal. Note semaphore in front of station. Top of water tank may be seen on far side of the train. (Courtesy New York, New Haven and Hartford Railroad Company)

with money, for it was April 1834 when the first little locomotive pulled its dinky coaches over the seven miles between Boston and Newton. Probably encouraged by having a railroad in operation, the management went to work in earnest and by the summer of the next year had its rails extending into Worcester. Not only was July 4, 1835, celebrated as Independence Day; the B&W had four trains, carrying 1500 passengers, rolling over the line.

Another early New England road was chartered June 22, 1831, as the "Providence—Boston Rail-road & Transportation Company," more familiarly known as the Boston & Providence. One of the early passengers, perhaps a frock-coated, beaver-topped "proper Bostonian," was not entirely pleased with his trip over the line on July 22, 1835, when he recorded in part, "This morning . . . I took passage on a railroad car to Providence. . . . Other cars were attached to the locomotive, and uglier boxes I do not wish to travel in . . . made to stow away some thirty human beings, who sit cheek by jowl as best they can. The poor fellows . . . squeezed me into a corner, while the hot sun drew from their garments . . . smells made up of salt fish, tar and molasses. By and by . . . twelve beaming factory girls were introduced, who were going on a party to Newport. 'Make room for the ladies!' bawled out the superintendent. 'Come gentlemen, jump up on top; plenty of room there!' . . . Some made one excuse, and some another. For my part, I flatly told him I had belonged to the corps of Silver Grays, I had lost my gallantry and did not intend to move. The whole twelve were introduced and soon made

The 801 was a Baldwin creation for the New Haven in 1904. Note guards over the drivers and the concave plates on pilot for snow removal. Baldwin, as well as other builders, used the 4-4-0 wheel arrangement from the 1840's well into this century. (Courtesy New York, New Haven and Hartford Railroad Company)

Engine 167 ready to pull out with "The White Train," which operated over the New York & New England (later New Haven) between Boston and New York. In the 1890's this was the most luxurious varnish string in the country and ran on a schedule of 5 hours, 40 minutes through the New England countryside. Because the cars were white it was generally known as "The Ghost Train." (Courtesy New York, New Haven and Hartford Railroad Company)

themselves at home, sucking lemons and eating green apples. . . . The rich and the poor, the educated and the ignorant, all herded together in this modern improvement in travelling . . . and all this for the sake of doing very uncomfortably in two days what could be done delightfully in eight or ten."

Later, this road was incorporated into the New York, New Haven & Hartford Railroad Company, with its over two thousand miles of rails stretching through Rhode Island, Connecticut, and Massachusetts.

Earlier, with reference to the locomotive *DeWitt Clinton,* we mentioned the Mohawk & Hudson Railroad, over whose rails it pulled the first steam train operated in New York State on August 9, 1831. This line originally ran between Schenectady and Albany, but the inclined plane at Albany was later abolished and the new route was laid out from Schenectady to Troy.

Dining car, where sumptuous meals (always including Cape Cod oysters) were enjoyed by proper Bostonians and others of the elite. (Courtesy New York, New Haven and Hartford Railroad Company)

The luxurious parlor car on The Ghost Train. (Courtesy New York, New Haven and Hartford Railroad Company)

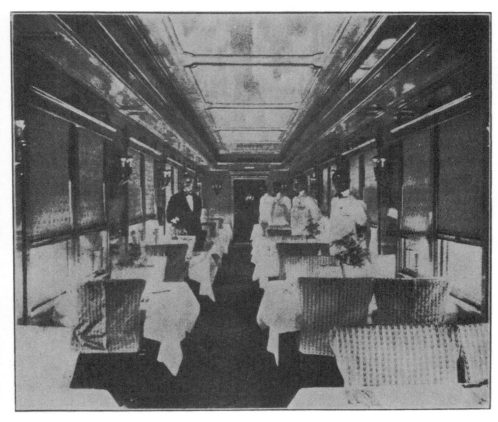

The boys in the diner await their dinner guests aboard the Yankee Clipper. (Courtesy New York, New Haven and Hartford Railroad Company)

The stack of the 1384 has just sent a cloud skyward as the big Pacific (class 1 4 F built by ALCO in 1916) gets the Yankee Clipper under way. (Courtesy New York, New Haven and Hartford Railroad Company)

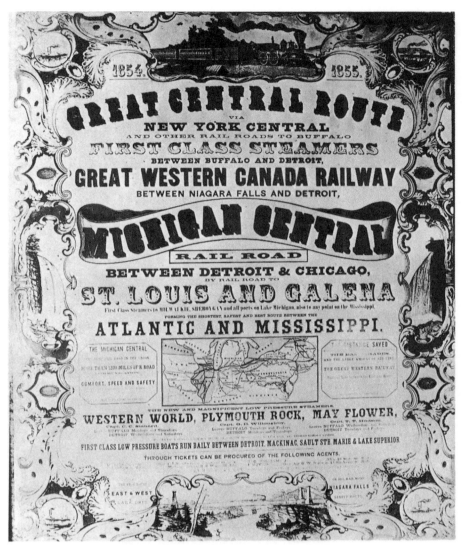

Old New York Central advertisement. (Courtesy New York Central System)

On April 29, 1833, charter was granted and three years later the Utica & Schenectady was in operation. On August 1, 1836, the Mohawk & Hudson had pulled two sections of excursionists from points east to the end of the line, where two new locomotives, each coupled to a ten-car-train, waited with steam up on the tracks of the Utica & Schenectady.

The first problem of its kind was now faced by two railroads: the working out of a joint running schedule for train connections between two different lines. The U&S suggested that the M&H schedule its through trains out of Albany for Utica at 8:00 A.M. and 2:00 P.M. Anxious to please its travelling public, the M&H thought these hours of departure "might occasion much inconvenience since they were the usual hours of breakfast and dinner." But by willing compromise of both roads, through service was effected without difficulty.

As often occurs, the solution of one problem posed another; some of the upstaters were severely criticizing the Utica & Schenectady "for running their trains on Sunday." The railroad published that it was "willing and desirous to discontinue the Sunday service as soon as proper arrangements could be entered into with the several railroad companies and the Post Office Department." Apparently "proper arrangements" could not be made, for the Sabbath runs continued.

Shortly thereafter the U&S again faced problems. These were met and overcome by the adoption of some rules the soundness of which was so apparent that roads all over the country adopted them. One read that westbound trains should run only on the north track, whereas eastbound trains should be upon the south track—according to timetable. Another was that conductors and engineers would

In June 1902, New York Central & Hudson River Railroad inaugurated perhaps the most famous train that ever rolled over rails—The Twentieth Century Limited. This was an all-Pullman, extra-fare train operating between Chicago and New York on a 20-hour schedule to compete with the Pennsy's Broadway Limited (between the same points and on an identical schedule); the fastest engines available pulled it.

Brooks-built 2-6-2 Prairies took over the job soon after inauguration and with their 190,000 pounds resting on 80-inch drivers got the job done; however, there were instances where they climbed the rails.

In late 1903 or '04, the Prairies were replaced with Brooks ten-wheelers. The 604 on the head end of The Century, built in 1900 for the Lake Shore & Michigan Southern (one of Mr. Vanderbilt's lines over which the Century rolled), weighed 172,500 pounds, carried a pressure of 200 psi and when the pistons in her 20x28 inch cylinders thrust the rods to her 80-inch drivers, she could and did really haul the train. This picture was made in late 1903 or early 1904. (Courtesy New York Central System)

The Brooks ten-wheelers gave excellent performance through the years, but as improvements were made they were replaced on the Century run by big Pacifics in the 'teens. Here we see the 3301 carrying green "rags" on one of the front sections as snarling flanges bite the curve along the palisades of the Hudson in the early twenties. (Reproduction of a painting given the author by the Central about 1923.)

compare watches daily with "The Standard Time at Schenectady." Another, that no train should arrive at a regular station ahead of time specified and that passenger trains had the right of way over freight and work trains. Still another made provision for the protection of a stopped train by a flagman by day and marker lights on the rear of all trains at night.

On July 3, 1839, the Syracuse & Utica started operations. Doubtless, many other roads were pestered by "dead heads," however, John Wilkinson, president of the road, seems to have been particularly annoyed by those riding free and kept a diary on the "evil" for several years. The entries in Wilkinson's diary for just a single week listed state officers, judges, congressmen, and other free-loaders to a grand total of nearly two hundred. Determined to put an end to the practice, Wilkinson inaugurated a rule whereby "After July 1, 1849 the only persons allowed to pass free are the officers and men in service of the company."

By 1843, traffic on the rails in upstate New York had grown to such proportions that the roads were considerably disturbed about "the consumption of intoxicants" by some of their operating employees. In January a joint meeting of representatives of the different lines was held and out of this came what was later to be known as the celebrated rule "G": "Resolved, that the several companies upon this Rail Road line will not employ persons in the business of transportation who *ever* drink intoxicating liquors." This was a good rule, but since rules are made to be broken, this was no exception.

By 1853 some eight railroads were working together, forming connecting links over 500 miles of track between Albany and Troy on the east and Buffalo on the west. Consolidation of these small and smaller lines was inevitable. On May 17, 1853, all of the lines entered into a merger, adopting a name that was to be known later as one of the greatest railroad systems in the country—New York Central.

THE ANTHRACITE ROADS

Ever since a wandering woodsman had accidentally stumbled into the stuff in the Wyoming Valley region of Pennsylvania, the natives had known about

105

Always on the lookout for the best to pull the famous century, the Central put 4-6-4 Hudsons by ALCO into service about 1927. The 5271 sifting down the mainline beside the Hudson River was built in 1929 or '30, carried her head of steam at 225 psi, and her 565,200-pound weight rested on 79-inch drivers. (Courtesy New York Central System)

"stone coal." However, so much difficulty had been experienced in using it as a fuel that it had been abandoned as worthless. But in 1771 the blacksmith Obadiah Gore set up his forge beside a spot where there was surface anthracite and used it in his fire. Stone coal was also known to be plentiful in the region of the Lackawanna Valley, but since this entire region of northeast Pennsylvania was wild, raw, and sparsely settled, other fuel was plentiful, and little, if anything, had been done to develop the use of anthracite commercially.

When the war of 1812 cut off the importation of bituminous coal from England, two enterprising Philadelphia merchants, Maurice and William Wurtz, conceived the idea of finding and marketing a substitute. Their quest finally led to the area around Carbondale where they bought up coal lands and engaged in mining in a small way. By the latter part of 1822, the brothers had a thousand tons of anthracite lying on the ground, but there were no transportation facilities to the cities to the east, which might buy their product.

John B. Jervis. (Courtesy Delaware & Hudson Railroad)

Old scene at loading docks on D & H Canal, Honesdale,
Pa. (Courtesy Delaware & Hudson Railroad)

Gravity train at Foster Horseshoe Curve, between Honesdale and Seeleyville, Pa. (Courtesy Delaware & Hudson Railroad)

Promoters in New York had heard of the rich deposits of "stone coal," and on April 23, 1823, obtained a charter for the Delaware & Hudson Canal Company, which would give them transportation means from the Carbondale District of Pennsylvania to New York City and other points. Chief Engineer Benjamin Wright soon made the acquaintance of the Wurtz brothers, and as the interests of the two groups were the same, the miners joined forces with the canal builders. Finding it impractical to construct a canal through the mountainous country between the headwaters of the Lackawaxen River and the Wurtz brothers' mines, Wright's report in 1825 stated in part, "There remains then only a good road, or railway. The latter, I think, will be preferred."

Wright resigned in 1827, and his assistant, John B. Jervis, became Chief Engineer and the first job he undertook was the survey of a railroad route from the canal terminus to Carbondale. Jervis had as his assistant at this time the 25-year-old canal engineer, Horatio Allen; both of these men were destined to later become famous as railroad men.

On October 9, 1829, the first shipment of anthracite was made over the line from the mines near Carbondale to Honesdale, connecting point on the canal. The little line of rails was now busily occupied hauling coal, and within a year the D&H owned nearly 300 "wagons," as the primitive coal cars were called.

On February 16, 1831, the New York Legislature chartered the Saratoga & Schenectady Railroad Company, a little line to run between these two points, "by the power of steam, of animals, or any mechanical or other power." John Jervis was to be

Designed by John B. Jervis, the first locomotive to be put into service by the Saratoga & Schenectady (acquired by D & H in late 1830's) arrived from the Stephenson Locomotive Works at Newcastle in 1833. *Davy Crockett* was a real horse. (Courtesy Science Museum, London)

Old scene at Scranton, Pa., terminal of D & H Canal Co. (Courtesy Delaware & Hudson Railroad)

Honesdale passenger station, a hundred years ago. (Courtesy Delaware & Hudson Railroad)

The yards at Carbondale about 1880. Dobbin still has his job as motive power. (Courtesy Delaware & Hudson Railroad)

An early passenger train at foot of plane at Honesdale.
(Courtesy Delaware & Hudson Railroad)

The loading docks were busy when this picture was made. Apparently all passenger cars had been put in the consist, and to accommodate, a flat car was coupled behind. The train is ready to be pulled up the plane by cable. (Courtesy Delaware & Hudson Railroad)

Chief Engineer, and by the middle of 1832 he had the road completed.

The horse furnished the first motive power, but not for long; soon the John Jervis designed locomotive *Davy Crockett* had arrived from the Stephenson works in England and on July 2, 1833, the engine made her maiden run between Schenectady and Saratoga. In a single week *Davy* moved 3500 passengers, at times heading a train of "eight carriages and three baggage wagons." Although at this time the road was almost strictly a passenger carrier, *Davy* proved her ability as a freight engine when she pulled fifteen tons of freight at a speed of seventeen miles an hour.

Meanwhile, the D&H was not concerned with the frivolity of passenger business and for many of its first years of operation was strictly a freight hauler. Becoming more aware of the possibilities of rail transportation, it slowly began pushing its rails out into neighboring sections of the state of its birth.

Before 1840, the D&H had acquired the S&S and started pushing its rails northward. Almost as the crow flies, it headed north through beautiful upstate New York, finally terminating on the Canadian Border at Rouses Point, where the Richelieu River opens into Lake Champlain.

With its general offices long since moved to Albany, almost at the center of its operations, this pioneer road which has operated under the insignia D&H since Horatio Allen opened the throttle of the Stourbridge Lion, first steam locomotive in commercial service on rails in America, has steadily

A 4-4-0 built by Dickson Locomotive Works, Scranton, Pa., heads President Grant's funeral train. Picture taken Tuesday, August 4, 1885. (Courtesy Delaware & Hudson Railroad)

Perhaps the conductor's solemn expression was brought about by the thin crowd that turned up at the station at Honesdale in 1896 to greet McKinley's campaign train. From the two brooms lashed to the rear end of the car, it must be presumed that Candidate McKinley also had intentions to "Clean up the mess in Washington." (Courtesy Delaware & Hudson Railroad)

This 2-8-0 engine was built by ALCO in 1930 for freight service. With boiler pressure of 500 psi, 20½ and 35½x 32 inch cylinders, drivers 63 inches in diameter, and a tractive effort of 70,300 pounds, this 80-foot-1-inch-long engine and tender weighing 583,500 pounds was really a workhorse. It was appropriately named for the D&H Chief Engineer, John B. Jervis, who surveyed and built the first part of the road in 1828. (Courtesy Delaware & Hudson Railroad)

The D&H proved its appreciation for Horatio Allen when in 1924 it put his name on the 1400. Built by ALCO, the engine and tender had a wheel base of 65 feet, 8 inches, with a total weight of 545,800 pounds. A boiler carrying pressure of 350 psi supplied steam to cylinders 23½ and 41 x30 inches. With drivers 57 inches in diameter, she put forth a tractive effort of 70,300 pounds. (Courtesy Delaware & Hudson Railroad)

The 4-6-6-4 engine 1519, built by ALCO in 1940, puts her 94,400 pounds of tractive effort to a freight drag in 1943. (Courtesy Delaware & Hudson Railroad)

Looking through her smoke deflectors, the 304 takes a curve near Waterford, N. Y., at the head of train #34, crack passenger train between Montreal and New York. (Courtesy Delaware & Hudson Railroad)

A big 4-6-6-4, the 1537, drags a grade on a fast frieght run
near Dyes, "late in the evenin'" of October 26, 1950.
(Courtesy Delaware & Hudson Railroad)

With a good head of steam, this 4-6-2 really rolls the wheels of train #34 near Comstock, N. Y., in midafternoon, March 30, 1948. (Courtesy Delaware & Hudson Railroad)

progressed. Always well managed, this fine railroad that cut its first teeth on the black diamonds of stone coal has always served, and served well, the populace along its hundreds of miles of rails from Pennsylvania to the Canadian Border.

On April 7, 1832, Pennsylvania had granted a charter to the Ligett's Gap Railroad, to operate a fifty-three-mile line from Providence (now Scranton) to Great Bend, on the Susquehannah River. No effort toward construction was to be made for fifteen years, but the charter was kept alive by one of the original incorporators, Dr. Andrew Bedford, who at his own expense had kept it renewed.

Men are always aroused by the actions of others, and in 1847, when the New York & Erie was creeping westward through New York, just across the state line, a group from the Scranton area of Pennsylvania decided to go into action. Foremost among them was George Scranton, who with associates was operating iron furnaces that had already sold rail to the Erie; the group was also interested in coal mines in the area. They approached Dr. Bedford, and arrangements were made for bringing the sleeping line to life.

Almost immediately, Chief Engineer Edwin McNeil started getting his roadbed down to receive the 6-foot-gauge line of rails (weighing 56 pounds to the yard) to be laid on hemlock ties. The mountainous terrain over which the rails would go presented some serious obstacles from the outset. Ligett's Gap was only two miles from the starting point, and when the line had reached Clark's Summit, seven miles from Scranton, it had lifted itself better than 500 feet. Trestles of rough timber, to be later filled with earth, spanned the valleys, and when Ark Swamp Ridge was reached the Tunkhannock Tunnel was blasted through for nearly a quarter of a mile.

Many mules and horses were employed during construction but being "particularly troublesome" at the many trestles, engineer McNeil thought a locomotive "would be most useful." Scranton thought well of the idea and, recalling a wheezing engine he had seen on the Cayuga & Susquehannah, sought to buy it.

Old Puff had been built by Walter McQueen in his shop at Albany in 1836 for the Ithaca & Owego, and since it was the builder's first engine (and probably his last) she had a few shortcomings, among which were joints which kept coming loose, allowing

steam to escape. This was almost a chronic condition that slowed the old girl's pace considerably. James Merrill, who worked for the I&O as a youth, later to become dispatcher at Scranton for the Lackawanna, recalled that frequently horse traders occupied the rear car of *Old Puff's* train, leading their stock at a walk beside and behind.

For two years *Old Puff* was on a schedule that had it leaving Ithaca at 7:00 A.M. and arriving at Owego at 11:00 A.M. Although the distance was only 27 miles, *Old Puff* met the schedule but three times. One of these rare occasions was right after a joint-tightening operation when she made it to Owego ten minutes ahead of time. She must have been in fine fettle on this run, for to celebrate the event she wouldn't be stopped and went right on through the depot.

Old Puff must have become tired and decided to end it all after she went through the station, for a little later she went through a bridge near Candor, killing her engineer and wrecking the bridge. She was dragged from her watery grave in the creek, put under a shed, and replaced with a horse, which Mr. Merrill proudly drove to *Puff's* former train.

Mr. Scranton's emissary found *Old Puff* resting quietly under the shed, put her on a raft at Owego, and floated her down the Susquehannah to Pittston, where she was hauled over a coal company's gravity road to Scranton. After several major operations the old girl was put to hauling ties and rails on the new construction of the Ligett's Gap.

Shortly after *Old Puff's* replacement by the horse, the C&S again turned to steam and sought "a good used locomotive." Recalling the difficulties with *Old Puff,* they wanted a real workhorse this time and, approaching the Reading Railroad, found one, which they christened the *Spitfire.*

By 1850 when the Ligett's Gap was nearing completion, *Old Puff* had become so contrary that she was junked. Her replacement was *Spitfire,* and even though she had totaled nearly two hundred thousand miles, she did a good job for her new owners.

In January 1828, New York State had chartered the Ithaca & Owego Railroad, enabling the line "to haul either freight or passengers . . . to cross streams (and) . . . allowing anyone with proper vehicle to use the tracks on payment of prescribed toll." A further provision of the charter stated, "if any person shall willfully or maliciously injure the said

118

Old Spitfire. (Courtesy Erie-Lackawanna Railroad)

Phoebe Snow. (Courtesy Erie-Lackawanna Railroad)

George W. Scranton. (Courtesy Erie-Lackawanna Railroad)

Railroad . . . the person so offending shall . . . pay to the corporation 3 times the amount of damages." In 1843 the Cayuga & Susquehannah Company took over the I&O (we presume the protective clauses in the charter, together with *Old Puff*, went along with the transfer).

In 1848, George Scranton and William E. Dodge had bought the C&S in order to transport coal from their anthracite fields. They got little but the right-of-way, but by October of 1849 over a quarter of a million dollars had been spent putting the road in working order. On December 17, 1849, the new engine, *G. W. Scranton*, was coupled to its train and made the initial run over the 6-foot-gauge line.

Even though the Ligett's Gap was not completed until late summer, a supplement to its charter on April 14, 1851, had changed its name to Lackawanna & Western. On October 15th all was ready for the first run, and engineer Francis A. Brown busied himself with his oil can around the 29-ton *Wyoming* as she stood with steam up awaiting the arrival of the Erie train at Great Bend. Finally arriving, the distinguished guests from New York got aboard and at the highball signal from conductor Marcus Blair the first Lackawanna train steamed toward Scranton. The next day, a long train loaded with "stone coal" pulled out of Scranton and, using the Erie tracks for a short distance from Great Bend, reached those of the waiting C&S at Owego, from whence it continued on to Ithaca.

After some further mergers the name was again changed to Delaware, Lackawanna & Western. For nearly fifty years the DL&W shunned passengers and was strictly a coal hauler. It not only hauled stone coal but used it for locomotive fuel, which was remarkably clean burning. The line capitalized on this feature around the turn of the century with the advertising character *Phoebe Snow*. Phoebe became as much a living personality as "Chessie," the C&O cat, and had many jingles written about her, such as "My gown stays white from Morn to night, upon the road of anthracite."

RAILS IN THE SOUTH

Virginia's First Railroad

Near the close of the sixteenth century a windstorm uprooted a big pine along Falling Creek near the little settlement of Midlothian, Virginia, laying bare a deposit of coal. Quick to recognize the possibilities of this unexpected bonanza, a few enterprising natives promptly commenced digging operations and hauled their black treasure by wagon to the banks of the James River at Richmond.

Through ensuing years the turnpike (still known as Midlothian turnpike) became a sea of mud in winter and a cloud of dust in summer, from the constant roll of the heavily laden coal wagons. This "inconvenience" to travelers brought frequent petitions to the legislature: "Do something about it." The constant prodding by the petitioners eventually brought action, and in 1828 a charter was granted to the Chesterfield Railroad Company "to run from an intermediary point between the coal pits of Nicholas Mills and Beverly Randolph, south of the Manchester Turnpike, to tidewater at the James River opposite Rocketts in the city of Richmond."

Apparently the original incorporators made no move toward building their road, and since Mills and Randolph were interested in getting their coal transported the twelve miles to Richmond at less than the then going-rate of 8 to 10 cents per bushel (more than a third of the price paid for coal on the docks at Richmond), they decided to do something about it. Accordingly, a new charter was obtained in February 1829, and Nicholas Mills became president. Almost immediately, the celebrated Col. Claudius Crozet, Napoleon's former engineering officer, was engaged to survey the proposed line.

By the fall of 1831, Moncure Robinson, a brilliant young engineer, later to become famous as a pioneer railroad builder, had the road completed. Strap-iron topped the wooden rails over the slight downgrade from Midlothian to Richmond. At the pits, loaded cars were raised on an inclined plane to the top of the embankment from whence they rolled down the 12-mile grade to the docks at Richmond. Crude brakes controlled the downhill speed of the loaded coal trains, all of which carried in their consist one "passenger car" on the rear—to accommodate the horses and mules that pulled the empties back to the mines.

In its first year of operation the Chesterfield moved 20,000 tons of coal, with earnings of $22,-000; in 1835–36, this pioneer hauler of coal moved 85,000 tons, with a revenue approximating one dollar per ton. The coal wagons had disappeared from the turnpike and the railroad had cut the freight rate from 8 to 10 to less than 3 cents per bushel.

The Captain holds his train long enough "to get a picture took" at Boonton, New Jersey, in 1895. Note old musket, fixed to top of headlight. (Courtesy Erie-Lackawanna Railroad)

Remains of old roadbed on Virginia's first railroad. (Courtesy Valentine Museum)

Whitmell Pugh Tunstall, the man who had the vision and gave his all to carry it to fruition. (Courtesy Southern Railway System)

In spite of the fact that no steam locomotive was employed, Virginia's first railroad did a prosperous business for the next twenty years. As frequently happens, its prosperity perhaps contributed to its undoing by giving encouragement to the promoters of the steam-powered line which almost parallel it. In 1851 the Richmond & Danville line was in operation, and in 1856 the little Chesterfield became a part of it.

Virginia's First East-West Railroad

" 'Tis a glorious triumph. . . . 'Tis the proudest day of my life." It was on March 8, 1847, that Whitmell Pugh Tunstall exaltingly spoke these words. The young Pittsylvania County attorney had battled in the Virginia Legislature since 1838 for a charter and at long last his tenacity had borne fruit. November 24th of the same year was even a bigger day, when the stockholders held their first meeting at Charlotte Courthouse and unanimously elected Tunstall President of the Richmond & Danville Railroad Company.

But frequently great chasms yawn between anticipation and realization; not only subscriptions but interest in the railroad itself was sadly lagging. In his first annual report on December 13, 1848, President Tunstall used all persuasive eloquence at his command to get the pocketbooks open. "Virginia, alone in her glory" he said, "seems unmoved either by instincts of interest, or the impulses of ambition. . . . If enterprising and gallant Georgia can send two roads . . . a distance of 500 miles . . . through a country from which she but yesterday drove the Indian, it does seem that Virginia might at least get to her own mountains."

This exhortation accomplished little, however, and constriction of the pocketbook continued to characterize prospective subscribers to R&D stock. In the annual report of December 12, 1849, other troubles were indicated. Landowners along the proposed right-of-way apparently had exalted ideas relative to values. Doubtless, President Tunstall was somewhat vexed when he commented in part, "Land which for ordinary purposes is valued at $2 per acre, and which would not be valued at more than that perhaps, if condemned for a graveyard; nor considered as of greater loss if sunk by an earthquake, is gravely put down at $30 to $40 per acre, if required for a railroad, and assessed at such prices if condemned by it. . . ."

Tunstall was a never-say-die fighter, however, and although progress was slow, construction pushed on. The year 1850 must have been a particularly trying one. President Tunstall's annual report in December referred to lawsuits, injunctions, inability to hire labor, and the scarcity and high price of feed for horses—in addition to the perennial difficulty of finances. In spite of these troubles, however, there was a note of cheer in the report that a stretch of thirteen miles of the road was "complete and in actual running order." (This thirteen-mile section out of Richmond almost paralleled the Chesterfield, and perhaps was largely responsible for the abandonment of that line's operations the following year).

But luck never remains static, and Tunstall's fourth annual report, in November 1851, was very encouraging. Chief Engineer Andrew Talcott had really pushed toward the goal, and the report proudly boasted that the 5-foot-gauge of strap-iron rails stretched all the way to Jetersville—44 miles west from Richmond. In addition, the company now owned three locomotives, 115 freight and three passenger cars; mileage operated for the year totaled 31,735. So elated was President Tunstall over this report of accomplishment that he added, "The rapid roll of the engines and cars, toward the interior, seems at last in some degree to have awakened that portion of the 'unterrified commonwealth,' and 'the mother of statesmen,' from their drowsy slumber and listless torpor."

For two more years this attorney-turned-railroader pushed his dream toward reality. His sixth report, in December 1853, contained the usual financial difficulties common to most of the pioneer roads, but the line had pushed its way 84 miles to Mossingford and grading was completed to South Boston—within 32 miles of the goal at Danville. This was to be the final report of the intrepid railroad builder; Whitmell Pugh Tunstall died of typhoid February 19, 1854.

Virginia's first east-west railroad was completed in the late spring of 1856 and regular scheduled train service was inaugurated in July. Old records of an April 1854 stockholder's meeting mention "Erecting a suitable monument to the memory of the late Whitmell P. Tunstall," but as far as known this was never done. Or was it? In August 1857, the most powerful locomotive on the line was completed in the company's shops. On the side of her cab was the name "W. P. Tunstall," and this engine

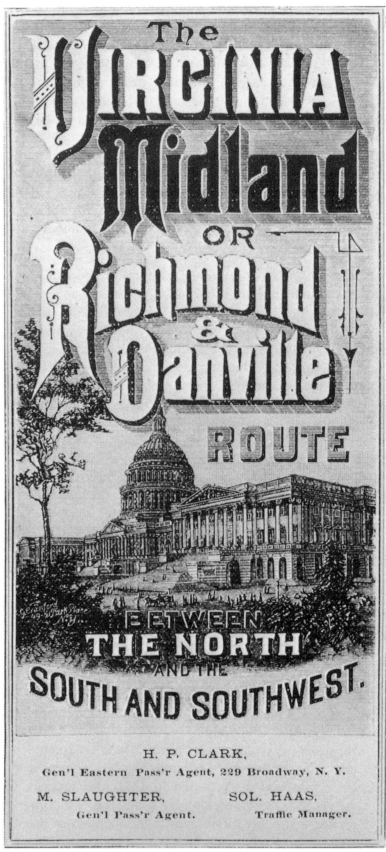

Old advertisement of R&D. (Courtesy Southern Railway System)

started serving the road for which her namesake had dedicated most of his mature life. What more fitting monument could there be to this indefatigable railroad pioneer?

The little strap-iron road was hardly dry behind the ears when it found itself plunged into a drama in which railroads had never before played a part— a war. Battered and broken by four years in the thick of the fighting of the Civil War, the R&D rose from the ashes, shook its bloody head, and struggled to its feet in 1865. Unquestionably, Whitmell Tunstall's vision and do-it-or-die spirit had permeated deep into the minds of those who carried the banner after him. By 1872 it had obtained control of both the North Carolina and the Northwestern North Carolina railroads. A few years later it added the Charlotte, Columbia & Augusta. After catching its breath and getting the feel of a real railroad system, it picked up the Virginia Midland in 1886 (the old Orange & Alexandria and Manassas Gap railroads). By 1890 the Richmond & Danville and East Tennessee, Virginia & Georgia, with their flocks of smaller roads, had been maneuvered under the same direction. Still interested in further expansion, it brought the Alabama Great Southern and Cincinatti, New Orleans & Texas Pacific into the fold.

What a pity Tunstall was not around to witness all that had happened since his hard struggle to get the little R&D from a dream to reality. But this was only the beginning, for in a reorganization in 1894 a new name came into the picture—The Southern Railway Company, parent of the great SOUTHERN RAILWAY SYSTEM.

Understandably, it is not possible in this brief account to comment upon the many pioneer lines that went into the makeup of this great railroad system; however, in just deference to the little pioneer line that was first to inaugurate regular service on an American railroad, it should be mentioned that for nearly three-quarters of a century the South Carolina Canal & Rail Road Company, more familiarly known as the Charleston & Hamburg, has been an integral part of the Southern.

With its network of over 10,400 miles of rails stretching from the District of Columbia on the east to the Mississippi River on the west, and south to the Gulf of Mexico, this great rail system really lives up to its maxim—THE SOUTHERN SERVES THE SOUTH.

When this picture was made in 1883 at Axton, Va., this Danville & Western Railway line had been open only two years. Today it is the Martinsville division of the Carolina & Northwestern Railway, a member line of the Southern Railway System. (Courtesy Southern Railway System)

All and sundry went down to the depot on summer afternoons when the 548 stopped her Cincinatti, New Orleans & Texas Pacific train at Rockwood, Tennessee. Picture taken about 1880. (Courtesy Southern Railway System)

RAIL ROAD CONNECTIONS FROM PHILADELPHIA TO NEW ORLEANS.

Places.	By what Road.	HOURS OF ARRIVAL.	HOURS OF DEPARTURE.
PHILADELPHIA......	Philadelphia, Wilmington and Baltimore............	4.55 P. M.	1.00 P. M.
BALTIMORE	Baltimore and Ohio..................................	5.30 P. M.	5.30 P. M.
WASHINGTON	Orange & Alexandria, and Virginia Central,	7.00 A. M.	7.30 P. M.
RICHMOND........	Richmond and Danville, and South Side............	4.30 A. M.	6.15 A. M.
LYNCHBURG........	Virginia and Tennessee.............................	12.30 P. M.	1.00 P. M.
BRISTOL..........	East Tennessee and Virginia.......................	12.30 A. M.	1.00 A. M.
KNOXVILLE........	Georgia and East Tennessee........................	10.30 A. M.	11.00 A. M.
DALTON..........	Western and Atlantic...............................	5.00 P. M.	5.30 P. M.
CHATTANOOGA......	Nashville and Chattanooga..........................	8.25 P. M.	9.20 P. M.
STEVENSON........	Memphis and Charleston.............................	12.20 A. M.	1.00 A. M.
GRAND JUNCTION....	Mississippi and Central............................	2.00 P. M.	2.30 P. M.
CANTON..........	New Orleans Jackson and Great Northern............	8.30 P. M. (1 day)	7.30 P. M.
NEW ORLEANS......	....	6.00 A. M.	

Passengers to New Orleans can continue on the Memphis and Charleston Railroad to Memphis, and proceed thence to New Orleans by Steamer, or to Vicksburg by Steamer, and thence via Railroad to New Orleans, or can leave the Memphis and Charleston Railroad at Grand Junction, and proceed by the Mississippi Central and New Orleans, Jackson and Great Northern Railroads to New Orleans.

Passengers who wish to go through direct, will leave Philadelphia at 1 P. M., and be sure to PURCHASE THEIR TICKETS VIA ORANGE & ALEXANDRIA R. R., and they will save from Three to Five Dollars on each Ticket to any of the within points.

BAGGAGE CHECKED THROUGH.

☞ The best of Eating Houses on the entire length of the route, and full time allowed for Meals.

NEW BOAT ARRANGEMENT FROM MEMPHIS.

In addition to the Regular Line leaving Memphis for the South every other day, on the arrival of the Train, the Company have arranged with nine other first class Steamers, to fill the intermediate days, making the line daily, and the only point to which Passengers can go and get a Boat South without delay. Meals and Berths on boats included in Fare.

☞ By this Route Passengers are allowed to stop over at any point, and proceed at their convenience.

GREAT SOUTHERN AND SOUTH WESTERN ROUTE

VIA

ORANGE AND ALEXANDRIA

RAIL ROAD

FROM WASHINGTON CITY TO RICHMOND

Danville,	Knoxville,	Chattanooga,	Huntsville,	Montgomery,
Lynchburg,	Dalton,	Nashville,	Memphis,	Columbus,
Bristol,	Atlanta,	Grand Junction,		

AND NEW ORLEANS.

THROUGH TO NEW ORLEANS IN 4 DAYS AND 12 HOURS.

THROUGH TICKETS

Can be obtained at the Offices of the Philadelphia, Wilmington & Baltimore Railroad Co., N. W. Cor. 6th & Chestnut Sts., and at the Depot, Broad & Prime Sts., Philadelphia.

JAS. LUCAS & SON'S STEAM PRESS.

Old advertisement featuring O&A. (Courtesy Southern Railway System)

Drawing taken from old Richmond and Danville Stock Certificate issued in 1856. (Courtesy Southern Railway System)

Old leaflet of North Carolina Railroad, showing mileage between stations but no train times. This advertisement was put out about 1855. (Courtesy Southern Railway System)

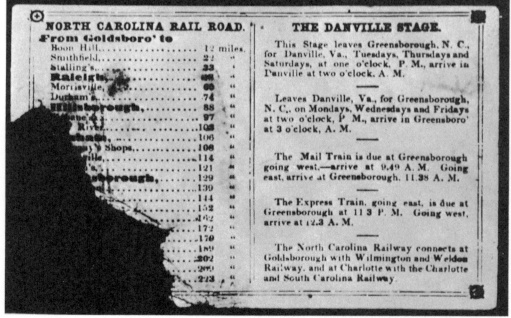

NORTH CAROLINA RAIL ROAD.
From Goldsboro' to

Boon Hill,	12 miles.
Smithfield,	22 "
Stalling's,	33 "
Raleigh,	48 "
Morrisville,	60 "
Durham's,	74 "
Hillsborough,	88 "
....	97 "
River,	105 "
....	106 "
..... Shops,	106 "
......ville,	114 "
......'s,	121 "
.....borough,	129 "
....	139 "
....	144 "
....	152 "
....	162 "
....	172 "
....	179 "
....	189 "
....	202 "
....	209 "
....	223 "

THE DANVILLE STAGE.

This Stage leaves Greensborough, N. C., for Danville, Va., Tuesdays, Thursdays and Saturdays, at one o'clock, P. M., arrive in Danville at two o'clock, A. M.

Leaves Danville, Va., for Greensborough, N. C., on Mondays, Wednesdays and Fridays at two o'clock, P. M., arrive in Greensboro' at 3 o'clock, A. M.

The Mail Train is due at Greensborough going west.—arrive at 9.49 A. M. Going east, arrive at Greensborough. 11.38 A. M.

The Express Train, going east, is due at Greensborough at 11 3 P. M. Going west, arrive at 12.3 A. M.

The North Carolina Railway connects at Goldsborough with Wilmington and Weldon Railway, and at Charlotte with the Charlotte and South Carolina Railway.

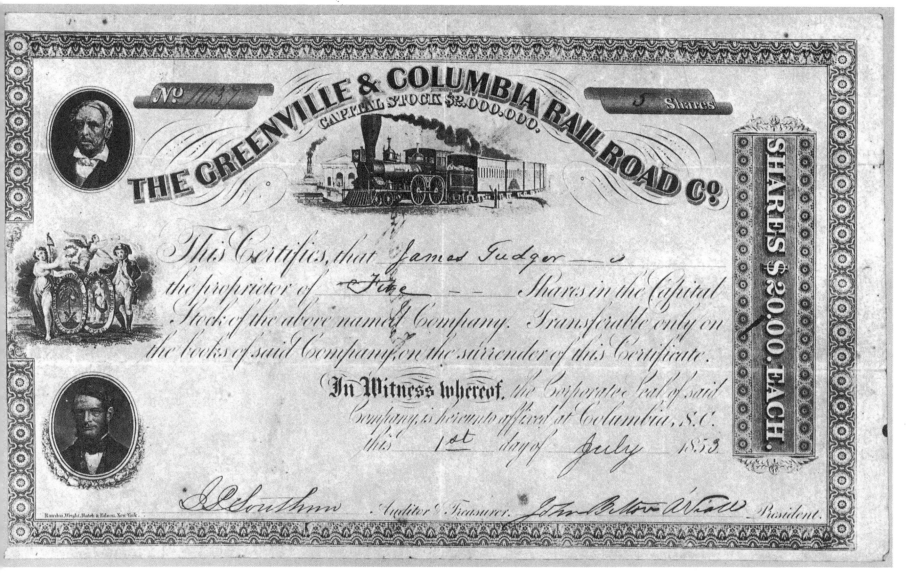

Stock certificate issued by G&C Railroad in 1853.
(Courtesy Southern Railway System)

Memphis & Charleston Railroad yard at Memphis, Tenn.,
sometime between 1880 and 1890. (Courtesy Southern Railway System)

A diamond-stacked wood-burner crosses Gashes Creek trestle about eight miles east of Asheville on Western North Carolina Railroad, one of the Southern's predecessor lines. Tree trunks, with the bark left on, were used for the upright timbers. (Courtesy Southern Railway System)

Office and depot of the Memphis and Charleston Railroad
sometime between 1880 and 1890. (Courtesy Southern Railway System)

The green and gold Pacifics, like the 1394 on the head end of the crack Crescent Limited, were the pride of the road and the South in the 1920's and up into the '30's. Put in service in 1923, perhaps no other 4-6-2 ever matched the symmetry and style of these proud creations of ALCO. (Courtesy Southern Railway System)

A stock certificate issued by the East Tennessee, Virginia & Georgia Railroad in June 1870. The ETV&G was a predecessor line of the Southern Railway Company. (Courtesy Southern Railway System)

Point Tunnel and viaduct over Mill Creek, located on Western North Carolina Railroad, one of the Southern's predecessor lines. (Courtesy Southern Railway System)

Virginia's First Steam Railroad

Even in 1829, farsighted men in Virginia and North Carolina had cast their eyes southward at what was taking place in South Carolina, and with bold vision went into action. On February 10, 1830, a charter had been secured for the Petersburg (Virginia) Railroad, to run its tracks 60 miles south into North Carolina to Weldon.

Virginia's first steam railroad did not have long to enjoy the exalted position, however, for in 1836 the Richmond & Petersburg had laid its 23-mile road south to connect with the little line running to Weldon.

The Wilmington & Raleigh had been chartered by North Carolina on January 3, 1834, but the people of Raleigh were not interested in lending financial support, and on March 19, 1840, it was operating into Weldon instead. With its name changed, in 1855, to Wilmington & Weldon, it gave through rail service (via Petersburg, Richmond & Petersburg, and Richmond, Fredericksburg & Potomac) from Wilmington to Fredericksburg (then terminus of RF&P). Since there were no connecting tracks between the three roads it was necessary for passengers from Wilmington to change cars at Weldon, Petersburg, and Richmond.

In 1869, Baltimore financiers acquired an interest in the three roads, along with some other lines in the two Carolinas, and under this unified management the "Great Atlantic Route" stretched all the way from Charleston to Richmond. Even with these connecting links, problems had arisen; trains coming from the South into Wilmington rolled over a 5-foot gauge, where their trucks had to be changed for the standard gauge North. This costly and inconvenient delay was not remedied until 1886.

In 1898, the little 23-mile line from Richmond to Petersburg swallowed its older and bigger sister running to Weldon; the consolidated lines were called Atlantic Coast Line Railroad Company of Virginia. The same year, a number of small lines in South Carolina merged into the Atlantic Coast Line Railroad Company of South Carolina. Pleased with the new setup, other roads came into the fold in 1900, and two years later a number of smaller lines, making up "The Plant System," were acquired to give the system a mainline from Richmond, Virginia, to Florida. Operating over more than five thousand miles of track, the Atlantic Coast Line Railroad Company is one of the best run roads in the country.

The eye is able to see long distances in level country, such as stretches southwestward from Portsmouth, Virginia, and men stricken with railroad fever easily visualized a line of rails extending to Weldon, North Carolina (77 miles away), southern terminus of Virginia's first steam railroad, the Petersburg. The visioning and talking stage soon inspired one of action, and on March 8, 1832, the legislatures of Virginia and North Carolina granted a charter to the Portsmouth & Roanoke Railroad for construction of a line between Portsmouth and the Roanoke River.

Walter Gwynn made a very interesting report on his survey to president Arthur Emmerson in late 1832. "The line which I have selected," he said, "commences at . . . the Western boundary of Portsmouth . . . and proceeds over an extremely . . . unbroken surface . . . to a few hundred yards north of the termination of the Dismal Swamp Land Company's Canal. Thence the character of the country changes and becomes somewhat bold. Undulations in the plane of the Rail Road are unavoidably made."

Meticulously describing in detail the summits encountered, as well as such metes and bounds as "Jerusalem," "Vick's Chapel," and "Buckhorn Run," Mr. Gwynn reached the end of his report with, "Descending from the summit, the line crosses the Petersburg Rail Road at about 300 yards south of Capt. Garey's [later Garysburg, 2 miles east of Weldon] . . . and terminates on the north bank of the Roanoke opposite Weldon. Its direction is S. 70.2 and its length seventy-seven miles, being only half a mile longer than the distance on a direct line between Portsmouth and Weldon." (This was really hitting the end of the line right on the button.)

Pleased with the line he had laid out, Gwynn added, "The engine which it is proposed to use will not exceed five tons weight, and its performance on the road will be equal to that of a six ton engine on a road with thirty feet grades. From this general view it will be seen that the face of the country is eminently suitable to the proposed work." One last recommendation was the use of "wood sills hollowed out in the middle so as to permit of the construction of a path over them, which will adapt it to use either horse or locomotive power, or both."

This last recommendation of Mr. Gwynn was that of a man with foresight, for when the wooden stringers capped with two-inch-wide strap-iron reached Suffolk (eighteen miles away) on July 27,

The *Edward Kidder* was a creation of the artistic William
Mason for the Wilmington & Weldon Railroad about 1870.
Note unusual trucks on tender, similar to those on Mason's
Highland Light. (Courtesy Atlantic Coast Line Railroad)

A 4-4-0 of a predecessor road of Coast Line. Note top ring
of stack has diameter as large or larger than the boiler.
(Courtesy Atlantic Coast Line Railroad)

133

A/P 5 A Pacific highballs through a high-green on a downgrade near Burroughs, Georgia, in 1928, as she hustles the Florida Special northward.

This de luxe train made its debut in January 1888 on a 30-hour schedule between New York and Florida. Even then it boasted incandescent lights, steam heat, and closed passageways between cars. A little later it was the first electrically lighted all-vestibuled train in the United States, electricity being supplied by a rubber belt from the axle of the baggage car to a generator inside. Interiors of the cars were finished in Spanish mahogany and birds-eye maple and lavishly decorated with French mirrors; cut glass chandeliers hung from carved "Queen Anne" ceilings.

Originally dubbed New York and Florida Special, this varnish job had her name changed to Florida Special about the turn of this century. Still rolling, this is the oldest de luxe train in continuous service on this continent. (Courtesy Atlantic Coast Line Railroad)

One of the first Atlantic types (4-4-2), which incidentally derived their name from having been first built for "Great Atlantic Route" in 1895. The 153 was built by Baldwin in 1896 or '97, and with 200 psi driving her pistons to 80-inch drivers, 80 miles an hour was old hat over the level stretches between Wilmington and Weldon. This picture well illustrates the greater diameter of trailers over leading trucks. (Courtesy Atlantic Coast Line Railroad)

134

The big Pacific 1531 hurtles the Palmetto Limited southward near Monteith, Georgia, in 1929. (Courtesy Atlantic Coast Line Railroad)

Icing refrigerator cars to keep Florida produce fresh for the Northern markets. (Courtesy Atlantic Coast Line Railroad)

With smoke pouring from her stack, the big 4-6-2 is in a hurry with the southbound Havana Special, just north of Hardeeville, South Carolina, on February 1, 1930. (Courtesy Atlantic Coast Line Railroad)

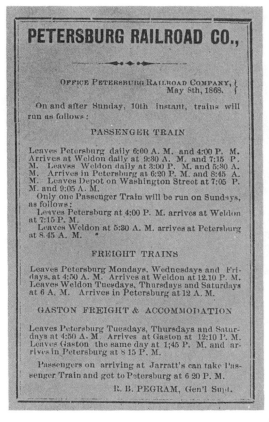

PETERSBURG RAILROAD CO.,

OFFICE PETERSBURG RAILROAD COMPANY,
May 8th, 1868.

On and after Sunday, 10th instant, trains will run as follows:

PASSENGER TRAIN

Leaves Petersburg daily 6:00 A. M. and 4:00 P. M. Arrives at Weldon daily at 9:30 A. M. and 7:15 P. M. Leaves Weldon daily at 3:00 P. M. and 5:30 A. M. Arrives in Petersburg at 6:20 P. M. and 8:45 A. M. Leaves Depot on Washington Street at 7:05 P. M. and 9:05 A. M.

Only one Passenger Train will be run on Sundays, as follows:

Leaves Petersburg at 4:00 P. M. arrives at Weldon at 7:15 P. M.

Leaves Weldon at 5:30 A. M. arrives at Petersburg at 8.45 A. M.

FREIGHT TRAINS

Leaves Petersburg Mondays, Wednesdays and Fridays, at 4:50 A. M. Arrives at Weldon at 12.10 P. M. Leaves Weldon Tuesdays, Thursdays and Saturdays at 6 A. M. Arrives in Petersburg at 12 A. M.

GASTON FREIGHT & ACCOMMODATION

Leaves Petersburg Tuesdays, Thursdays and Saturdays at 4:50 A. M. Arrives at Gaston at 12:10 P. M. Leaves Gaston the same day at 1;45 P. M. and arrives in Petersburg at 8 15 P. M.

Passengers on arriving at Jarratt's can take Passenger Train and get to Petersburg at 6 20 P. M.

R. B. PEGRAM, Gen'l Supt.

Wilmington & Weldon Railroad.

R. R. BRIDGERS, Pres. S. L. FREMONT, Ch. Eng. & Sup.
W. M. POISSON, General Ticket Agent.

Mail.	Mil's	STATIONS.	Mil's	Mail.
A. M.		LEAVE ARRIVE		
		WILMINGTON. 3	162	
	9	North East	153	
	11	Marlboro'	151	
	14	Rocky Point	148	
	22	Burgaw	140	
	29	South Washington	133	
	33	Leesburg	129	
	38	Teachey's	124	
	42	Rose Hill	120	
	48	Magnolia	114	
	55	Warsaw	107	
	59	Bowden's	103	
	63	Faison's	99	
	70	Mount Olive	92	
	75	Dudley	87	
	84	**GOLDSBORO** 2	78	
	95	Nahunta	97	
	102	Black Creek	60	
	108	Wilson	54	
	116	Joyner's	46	
	125	Rocky Mount 4	37	
	133	Battleboro'	29	
	137	Whitaker's	25	
	143	Enfield	19	
	149	Ruggles	13	
	154	Halifax	8	
P. M.	162	**WELDON.** 1	0	
		ARRIVE LEAVE		

¹Connects with Raleigh & Gaston, Seaboard & Roanoke, and Petersburg Railroads.
²Connects with North Carolina and Atlantic and North Carolina Railroads.
³Connects with Wilmington and Manchester Railroad. Also, with Steamers sailing from Wilmington.
⁴Tarboro' Branch.—Trains run between Rocky Mt. and Tarboro', connecting with the Main Line.

Richmond and Petersburg

RAILROAD COMPANY.

On and after Wednesday, the 27th instant, the trains on this road will run as follows:
Leave Richmond at............4 A. M. and 2 P. M.
Leave Petersburg at.....9;15 A. M and 8:45 P. M.
The 4 A. M. Train will not leave Richmond on Mondays, and the 6:45 P. M. Train will not leave Petersburg on Sundays.
Passengers for Norfolk will take the 2 P. M. Train. Fare to Norfolk $4 Baggage checked through.
Passengers for Clover Hill will take the 4 A. M. Train on Wednesdays and Fridays, connecting at Chester with the Coal Train.

E. H. GILL,
Engineer and Superintendent,

WILMINGTON, CHARLOTTE & RUTHERFORD R. R.

R. H. COWAN, President, Lincolnton, N. C.
WM. I. EVERETT, Supt., Wilmington N. C.

Passenger Train on this Road leaves Wilmington on Tuesday, Thursday and Saturday, at 7 o'clock A. M.
Arrive at Sand Hill same days, at 3 P. M.
Arrive at Wadesboro' (Stage,) at 12 midnight.
Leaves Wadesboro' (Stage,) on Tuesday, Thursday and Saturday at 2 P. M.
Leaves Rockingham (Stage,) on Monday, Wednesday and Friday, 4:30 A. M.
Leaves Sand Hill (Cars,) Monday, Wednesday and Friday, at 7 o'clock, A. M.
Arrive at Wilmington same day at 3 P. M.

W. I. EVERETT,
Gen. Sup't

Early advertisements of Coast Line predecessors. (Courtesy Seaboard Air Line Railroad Company)

Early advertisement of Richmond & Danville Railroad.
(Courtesy Seaboard Air Line Railroad)

1834, the motive power was old Dobbin. The editor of *Norfolk American Beacon* was one of the enthusiastic passengers on that first run and the next day carried an account of the trip to Suffolk in a happy vein: "After the enjoyment of 5½ hours, we took leave of our worthy host, and were wafted along this noble road, at a pleasant rate to our homes, in time to refresh ourselves with a good cup of Tea, and retire to bed assured of a good night's repose, by the healthful exercise of the car riding, and the pleasing incidents of our trip. We invite all who enjoy refreshment and recreation from the toils of business and domestic cares . . . to take a ride to Suffolk on the Rail Road."

But this was to be a real railroad, and in less than sixty days after the editor's inaugural train ride his paper announced: "On Wednesday, September 24, 1834, The Locomotive Engine John Barnett, with its train of Coaches and Cars, will commence running between Portsmouth and Suffolk." (Whereas old records of Seaboard indicate that this engine was built in America, its builder or description is unknown.)

At this time another line, far to the south, which would someday become a link in a great rail system, was aborning; Florida's first railroad, the Talla-

hassee, was under construction. On a bright May morning in 1836 it had been completed, and to the accompaniment of band music great throngs of enthusiasts cheered as two mules threw their weight into the collars and the dinky little coach, filled to overflowing, rolled forward on the 22-mile stretch of track toward Port Leon on the Gulf of Mexico. The special held her schedule for the first fifteen miles when the motive power decided it had had enough of railroading and balked. Unyielding to vigorous persuasion, the mules were unhitched, a pair of horses were borrowed from a farmer, and the first train to move over rails in Florida completed its 22-mile run the same day it started.

Meanwhile, the Raleigh & Gaston Railroad had been chartered by the state of North Carolina and the temporary services of Moncure Robinson (builder of Virginia's first railroad and RF&P) were obtained as Consulting Engineer. Although the first spade was turned at Gaston on November 1, 1836, it was mid-March 1840 before President T. P. Devereux saw his 86-mile line creep into Raleigh.

Regular service was inaugurated on March 21, 1840, and the *Raleigh Register* reported, "About six o'clock of that day, the first steam locomotive,

137

A replica of the *Raleigh*, now in her "roundhouse" in
the North Carolina Historical Museum at Raleigh, N. C.
(Courtesy Seaboard Air Line Railroad Company)

138

Following the *John Barnett,* the 10-ton locomotive *Raleigh,* built in England, was put in service on the Portsmouth & Roanoke. A contemporary drawing shows the little 0-4-0, with her engineer standing beside the woodpile, pulling her one-car train. (Courtesy Seaboard Air Line Railroad Company)

ENERGY
GOVERNMENT LOCOMOTIVE, AFTERWARDS SEABOARD & ROANOKE R.R. CYLINDERS 15"x24" DRIVERS 4'6".
BUILT AT PATERSON, NEW JERSEY. 1862.

The dressed-up *Energy* was built by Rogers in 1862 for the U.S. Government. Later acquired by Seaboard & Roanoke. The fluted dome, elaborately scrolled bell hanger, hand painted headlight, and other fancy work came with the purchase. With her balloon stack she looks as though she might have lived up to her name. (Courtesy Seaboard Air Line Railroad Company)

Forty years after the *Tornado,* the R&G had gone to real
class in its motive power. The 214 even boasted air brakes.
(Courtesy Seaboard Air Line Railroad Company)

The builder of *Tornado,* Raleigh & Gaston's first locomotive, is not known, but she was a horse in her day—
1840 and later. (Courtesy Seaboard Air Line Railroad
Company)

Turntables served as pedestals as well as for turning engines. The 420 was built for SAL predecessor Carolina Central in the 1880's and served well even into this century. (Courtesy Seaboard Air Line Railroad Company)

Picture used to advertise "The Atlanta Special," the all-Pullman inaugurated in 1895 between New York and Atlanta over the route of "The Seaboard Air Line." It is doubtful that the speed indicated on the picture was her average; however, it must be said that the train in all probability did roll at this high speed on the stretch over the Carolina Central tracks shown in the sketch below. (Courtesy Seaboard Air Line Railroad Company)

141

TIME TABLE

FROM

NEW YORK to ATLANTA, GA.

Trains Leave.	MILES.	May, 1868.	MILES.	Trains Arrive.
A. M. 8 40	0	..New York..	1136	5 12
P. M. 12 03	88	.Philadelphia.	1048	P. M. 1 30
12 55	116	..Wilmington..	1020	12 15
3 45	186	...Baltimore...	950	9 45
7 30	226	..Washington.	910	7 45
11 20	281	.Aquia Creek.	855	A. M. 1 45
A. M. 5 00	356	..Richmond...	780	8 50
6 50	378	...Petersburg..	758	7 25
10 35	441	...Weldon....	695	3 30
P. M. 3 20	538	.RALEIGH..	598	9 35
7 17	620	..Greensboro'	516	5 05
9 36	670	...Salisbury...	466	A. M. 2 07
12 00	713	..Charlotte..	423	11 36
A. M. 6 00	822	...Columbia...	314	4 00
8 00	847	..Kingsville...	289	P. M. 2 20
11 10	890	..Branchville..	246	11 00
P. M. 3 45	965	...Augusta...	171	A. M. 6 00
A. M. 4 00	1136	....Atlanta...	0	6 45 P. M.

Passengers going South From Weldon have the choice of two routes, viz:	Passengers going North From Weldon have the choice of three routes, viz:
1st. Via Raleigh, Charlotte and Columbia to Kingsville, S. C.	1st. Via Petersburg, Richmond, Washington, and Baltimore.
2nd. Via Goldsboro, Wilmington and Florence to Kingsville, S. C.	2nd. Via Seaboard and Roanoke Rail Road and Bay Line of steamers to Baltimore.
	3rd. Via Seaboard and Roanoke Railroad and Annamessic line.
Fare same each route.	Fare the same each route.
Passengers arrive in Augusta and Atlanta the same time by each route.	Passengers arrive in Philadelphia and New York about the same time by each route.

An 1868 time card. (Courtesy Seaboard Air Line Railroad Company)

Raleigh & Gaston Railroad.

W. J. Hawkins, President.

A. B. Andrews, Master of Trans.; W. W. Vass, Treas.

J. M. Pool, Gen. Tick. Agt.; Thos. Badger, Chf. Cl'k.

Armstead Jones, Ticket Agent.

RALEIGH, N. C.

Trains Leave.			Trains Arrive.
Mail.	Mil's	STATIONS.	Mil's	Mail.
A. M. 9 35	0	RALEIGH 1	97	P. M. 3 15
9 57	6	....Mill Brook....	91	2 58
10 10	10	....Huntsville....	87	2 47
10 29	16	........Wake........	82	2 30
11 08	27	...Franklinton...	70	1 55
11 36	36	....Kittrell's....	61	1 32
12 04	44	...Henderson...	54	1 10
12 43	54	.....Junction.....	44	12 43
12 52	57	....Ridgeway..	41	12 34
1 12	61	....Warrenton...	36	12 17
1 25	66	......Macon......	34	12 07
1 59	76	....Littleton....	21	11 37
2 29	85	....Gaston 2....	12	11 11
3 05	97	....WELDON 3..	0	10 35
P. M.		ARRIVE LEAVE		A. M.

CONNECTIONS.

1. Connects with the North Carolina Railroad.

2. Connects with Petersburg Railroad.

3. Connects with Wilmington and Weldon Rail Road.

3. Connects with Seaboard and Roanoke Railroad.

Old "arrangement," *Tornado* blew in on. (Courtesy Seaboard Air Line Railroad Company)

Seaboard & Roanoke Railroad Co.

E. G. Ghio, Superintend't of Trans., Portsmouth, Va.

Leave.			Arrive.
Mail.	Mil's	STATIONS.	Mil's	Mail.
A. M. 6 00	0	....PORTSMOUTH 3....	80	P. M. 7 30
6 56	17	......Suffolk......	63	6 33
7 27		....Buckhorn....		6 08
7 44	31	...Carrsville...	49	5 51
8 10	37	...Franklin 2...	43	5 36
8 27	41	.....Nottoway.....	39	5 20
8 53	50	....Newsom's....	30	5 02
9 08	54	.....Boykins.....	26	5 47
9 17	57	....Branchville....	23	4 36
9 35	63	..Margarettsville..	17	4 19
9 55	70	.....Seaboard.....	10	4 00
10 30	80	....WELDON 1....	0	3 30
		ARRIVE LEAVE		

1. Connects at Weldon with the Raleigh & Gaston, Petersburg, and Wilmington & Weldon Railroads.

2. Connects with steamers for Plymouth & Edenton.

3. Connects at Portsmouth and Weldon with steamboats.

Baltimore Steam Packet Company.

John M. Robinson, President, Baltimore, Md.

For Baltimore and all Points North and West.

One of the steamers of the Baltimore Steam Packet Company, will leave their wharf, east Wide Water St., Norfolk, at 6.15, P. M., daily, (Sundays excepted) and Portsmouth, on the arrival of the evening Passenger Train of the

Seaboard & Roanoke Railroad,

at 7.30 P. M., touching at Old Point. The Company are now running their fine steamers LOUISIANA, GEORGE LEARY and ADELAIDE, all in thorough order, and remarkable for their speed and safety. State rooms can be engaged during the day.

The time card *Energy* pulled her trains on. (Courtesy Seaboard Air Line Railroad Company)

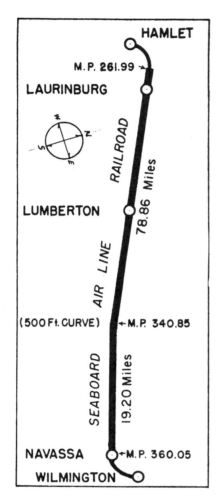

Longest straight stretch of railroad in the United States.
(Courtesy Seaboard Air Line Railroad Company)

SAL light Pacific built by Baldwin, 1912, on ready track in the late 'teens. (Courtesy Seaboard Air Line Railroad Company)

This engineer wouldn't trust just one rabbit foot and insisted on the whole rabbit riding in front of the smoke box of the 836, ready to pull out with the crack Orange Blossom Special. Engine built by ALCO, 1913. (Courtesy Seaboard Air Line Railroad Company)

A straight stretch of roadbed Walter Gwynn laid out over a hundred years ago along the Seaboard. (Courtesy Seaboard Air Line Railroad Company)

Heavy power with speed to match: the 249, a big 4-8-2, gracefully stands at the head of the Orange Blossom Special. Her bell is ringing and within moments she will pull out of Acca Yard, Richmond, and dust the rails as she heads south toward Florida. Designated Mountain type, 249 was built by Baldwin, 1925. (Courtesy Seaboard Air Line Railroad Company)

Gold spike and cup to commemorate the completion of 200 miles of track that linked 18 railroads into the corporate system now known as Seaboard Air Line Railroad Company. (Courtesy Seaboard Air Line Railroad Company)

that ever snorted amongst the hills of Crab-tree, reached the limits of our City, and was enthusiastically welcomed with every demonstration of joy. The bells rang, the artillery roared and the people cheered. . . . We hail the rumbling of the first locomotive, as the glad omen of future prosperity. . . ."

By 1853 difficulties had long since overtaken the Portsmouth & Roanoke, and it had emerged from reorganization in 1846 with a new name, Seaboard & Roanoke. The Raleigh & Gaston had made connection with it at Weldon and there was now through rail service over the 175 miles from Portsmouth to Raleigh.

By 1893, the Seaboard & Roanoke, along with five other lines, had become associated as "Seaboard Air Line," with continuous rail service from Portsmouth to Atlanta, Georgia, thus setting the stage for the right man to put together a railroad system to compete with "The Great Atlantic Route" (ACL). And the right man stood at the stage door, ready to make his entry.

A thirty-year-old Richmond banker had become president of the Georgia & Alabama Railway in 1895, and with clear vision of the possibilities present set his plans in motion. With enthusiasm and ability, John Skelton Williams tackled the intricate job of welding into one corporate entity the associated roads plus other southern lines, and on July 1, 1900, had put together a system operating over 2600 miles of railroad through six southeastern states from Virginia to Florida.

Seaboard Air Line Railroad Company now operates over more than 4000 miles of rails "Through The Heart Of The South."

The Connecting Link

Opportunity ever beckons to those who see and seize it by the forelock. For the first quarter of the nineteenth century passengers between Richmond and Washington could make the approximately 100-mile trip by stagecoach in about 38 hours. Freight was carried by Conestoga wagon, and the United States Mail, then known as "The Great Mail," was hauled in carts. "Express Mail," at much higher rates, was carried on fast horses which were changed about every fifteen miles. (Perhaps this was the first Pony Express.)

In late 1833 Virginia's first steam railroad, the Petersburg, was slowly creeping southward toward Weldon, North Carolina, while to the North the Baltimore & Ohio was feverishly extending a branch to Washington. It was at this time that Nicholas Mills, who had been profitably operating Virginia's first railroad, the Chesterfield, for two years, met with his banker friend, John A. Lancaster, took a good look at the prospects, and lost no time in putting things together and getting into action.

On February 25, 1834, the Virginia Legislature granted a charter to the Richmond, Fredericksburg & Potomac Railroad Company for the construction of a railroad "from Richmond to a point on the Potomac River where connection can be made with steamboats for Washington." Perhaps because Mr. Mills employed only horse and mule motive power on his road, or was generally skeptical of steam locomotives, he authorized the president and directors "to purchase all machines, wagons, vehicles, carriages and teams of any description whatsoever, which may deem necessary or proper for the purposes of transportation." There were some unique features in this charter, one being that the roadway and all other property of the company, as well as all profits from operation, should be free from any and all taxes. Even more unique was the provision that for thirty years (later extended) no other railroad could be constructed between Richmond and Washington.

Although it must be said that the Commonwealth of Virginia had encouraged transportation ventures such as canals and turnpikes since 1784, it would seem that shrewd political minds grasped opportunistic possibilities in this charter, for the Commonwealth subscribed to two-fifths of the capital stock. Others had also seen the opportunity, and the state had to be content with 2752 shares—which it still owns.

Shortly after the first organizational meeting on June 20, 1834, at which Lancaster was elected president and Nicholas Mills one of the directors, Moncure Robinson (to become president in 1840), the young engineer who had constructed Mr. Mills' railroad, was engaged as Chief Engineer, with instructions to commence operations at the earliest possible date. By the end of January 1836, Robinson had his wooden stringers, capped with light strap-iron, extending northward for approximately twenty miles to the South Anna River.

As was the case with most budding railroads of

On June 2, 1900, John Skelton Williams, Jr., then three years of age, was steadied by Mr. Williams, Sr., as the youngster pounded away at the spike. Indeed a momentous occasion. (Courtesy Seaboard Air Line Railroad Company)

A post rider with "Express Mail" walks his horse over a stretch of "corduroy road" near Fredericksburg, Virginia, about the turn of the nineteenth century. (Courtesy Archives Virginia State Library)

Stagecoach, loaded and ready to continue north from Hanover, Virginia, toward Washington, about 1800. (Courtesy Archives Virginia State Library)

148

the day, no sooner had some track been laid and a little furniture obtained than an excursion over the line became a must. It is unknown whether the *Roanoke*, purchased second-hand from the Petersburg, or a new locomotive purchased in England pulled this first train over the RF&P on February 13, 1836. Captain Blair Bolling, an officer of the war of 1812, was one of the passengers, and fortunately for posterity he recorded the event in his diary:

"The Managers of the Richmond, Fredericksburg and Potomac Creek Railroad, opened twenty miles of it, which is just completed, and in order to give it notoriety as well as to evince a liberal spirit, invited the Governor and Council, Judges of the several courts, Mayor and Aldermen of the City and Legislature, and such other individuals as they thought proper, amongst which latter class I was so fortunate as to be included. A company of about one hundred and sixty persons assembled and embarked on board the cars propelled by a Locomotive Engine about eleven o'clock A.M. and proceeded in

fine style amidst the shouts and applause of an admiring and an amazed multitude. We arrived about one o'clock at our place of destiny within three quarters of a mile of the South Anna River where we found a light but neat building, one of the appendages of the railroad and transferrable along it, upon a car, in which was a table spread, and loaded with the finest wines and liquors, to partake of which a cordial invitation was extended to the whole company, who accepted and partook apparently with enthusiastic delight, and very soon began to exhibit its exhilarating effects in their animated countenances, voices and movement. In about an hour we were invited to a saw mill operated by steam about one hundred yards distant, where we found a most sumptuous dinner spread for the company who partook of it, and as soon as the eating was over we were visited with a profusion of champagne, that soul inspiring draught which, as it is wont to do, soon gave birth to many a jovial song and the animated laugh, and terminated the saw mill scene with great hilarity and conviviality. We then re-embarked and returned home, with speed, without accident and with grateful acknowledgements."

Three handsome and powerful Pacifics, built by Baldwin in 1927, wait their clearance signal to follow No. 325, which has just started her train for Washington, 1928. (Courtesy Richmond, Fredericksburg & Potomac)

Eighth and H Streets (now 8th and Broad Streets), Richmond, Virginia, as it looked in 1836, when Richmond, Fredericksburg & Potomac Railroad's first passenger station occupied a corner. (Courtesy Richmond, Fredericksburg & Potomac)

150

Old Byrd Street Station was a handsome edifice when it was opened jointly by RF&P and R&P on April 10, 1887. Picture made about 1905 (man standing in left foreground is conductor of the "Summer Car"). At that time streetcar conductors were required to leave the car when it approached a railroad crossing (and there were many), stand on the railroad tracks, look both ways, and if no train was in sight, signal the motorman to proceed. (Courtesy Richmond, Fredericksburg & Potomac)

Broad Street Station, at Richmond, was completed and put
into joint operation by RF&P and ACL on January 6,
1919. Picture made in summer of 1919. (Courtesy Richmond, Fredericksburg & Potomac)

No. 302 lays into a well banked curve with her southbound Limited in the late 1930's. (Courtesy Richmond,
Fredericksburg & Potomac)

152

John Lewis, Superintendent of Motive Power, takes delivery of *General Robert E. Lee* (Engine No. 551) at Philadelphia in 1937. With steam pressure of 260 pounds, 27x 30-inch cylinders, 77-inch drivers, and a tractive effort of 62,800 pounds, these highly finished engines were the acme of motive power in the South at this time, both in looks and performance. Intended mainly for freight service, they averaged approximately 25 round trips per month between Richmond and Potomac Yard. Five of these locomotives were built for the road in 1937, all bearing the names of Confederate Generals. In 1938, six almost identical engines went into passenger service of the road—these bearing the names of Virginia governors. (Courtesy Richmond, Fredericksburg & Potomac)

153

Old Richmond & Petersburg station at 8th & Canal Streets, Richmond, built about 1838. Until 1867, when this station was operated jointly by RF&P and R&P (later ACL), through passengers and their baggage were transported the five blocks between the stations by omnibus and wagon. (Courtesy Richmond, Fredericksburg & Potomac)

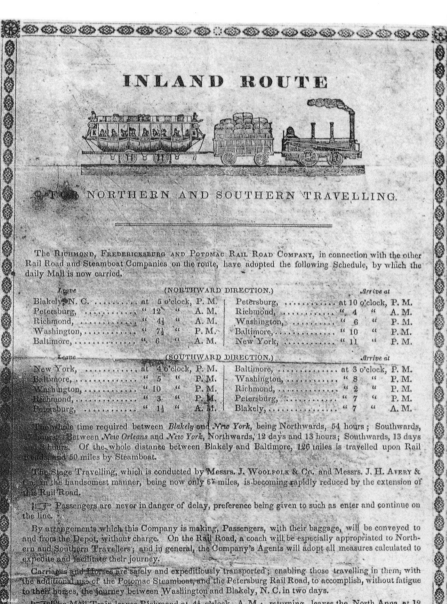

INLAND ROUTE

FOR NORTHERN AND SOUTHERN TRAVELLING.

The RICHMOND, FREDERICKSBURG AND POTOMAC RAIL ROAD COMPANY, in connection with the other Rail Road and Steamboat Companies on the route, have adopted the following Schedule, by which the daily Mail is now carried.

Leave	(NORTHWARD DIRECTION.)	Arrive at
Blakely, N. C. . . . at 5 o'clock, P. M.	Petersburg, ... at 10 o'clock, P. M.
Petersburg, ... " 12 " A. M.	Richmond, ... " 4 " A. M.
Richmond, ... " 4½ " A. M.	Washington, ... " 6 " P. M.
Washington, ... " 7½ " P. M.	Baltimore, ... " 10 " P. M.
Baltimore, ... " 6 " A. M.	New York, ... " 11 " P. M.

Leave	(SOUTHWARD DIRECTION.)	Arrive at
New York, ... at 4 o'clock, P. M.	Baltimore, ... at 3 o'clock, P. M.
Baltimore, ... " 5 " P. M.	Washington, ... " 8 " P. M.
Washington, ... " 10 " P. M.	Richmond, ... " 2 " P. M.
Richmond, ... " 3 " P. M.	Petersburg, ... " 7 " P. M.
Petersburg, ... " 1½ " A. M.	Blakely, ... " 7 " A. M.

The whole time required between *Blakely* and *New York*, being Northwards, 54 hours ; Southwards, . . hours. Between *New Orleans* and *New York*, Northwards, 12 days and 13 hours; Southwards, 13 days . . . 13 hours. Of the whole distance between Blakely and Baltimore, 126 miles is travelled upon Rail Roads, and 50 miles by Steamboat.

The Stage Travelling, which is conducted by Messrs. J. WOOLFOLK & Co. and Messrs. J. H. AVERY & Co. in the handsomest manner, being now only 67 miles, is becoming rapidly reduced by the extension of this Rail Road.

☞ Passengers are never in danger of delay, preference being given to such as enter and continue on the line.

By arrangements which this Company is making, Passengers, with their baggage, will be conveyed to and from the Depot, without charge. On the Rail Road, a coach will be especially appropriated to Northern and Southern Travellers; and in general, the Company's Agents will adopt all measures calculated to expedite and facilitate their journey.

Carriages and Horses are safely and expeditiously transported ; enabling those travelling in them, with the additional use of the Potomac Steamboat, and the Petersburg Rail Road, to accomplish, without fatigue to their horses, the journey between Washington and Blakely, N. C. in two days.

☞ The Mail Train leaves Richmond at 4½ o'clock, A. M.; returning, leaves the North Anna at 12 o'clock, M. The alternate Trains for Passengers and Freight, leave the North Anna at 7 o'clock, A. M. and 4, P. M.; and Richmond at 9 o'clock, A. M. and 1, P. M.

All possible care will be taken of baggage, but it will be carried only at its owner's risk.

RAIL ROAD OFFICE, Richmond, May 30, 1836.

An 1836 advertisement of Richmond, Fredericksburg & Potomac. (Courtesy Richmond, Fredericksburg & Potomac)

Regular service over the twenty-mile stretch of rails was inaugurated the following day, and on January 23, 1837, the line had been completed into Fredericksburg. The bud had begun to flower, business had been good, and a contract to carry "The Great Mail" at $200 per mile per year had been secured. Six British-built locomotives (*American, Fredericksburg, Jefferson, Potomac, Richmond,* and *Washington*) were kept busy pulling the rolling stock, which consisted of 5 passenger cars (each seating 24 passengers), 2 baggage cars, 1 horse car, 20 boxcars, and 3 coal cars. A depot and shop had been constructed in Richmond. But the dark clouds of the panic of 1837 soon floated over the horizon and as American pocketbooks constricted it was necessary for Moncure Robinson to go to London to endeavor to negotiate a loan. The engineer-turned-investment-salesman must have been a good one, for he exchanged bonds for $324,005.61. By 1861 the line had reached Acquia Creek, from which steamboats plied to the Potomac River, and here it was to remain until after the Civil War. Not until July 2, 1872, did it operate through rail service between Richmond and Washington.

Only 116 miles long, the Richmond, Fredericksburg & Potomac is a most important railroad; in addition to its own profitable business it serves as the connecting link between North and South for the great systems of ACL and SAL.

Acorns to Oaks

When an acorn falls, the sturdiness of the oak that may spring from it can never be predicted. On January 26, 1836, one fell at Petersburg, Virginia—in the form of City Point Railroad. As acorns go, this was a small one, and sprouted a line only 9 miles long, to City Point on the James River.

This was a runt, as evidenced in 1838, when it boasted only twelve employees—a Superintendent of Transportation, one engineer, one "Captain of the Train," an "Overseer of the Road," a locomotive fireman, one watchman, and six laborers. Its furniture consisted of two 6-wheel locomotives (valued at $13,000), twenty-eight 4-wheel freight cars, two 4-wheel passenger cars, and one handcar. But on September 7 throngs of people from the little town and the surrounding countryside cheered as the first little train pulled out of Petersburg. Thirty minutes later it had negotiated the nine miles over wooden rails, which were capped with strap-iron and resting on stone ties, and stopped at City Point.

Money, the heart and backbone of any project, was hard to come by. Recovery had been slow from the great panic of 1837, which had reached in all directions. In 1839, the road's president reported in part, "Cost of work . . . unnecessarily great from causes difficult to state accurately." He hoped that the directors "were not intimidated . . . as to final success . . . that by economy and . . . diligence the affairs of the company will recover from embarrassment."

In 1842 a new president was not only harrassed with the "embarrassment" he had inherited but also "a pressing debt about to foreclose on the best locomotive of the road, owned at present by Messrs. James, Morson and Spencer of Petersburg, who are bound for payment of $3,000 on the first of March next, to Mr. Norris who released the engine to them for their bond, and unless this can be paid against this day, these gentlemen may be under necessity to make sale of the engine, which would put a stop to the road." (The locomotive referred to was the *Powhatan,* built by William Norris of Philadelphia in 1838.)

Old records do not tell us what happened to the locomotive but four years later, in 1846, another new president solemnly reported, "Business daily diminishing with the prospect before the company . . . entirely unable to prop its credit . . . and equally unable to renovate the road. The period cannot . . . be far distant when the affairs must be wound up and the road . . . fall into other hands or go down altogether."

Unable to "prop its credit" the sickly little road "fell into other hands" the next year and was reorganized as the Appomattox Railroad. After another sinking spell it was reorganized again as the South Side Railroad. Revived by these transfusions, the little line with its five-foot tracks began to creep westward through Burkeville and toward Lynchburg. The terrain offered no difficulty to construction until the great flats, lying hundreds of feet below the bluffs of the Appomattox River, just east of Farmville, were reached in 1853. Lighting into the problem, Chief Engineer C. O. Sanford solved it by raising a timber truss bridge supported on brick piers 125 feet high to span more than a half mile. In November 1854 the line had completed its slow but steady crawl and trains were operating over the

The *Washington*, built by William Norris in July 1836, was identical to the *Powhatan*, built for the City Point Rail Road in 1838. (Courtesy Norfolk & Western Railway Company)

The "high bridge" spanning the great flats of the Appomattox River. (Courtesy Norfolk & Western Railway Company)

The Roanoke yards of N&W. (Courtesy Norfolk & Western Railway Company)

A yard goat making up passenger train at Roanoke passenger station in the late 1880's. (Courtesy Norfolk & Western Railway Company)

124 miles between Petersburg and Lynchburg.

In the fall of 1830, years before the little City Point had even sprouted, people in the hill city of Lynchburg had seen the possibilities of rails stretching westward—although probably none of them had ever seen a railroad. So much pressure was brought to bear that the legislature passed an act on April 5, 1831, incorporating the Lynchburg & New River Railroad. But they were unable to agree on the route (and doubtless were concerned about the three million dollars to be raised for construction), and the proposed road followed some others and died aborning.

But the idea remained alive, and some of the more farsighted promoters could visualize an overland railroad stretching all the way to the Mississippi. After some dry runs, charter was finally obtained in 1848 for the Virginia & Tennessee Railroad, "to run from the city of Lynchburg to the Tennessee line at Bristol."

It took nearly two years to get their ducks lined up, but the Hill City boys were in earnest this time, and on a cold day in January 1850, Governor Floyd's pick struck the first blow into some frozen ground to start the line. These hearty fellows had undertaken a real engineering feat at the time, for the road had to go around, up, and through mountains. There was no pattern to go by, maps were inaccurate, and there was no earth-moving machinery—only men, mules, and sweat. Men with hearts of oak and brawn to match the granite ramparts opposing them, set to. Dynamite had not yet been invented and rock-cuts, fills, and three tunnels were blasted with black powder.

Rough country slowed but never stopped this mountain railroad, and on November 1, 1852, rails had been spiked down 53 miles west of the starting point, at Big Lick, then hardly more than a crossroad with its 600 inhabitants, but later to become the city of Roanoke. In the wintry blasts of December, the rails passed through Salem and headed ever westward through the Roanoke River Valley. At a snail's pace it slowly pushed up the eastern continental divide to Christiansburg, then across the mountain plateau toward Tennessee. Weary, out of money, and with only transportation of salt and plaster from its Glade Spring Salt Works branch to sustain it, the line just about gave out, but guts and the will to carry through saw the last rail spiked down at Bristol on October 1, 1856—204 miles from Lynchburg.

In spite of the fact that railroad enthusiasts at Petersburg could now see lines of rails stretching north, south, and west from the "Cockade City," they were restless. There was no line running East and the old seaport of Norfolk seemed to have been left in the lurch. Rail lines coming west out of Norfolk had been discussed, but such contemplations had remained in the talking stage until March 17, 1851, when some of the more enterprising citizens secured a charter for the Norfolk & Petersburg Railroad.

Raising the funds needed for getting the project started and under way posed the usual problem, but to this had been added another. Nearly two years of surveys had proved disappointing, since the route seemed impassably blocked by the dense and almost bottomless Great Dismal Swamp. At the first meeting of stockholders, held in 1853, an atmosphere of gloom prevailed until someone mentioned the name of a young engineer who might be able to come up with a solution to the problem staring them in the face.

Late in 1853 the twenty-seven-year-old William Mahone, who after graduating in engineering from Virginia Military Institute had served with the Orange & Alexandria Railroad and later built the Fredericksburg and Valley Plank Road, was called in to "look at the problem." Expressing the opinion that the job could be done, young Mahone was employed as Chief Engineer at the then princely salary of $2500 a year.

Aware of tight finances and with a shortage of labor, the young engineer waded into his difficulties. A 100-foot-wide right-of-way was cleared and a deep matrix was laid; swamp trees were then limbed and thrown to the center in such a manner as to make a corduroy mat. An embankment of earth was then placed on top of the mat, which furnished a stable foundation, and this right-of-way was pushed across the swamp for a distance of ten miles. So sound was Mahone's engineering and so thorough his construction that today, over one hundred years later, his roadbed across Dismal Swamp still carries the tonnage of one of the heaviest traffic railroads in America—and with amazingly little maintenance.

Coming out of the swamp near Suffolk, this engineering genius looked through his glass toward Petersburg. When the line was completed in 1858, a fifty-two-mile stretch of its eighty miles was the longest piece of straight railroad track in the world. The directors were so impressed with the rare ability

The *Roanoke,* named for the county bearing the name, was the eighth locomotive owned by the Virginia & Tennessee and was placed in regular service in January 1854. (Courtesy Norfolk & Western Railway Company)

Interesting old picture of gang that worked section 7. (Courtesy Norfolk & Western Company)

Engine #30, hot as a firecracker and ready to head west out of Radford in 1886. This run would cross the New River over bridge to right, whereas Tennessee-bound trains crossed over bridge to left. The village of New River is in the background. This was in all probability "That New River Train" made famous by ballad singers in the hills. (Courtesy Norfolk & Western Railway Company)

160

Hefty engineer of the 91 poses in gangway while members of train crew take their stance for a picture. Train probably stopped near Roanoke in the 1880's. (Courtesy Norfolk & Western Railway Company)

Chief Engineer, William Mahone, at the glass in Dismal Swamp. (Courtesy Norfolk & Western Railway Company)

The brilliant early railroader, Gen. William H. Mahone. (Courtesy Norfolk & Western Railway Company)

Locomotive built by William Mason in 1871, shown in transit. Used on the Atlantic, Mississippi, and Ohio Railroad. (Courtesy Norfolk and Western Railroad)

The husky 1201 has westbound train #41 right on the advertised as she busts through a snowstorm near Pulaski, Virginia, in 1937. (Courtesy Norfolk & Western Railway Company)

This picture is thought to be of candidate Rutherford Hayes' campaign train stopped at Columbus, Ohio, in 1876. Sciotia Valley Railroad was N&W predecessor. (Courtesy Norfolk & Western Railway Company)

of the man who had built the road that they made him its head in 1860.

The now thirty-two-year-old railroad president had hardly taken his seat of office when the outbreak of the Civil War called him to the colors as a lieutenant-colonel. Within a week he had been promoted to full colonel and before the end of the year to brigadier general. Serving the Confederacy with characteristic drive and ability on the battlefields of Bull Run, Gettysburg, Chancellorsville, and Wilderness, the railroader-turned-soldier distinguished himself at the Battle of the Crater at Petersburg in the late summer of 1864; and for this achievement was promoted to major-general at the close of the engagement.

General Mahone was what has been correctly termed "a born railroader," and returning to the

presidency of his now devastated N&P in 1865, he immediately plunged into the desperate fight of restoring his road to operating condition. Its western connection to Lynchburg, South Side, was in even worse condition and, recognizing Mahone's fighting ability and skill as a railroader, its directors asked him to accept the presidency of that road in December 1865.

Even with so much to demand his attention, General Mahone had dreamed much about a consolidated railroad all the way across Virginia and into Kentucky and West Virginia, where valuable coal deposits were reported. Working toward the fulfillment of his dream, he convinced the stockholders of the Virginia & Tennessee of his ideas to such an extent that in October 1867 they elected him president of that road.

Now president of three railroads that stretched 408 miles from Norfolk, Virginia, to Bristol, Tennessee, this intrepid glutton for punishment really had problems. All of his railroads were war-torn and in

164

Nearly a million pounds of engine, the 2181 of the Y6b
class, puts her 152,000 pounds of tractive effort on a time
freight in 1949. (Courtesy Norfolk & Western Railway
Company)

With a good head of steam, the 2173 rolls her coal drag
east along the New River. (Courtesy Norfolk & Western
Railway Company)

Locomotive service area at Portsmouth, Ohio. (Courtesy Norfolk & Western Railway Company)

A unique front-end view of a Y6 as the 2130 heads east
out of the Roanoke yards with a coal drag "a mile long."
(Courtesy Norfolk & Western Railway Company)

A Y6 and Y6a at "the filling station" on a snowy day.
(Courtesy Norfolk & Western Railway Company)

An unusual night scene. A big class A throws smoke toward the snowy sky as the 1228 gets her time freight on the move. (Courtesy Norfolk & Western Railway Company)

A big Y6 rolls a time freight across the James River at Natural Bridge Station in 1950. (Courtesy Norfolk & Western Railway Company)

Bustin' into tomorrow around mountains of solid granite near Radford, Virginia. (Courtesy Norfolk & Western Railway Company)

shambles; money was scarce and at times nonexistent, and even had there been plenty of money new equipment was unavailable. Facing the problem squarely, Mahone got together what pieces were left, patched them up, and made them do. In one instance two engines that had dropped through a burned bridge into the Appomattox River during the war were pulled from their watery grave, re-

paired, and put into service again. Old records reveal that, due to shortage of funds, workmen were sometimes paid off in salt pork, corn meal, and a promise they would someday be paid in money.

A man of lesser talent and boldness would have given up in despair, but not General Mahone. This gritty railroader not only got his roads into operation but soon had them operating at a profit, and in November 1870 brought all three into consolidation by organizing the Atlantic, Mississippi & Ohio. By

170

With his fist clenched to go through the hoop, a front brakeman leans to for orders, on the fly. (Courtesy Norfolk & Western Railway Company)

The 2151 is really working as she drags her time freight eastward at Maybeurry, West Virginia. In a moment the powerful Y6 will clear the trestle but continue on the grade for some distance. William Alley, who shot this picture in 1940, was standing on the abutment just in front of the approaching engine. Mr. Alley stated to the author that the trestle spans a valley below for a distance of approximately one thousand feet; that in 1937, a similar engine at the head of a westbound time freight climbed the rails (on the downgrade) moments before the engine went on the trestle, taking 53 loaded cars with her, and as she landed in the valley below, the boiler exploded and blew fragments for a distance of a quarter mile. (Courtesy William L. Alley, Jr.)

this time new railroad equipment was available—if there was money to pay for it. Lacking sufficient operating capital, Mahone arranged with British capitalists to float a loan, and new locomotives and other necessary equipment were purchased. Interest was being met and the future looked bright—when lightning struck.

In 1873 a financial crash which brought on a panic involved the whole country. Business for the three-year-old railroad system fell away and earnings failed to meet obligations. In spite of heroic efforts, the AM&O was thrown into receivership in early 1876. Mahone was not appointed one of the receivers, and in 1881 the road was sold at auction to Philadelphia financial interests, who promptly reorganized it as Norfolk & Western Railroad Company. Never again was General Mahone to be actively connected with the railroads to which he had brought so much talent and given the best years of his life.

Under new ownership the road began to expand and by 1883 had pushed a branch line 70 miles from Radford into West Virginia and reached the great coal fields surrounding what is now Bluefield. The railroad that General Mahone had put together had really reached pay dirt. Not only had it found what was to fuel its locomotives for nearly three quarters of a century, but something that would eventually make it a railroad with more freight cars per mile of line and the highest average ton-miles per freight train hour than any railroad in America.

Roses bloomed until another big panic struck in 1893. Unable to meet all its obligations promptly, the road asked to be put into receivership the following year. Belt tightening, good management, and coal soon brought them out, however, and in 1896 reorganization gave birth to that sturdy oak, known since as Norfolk & Western Railway Company, with rails stretching over two thousand miles from Dismal

172

Operator at BH Tower waves a big Y6 ahead as she rolls
a time freight westward into the night. (Courtesy Norfolk
& Western Railway Company)

Excellent study of a Class A. This engine was built in the N&W shops in 1936 and was the second of this class. Used on the flatter portions of the road (east of Roanoke and west of Williamson, W. Va.), the 1201 and her sisters were the longest locomotives built by N&W (121' 9¼" with tender), weighed 951,600 pounds, and, set up on roller bearings, had a tractive effort of 114,000 pounds. With their 70-inch drivers they frequently attained speeds of better than 70 miles an hour. Used in freight service. (Courtesy Norfolk & Western Railway Company)

No, it's not a Christmas tree, the N&W just wanted all and sundry to know there was plenty of light around the Roanoke roundhouse. (Courtesy Norfolk & Western Railway Company)

Part of the Roanoke shops as they looked in the 1950's.
(Courtesy Norfolk & Western Railway Company)

The completed masterpiece from the shops of the N&W
has rolled off the assembly line and stands on the ready
track in 1941. (Courtesy Norfolk & Western Railway
Company)

Here we see the forerunner of the famous class J passenger engines, the 600, on the assembly line in the Roanoke shops in 1941. These 109′ 2″-long locomotives with their tenders weighed 872,600 pounds and had a tractive effort of 80,000 pounds. With streamlined torpedo jackets shrouding their boilers, stream-styled cowls over the coal bunkers of their tenders, 70-inch drivers, and set up on roller bearings, nobody ever found out their ultimate speed. Truly, these beautiful, dependable, and performing locomotives represented the acme of steam motive power. (Courtesy Norfolk & Western Railway Company)

On the head end of the crack Powhatan Arrow, the 607 keeps rails from rusting as she highballs along a stretch of well ballasted road beside the New River. A great train, pulled by a great engine on a great railroad. Should the ghost of Gen. Mahone have stood by as she passed, he would have pulled himself erect, kicked his heels together, and saluted the culmination of what he started so long ago. (Courtesy Norfolk & Western Railway Company)

THE JAMES RIVER AND KANAWHA CANAL, RICHMOND, VIRGINIA.—[Sketched by J. R. Hamilton.]

Swamp through Virginia, West Virginia, and Ohio, and making short sorties into Kentucky, Maryland and North Carolina.

Some Country Boys Build a Railroad

Financiers and promoters in cities were not the only men with visions of rails stretching through the land. Most of the little pioneer lines were born to connect two or more cities, but others came to life literally in the country. On September 14, 1835, a small group of planters met at the little county seat at Louisa Courthouse, Virginia, to discuss the possibility of a railroad, and at this meeting raised or pledged the sum of $590 "for surveys of the route." Evidently the surveys were encouraging, for on February 18, 1836, a charter was granted to the Louisa Railroad, naming Frederick Harris as president. These country boys went to work with vim, and by December 20, 1837, the line had been completed and was in operation from Frederick's Hall (President Harris' plantation) to Hanover Junction (now Doswell), 21 miles east, to connect with the tracks of the RF&P.

Crop failures, droughts, and other vicissitudes of nature mean little to the hardy men who wrest their livelihood from the soil, and apparently the great panic of 1837 had little effect upon the determination of these men to build their railroad. Most countryfolk are frugal by nature, and coupled to that is the fact that cash-in-hand is hard to come by and should be respected. So these farmers-turned-railroaders made a deal with the RF&P whereby that road would "perform all transportation service on the line of the Louisa Railroad." This arrangement made it possible for the Louisa to employ its capital in extension of the road, rather than have it tied up in motive power and rolling stock, and was in effect until 1847. Taking another look in the till, President Harris reduced his salary from 1500 to one thousand dollars annually in 1837 (perhaps news of the panic had filtered in).

After settling the transportation deal, the little road continued its way in a westerly direction from its starting point without untoward incident until November 1839, when some gunpowder exploded in a freight car about two miles west of Louisa "killing a brakeman and stunning the engineer and fireman." This shocking event brought an order from President Harris "that no more explosives would be hauled by the road." This same year the road secured a government contract to carry mail (at $75 per mile per year).

In 1845 a new president was elected, Edmund Fontaine, a most able man under whose guidance the determined little railroad continued its westward crawl. Within a few years it had reached the Blue Ridge Mountains, where Col. Claudius Crozet was engaged from 1849–1853 in construction of the then longest railroad tunnel (under Afton Mountain) in America for the state-owned Blue Ridge Railroad.

In 1850, when the name of the Louisa was changed to Virginia Central Railroad, the line operated its own equipment and could boast five locomotives, among them the *Frederick Harris, Charles*

Frederick's Hall Mansion, home of the first president of
Louisa Rail Road (Photo by Lance Phillips)

Station at Frederick Hall, where the Louisa Rail Road
started. Poindexter's Store (seen between railroad buildings) has been in operation over a hundred years. (Photo
by Lance Phillips)

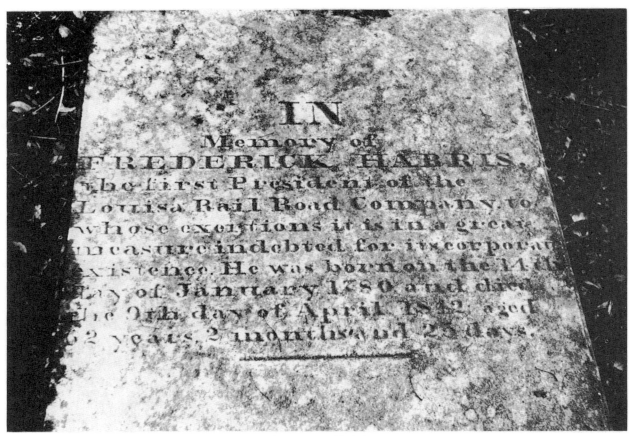

Memorial stone to Mr. Harris. (Photo by Lance Phillips)

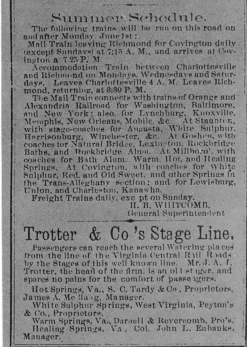

Advertised schedule of Virginia Central, about 1855. (Courtesy Seaboard Air Line Railroad Company)

The Brooks-built 73 at the head of her train on the Hocking Valley & Toledo (C&O predecessor) in 1879. (Courtesy Chesapeake & Ohio Railway Company)

The *Columbus,* a beautiful and neat little 4-4-0, built by Hinkley and Williams, Boston, at a roundhouse on the HV&T in 1868. (Courtesy Chesapeake & Ohio Railway Company)

First locomotive built by Muskegon Iron Works for the Chicago & West Michigan (C&O predecessor). (Courtesy Chesapeake & Ohio Railway Company)

Day coaches on the C&O looked like this during the last half of the nineteenth century. If the author's memory is up to par, they still looked like this around the turn of this century. Finished outside in a bright orange-yellow, with plush upholstery of a slightly darker hue inside, they made up a really "doggy" train when compared with the olive drab of some of the other lines coming into Richmond. We never saw "The White Train" on the New York & New England, but we'll wager it had nothing on the Chesapeake & Ohio's yellow ones. (Courtesy Chesapeake & Ohio Railway Company)

No, it isn't one of the Erie's diamond cars. The diamond-shaped window decoration was to add luxurious looks to a C&O Pullman about 1900 or a little later—and they were palaces in their day. (Courtesy Chesapeake & Ohio Railway Company)

An Atlantic-type engine begins to open up with C&O's #12, westbound over the James River Division (old Richmond & Allegheny). The photo was made in the summer of 1912, just outside of Richmond with the old canal in the foreground and historic Hollywood Cemetery as a backdrop. (Courtesy Chesapeake & Ohio Railway Company)

An older sister of the 491, the 432, romps down the mainline near Thurmond, West Virginia, with the westbound FFV in the early '30's. (Courtesy Chesapeake & Ohio Railway Company)

The 1654 lays to on a grade near Alderson, West Virginia, with an eastbound coal drag of over 5000 tons in 1943. These articulated engines (class H8 2-6-6-6) were built by Lima for the C&O from December 1941 into 1949. Carrying 260 psi to four 22½x33-inch cylinders, the 67-inch drivers produced a tractive effort of 110,200 pounds. These mighty powerhouses with their tenders weighed in at 1,098,540 pounds. The grade is heavy as well as the consist but the 1654 could take more than either had to offer. (Courtesy Chesapeake & Ohio Railway Company)

A close-up of the 491, a powerful and fast passenger locomotive used by the C&O on its mountain divisions. Incidentally, the engine is on the head of the road's crack eastbound Sportsman, stopped at White Sulphur about 1938. (Courtesy Chesapeake & Ohio Railway Company)

Y. Kimbrough and *Westward Ho,* two switching engines, five passenger coaches, three baggage cars, and one hundred 4-wheel and twenty-three 8-wheel freight cars. Although not experiencing the mushroom growth of some of the early roads, in 1861 the Virginia Central carried 166,000 passengers 108,534 miles. In addition it hauled 50,600 tons of freight, including 3819 barrels of whiskey and 982 kegs of gunpowder (President Fontaine had apparently rescinded Mr. Harris' order of 1839). The country boys had moved slowly but they were really railroading now.

War-ravaged and weary in 1865, the game little road had a capital of $3,400,000, owed $1,900,000, and had in its treasury one hundred dollars—in gold. Two years later Virginia Central's rails joined with others to give birth to the Chesapeake & Ohio.

A Palmetto Bud

Like fire on the loose in dry tinder the railroad fever had attacked its victims up and down the Atlantic seaboard. Alert business men in Charleston, South Carolina, had been quick to see that the seaport city's commerce was dwindling due to the growth of many little towns across the state. The Santee Canal had been in operation from Charleston westward to the middle of the state since 1800, and there were many advocates of additional waterways. There were others, however, who saw the only solution in a railroad. Taking no chances of missing out on a waterway, should the majority desire this method of transportation, a group sought a charter in 1827, and on January 30, 1828, such was issued to the "South Carolina Canal and Rail Road Company." The proposed operation was to be in a generally northwesterly direction from Charleston to Hamburg (on the South Carolina side of the Savannah River, just across from Augusta, Georgia), a distance of 136 miles.

At the formal organizational meeting on May 12, 1828, $350,000 (half of the authorized capitalization) was subscribed, and William Aiken was named president. Chafing to get the project under way, President Aiken arranged for two separate surveys —one by the civil engineer, J. B. Petival, the other by a detachment of the U.S. Corps of Engineers under Col. William Howard. These farsighted business men realized that such a new and at that time gigantic venture should be guided by only the most capable hands, and accordingly the directors cast around for the very best talent available. They were fortunate indeed, for in July 1829 they found the man for the job.

When twenty-seven-year-old Horatio Allen accepted the challenge to build the road as the new company's Chief Engineer, there was some unfinished business requiring his attention in Pennsylvania—"the taming of the Lion" for the Delaware & Hudson, which delayed his presence in Charleston until September. Having seen the promise of the railroad era to come, this former canal engineer had crossed the Atlantic in 1828 to study English railroads. Taken in tow by George Stephenson, Allen not only had the opportunity to view the Liverpool & Manchester road then under construction, but also to get first-hand knowledge of the operation of steam locomotives in daily use on the Stockton & Darlington. His keen eye, inventive mind, and passion for detail were to place him in an outstanding position as a builder and operator of railroads in America in the years ahead. Thus, the dream of these Charleston business men of the most ambitious railroad project yet undertaken in the world, was to come into reality through this young engineer's professional competence.

It is probable that not more than 10 per cent of the subscribed capital had been paid in at this time, and in addition to the usual difficulty of financing such a venture there was an imposing engineering problem. Since the coastal area of South Carolina is low and the ground soft, there would be difficulties in getting the road laid through some of the low country it was to follow. However, the versatile and able young engineer proved equal to the task.

Allen made some experiments with the use of piles and found a method that seemed satisfactory. When finally completed to Hamburg, the 136 miles of railroad was literally a timber bridge of heart pine, at some places resting on the surface but for the most part five to six feet above ground. This was not the type of construction Allen would have preferred, for he knew and so advised the directors that future problems would arise from decay of the timber; but well aware of the limited resources at his disposal, he also knew it was the only kind of road he could build. When it was formally opened on October 3, 1833, the entire road had less than 20,000 cubic yards of embankment, less than 30 miles of shallow cuts, and only one timber bridge (over a 400-foot-span of the Edisto River).

As the company's resources increased, earth was

filled around the piling and trusswork, with the result of added firmness, reducing the problem of settling. Railroad builders who viewed Allen's handiwork marvelled at the moderate cost of the substantial road. Ten years after completion portions of embankments were washed out by flood, and in 1843 President Tupper stated, "Repairs were made in about six days. . . . Had the superstructure been on an embankment only, it would have been months before the repairs would have admitted passage of an engine. . . . For this mode of construction the Company is indebted to the judgment and skill of Horatio Allen, Esq., Chief Engineer. . . . In planning and building a road of the cheapest possible construction, as it was then well understood that the means could not be obtained for a more costly work . . . it is believed that no other man could have more completely met the wishes of the Company." This was indeed a compliment to the intelligence and inventive mind of the young engineer who had perhaps brought more practical experience and observation of railroads to this ambitious project than would have been available from any other. And in this day it must be realized that Horatio Allen was called upon to make engineering decisions for which no precedent existed—decisions that would follow him the rest of his professional life.

We have earlier referred to this road's first two locomotives, the *Best Friend* and *West Point*, and al-

though history does not tell us so, it is quite natural to assume that Allen was a most interested spectator at *Best Friend*'s epochal run. His knowledge of and interest in steam locomotives was evidenced on May 16, 1831, when he suggested some improvements in boilers and flues and an increase in the capacity of the steam chamber. At the same time he felt that a more powerful engine would better serve the road. This naturally meant more weight on the iron-capped wooden rails and to take care of this he suggested the locomotive be placed on eight wheels, for better distribution of weight. Foreseeing the difficulty an 8-wheel engine would have in rounding curves and passing over irregularities in the track, Allen proposed to overcome this by connecting only the center of the axle of each pair of wheels to the locomotive frame; thus each axle could move independently in rounding a curve.

Accordingly, the West Point Foundry was authorized to build such an engine as proposed, and in January 1832 the *South Carolina* arrived in Charleston. At a stockholders' meeting in May, the directors reported, "The advantages which it [*South Carolina*] possesses over those first procured is obvious. Its power is very great. . . . The board being fully satisfied of the preference due it, have ordered four similar engines, which will be procured by Mr. Allen. . . ." During 1833 the West Point Foundry delivered the *Barnwell*, *Edisto*, and *Hamburg*.

The locomotive "South Carolina," placed in service in 1832 on The South Carolina Canal and Rail Road Company (now part of the Southern Railway System). (Courtesy Southern Railway System)

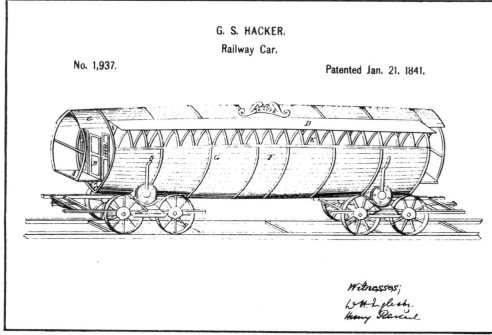

This extremely interesting railroad car, known as the "barrel car," was patented and built by G. S. Hacker, Master Carpenter of the South Carolina Canal and Rail Road Company, in 1841, and was used on that railroad for a short period of time. (Courtesy Southern Railway System)

188

From the beginning of his association with the road, even while constructing it, Allen had shown such keen interest in motive power and in the general operation of the railroad that it was only natural that he should be appointed operating manager, and early in 1834 this versatile railroader assumed the title of Superintendent of Transportation, in addition to that of Chief Engineer. Almost immediately he put together an organization with three general departments—Road, Machinery, and Transportation. Going a step further, Allen established two divisions of his road, Eastern and Western, with a General Superintendent in charge of each.

By July 1834, nine locomotives, nearly 40 passenger cars, and 90 freight cars were in regular service on the line. Three of the engines were pulling mixed trains "to and from Aiken daily, a distance of 120 miles, in nine hours, stoppages for two meals, for wood, water, etc., included. Each engine in succession lies by every third day at Charleston." Each locomotive pulled four passenger carriages and at least one baggage car in its train. In addition to the passenger carriages, the *Aiken* carried one freight car in its consist; the *Horry* two; and the *Edgefield* four. The engines, *Hamburg, Charleston, E.L. Miller,* and *Native* were put into regular freight service, pulling from eight to 25 cars each between Charleston and Aiken, the round trip requiring three to four days.

Horatio Allen was really running a railroad now and quickly discovered the need for scheduled operations and keeping his trains on time. There was no standard time then, only sun time, and that varied nearly seven minutes between Charleston and Hamburg. However, to such a railroad genius as Allen this was just another obstacle to get over, and get over it he did.

In his memoirs he states, "With the view of attaining the greatest possible regularity in the time of running of passenger engines, regulations have been established fixing the hour of departure from the six more important points on the line, as well as that of the earliest time at which they be permitted, under a penalty of five dollars, to arrive at the following one.

"The only difficulty that has been found in carrying this into practice has arisen from the want of a uniform standard of time at the different points. This we have removed by placing clocks at the Depositories at Charleston, Summerville, Branch-

ville, Blackville, Aiken and Hamburg, which being well regulated and readily accessible to the Engineer and Agent will enable them to regulate their movements on the road with great accuracy."

There can be no question that the successful building and operation of America's most ambitious early-day railroad project was due primarily to the genius of Horatio Allen. The job he had undertaken had been done, and done well; now, true to his breed of man, Allen looked for the challenge of new fields to conquer. After another extended tour of Europe he returned to America and with his old friend, John B. Jervis, built the Croton Aqueduct, New York's first large-scale water supply system. This tremendous undertaking completed, Allen was literally drafted into railroading again, when in 1843 he became president of the New York & Erie Railroad. But this man was an accomplished engineer, and disheartened at the financial dilemma which was part and parcel of Erie since its beginning, Allen resigned the presidency in 1844. When Erie finally reached the Great Lakes in 1851 he was its Chief Engineer.

Feeling that his work with Erie had been accomplished and again looking for new fields to conquer, 1870 found him Chief Consulting Engineer for a cable suspension bridge across the East River between Manhattan and Brooklyn; today the Brooklyn Bridge stands as another monument to his skill.

The high-iron road he built from Charleston to Hamburg still lives. Although the name has long since changed, it is an integral and vital part of the over 10,000 miles of steel rails in the great Southern Railway System, which stretches its network throughout the South.

A Little Line in the Deep South

In 1828, a Morris Hoffman of New Orleans journeyed to far-off Quincy, Massachusetts, "to view the railroad" (Granite State, first railway in America). He also stopped in Baltimore "to view the B&O" (which was scarcely a year-old) and "consulted and advised with engineers . . . and engagement was made with General Swift . . . to come to Louisiana and examine the ground over which it was proposed to run the road."

Returning to New Orleans, Hoffman organized the New Orleans Railroad Society. On the crest of the wave of public interest in railroads, the

Flanked here by the "Best Friend of Charleston" (first steam locomotive to operate on regular scheduled service on the American continent) and a modern 4-unit Diesel at Chattanooga, Tenn., Southern engine No. 6330 had just finished the last run to be made by a steam locomotive on the Southern Railway System. This final run was made on June 17, 1953. (Courtesy Southern Railway System)

Pontchartrain Railroad Company was chartered on January 20, 1830, to operate "From the city of New Orleans to some suitable point on Lake Pontchartrain or Bayou or other stream leading to said lake, not exceeding ninety feet wide, with as many sets of tracks as the said company may deem proper." Other charter provisions permitted the company to fix rates; however, passenger fares could not exceed 37½ cents each way, freight charges could not exceed 50 cents per ton, and "building material and firewood [shall] be transported for 30 cents per ton."

General Swift duly arrived and got the road built; and with fitting ceremonies, in which the Governor, members of the Legislature, and other dignitaries participated, the road was officially opened April 23, 1831. However, old records state "From experience of the B&O road, it has been considered expedient to use horses rather than steam engines. A velocity of 12 miles per hour can be obtained with horses. The order for the steam locomotive engine was countermanded."

Soon wishing to modernize, the road ordered a locomotive built by John Shields of Cincinnati, but when it arrived no one could be found who knew how to run it and the engine was relegated to stationary use. Possibly skeptical of American-built locomotives, the directors put the British-built *Pontchartrain* into service on September 17, 1832, when it hauled twelve coaches carrying three hundred passengers from the city to the lake shore. Within a few days it had struck and killed a Negro boy; within a week it had turned over in a ditch after hitting a cow.

By 1838, a resort hotel had been built at Milneburg, as the lake terminus was now called, and the prospering railroad owned four locomotives. The resort, later known as Bordeau Gardens, was a favorite watering place of pleasure loving citizens of New Orleans. The trip there by rail became so popular that at times it was necessary for the conductor to have a police escort to assist in collecting fares. Some of the passengers became so boisterous that the first train to arrive in the morning carried an empty boxcar in its consist which was set off on a siding. By nightfall this boxcar, which was really a bastille-on-wheels, was coupled to the rear of the train, where its contents of disorderlies and drunks was transferred "with considerable disturbance of the peace" to the jail in New Orleans.

On February 26, 1848, William Norris, Philadelphia locomotive builder, telegraphed the road:

". . . can ship at once a superior engine, $7000, four, six, eight and twelve months with interest. Answer by telegraph." It cannot be definitely established, but this telegram is believed by some to refer to *Smoky Mary,* the little engine that as far back as can be remembered made eight round trips on weekdays and twelve on Sundays at the head of her train over the 4½ mile road—running backward on the return trip to New Orleans, since there was no turntable at the other end.

When engineer John Galivan brought his train to a stop in New Orleans at 6:25 P.M., March 15, 1932, his pride and joy for 37 years, *Smoky Mary* had made her last run. *The Mobile Press* of March 16th stated in part, *"Smoky Mary* was known to every resident along the route. . . . 'She was just like one of the family!' wailed Mrs. F. Roma, 70, who rode the last trip."

For three more years the Louisville & Nashville, which had taken the Pontchartrain under its wing in 1880, operated freight trains "irregularly" over the track until 1935.

West of the Appalachians

Although the railroad fever first raged on the Atlantic seaboard, no part of America was immune from its attack. In the year of the great panic, 1837, a profligate legislature of Illinois (Abraham Lincoln was a member) had apparently gone wild and voted huge sums to build canals, highways, and railroads. Of twelve million dollars voted for internal improvements, nearly two million was allocated for the Northern Cross Railroad, proposing a line from Quincy, on the east bank of the Mississippi, through Springfield to the Indiana state line. On July 10, 1837, grading contracts were let, completion to be by January 1, 1840. The contract price was $8430 per mile "for mud sills, crossties and strap-iron rails (2½ by ⅝ inches weighing 13 pounds to the yard) laid on longitudinal stringers . . . the rails to be spiked to the stringers with 20 penny nails."

On May 8, 1838, the first rail was spiked down and on November 8th of the same year the *Rogers* (built by Rogers, Grosvener, and Ketchum of Paterson, New Jersey) pulled its first train to Morgan City (12 miles away) in two hours, "to the amazement of hundreds of spectators gathered to see the first real train to operate in the entire Mississippi Valley."

By 1840 three million dollars had been spent,

The *Rogers*. (Courtesy Wabash Railroad)

"Smoky Mary," on the tracks of the Pontchartrain in the
early part of the present century. (Courtesy Louisville &
Nashville Railroad)

This fashionably attired lady was built in 1867 for the Toledo, Wabash & Western (Wabash predecessor). Unfortunately, it is not possible to identify the crew, who posed with their charge at the Toledo roundhouse. (Courtesy Wabash Railroad)

The engineer and a VIP of the road pose for a picture about 1870. (Courtesy Wabash Railroad)

but it took another state appropriation to get the line to Springfield by 1842. The state's finances had now become so muddled that the railroad rested at Springfield for five years. Many thought the little line dead, but in 1847 private promoters revived and reorganized the sleeper, changing its name to Sangamon & Morgan Railroad. The little *Rogers* and a sister locomotive, as well as the rolling stock, had been worn out in state service, so while the line awaited new motive power the two remaining cars were pulled by oxen.

The name was again changed in 1855, to Great Western Railroad, and by 1856 had crept to the Indiana state line, where it connected with the tracks of the Lake Erie, Wabash & St. Louis line. Business must have been poor, for in 1857 Robert Schuyler, a "Railroad Magnate in New York," bought the Great Western for $100,000.

Possibly some of the trials and tribulations of this early road were brought about by lack of rules, for soon after Mr. Schuyler acquired it "Rules For Running Trains" were put into effect. They read, in part:

The dampers of the ash pans must be closed when crossing bridges . . . at a speed of not more than 6 miles an hour.

If any part of the train becomes detached when in motion . . . it is the duty of the brakeman to stop the detached part to prevent a collision with the part in advance.

Throwing wood from tenders . . . is strictly forbidden.

Baggage and brakemen will not pass through the passenger cars when they are in motion. . . .

Smoking, reading or conversing while on their trains is strictly forbidden.

Great care must be taken to avoid running over stock, and too frequent occurrences of this kind will be considered evidence of incompetency on the part of enginemen and conductors.

This pioneer road later joined its rails with others to become the Wabash Railroad.

Internal improvements, which included railroad construction, had been talked about and ballyhooed in Illinois since 1832. So much heat had been generated that on January 18, 1836, the Central Railroad Company was incorporated to build a road "from the mouth of the Ohio to a point on the Illinois River at or near the termination of the Illinois-Michigan Canal." This railroad, however, was destined for a long sleep within its corporate papers before any construction started.

Abraham Lincoln and other members of the Illinois Legislature of 1837 had frenziedly voted appropriations and for the vast works envisioned in "The Internal Improvement Act." Without estimates of cost or knowledge of need from surveys, four million dollars was appropriated for the Illinois-Michigan Canal, three and a half million for the Central Railroad, more than a million and a half for the Northern Cross Railroad, and still more millions for some dozen other railroads. But panics—later known as depressions and more recently as recessions—have a way of dealing with the folly of men, and the big one of 1837 brought financial chaos to the state, resulting in acts of the legislature of 1840 that stopped all railroad construction in the state. (Out of it all had come only 26 miles of the Northern Cross Railroad.)

Not until fourteen years later, when Lincoln's rival, Stephen A. Douglas, got to the United States Senate and helped push through the Federal Land Grant, did the Central Railroad rouse from its long slumber. In February 1851, the Illinois Legislature chartered the Illinois Central Railroad Company, granting it two and a half million acres of public lands allotted to it by the Federal Act. Soon thereafter Chief Engineer Roswell B. Mason and his young assistant, Grenville M. Dodge, were busy constructing the road. (Dodge would later become famous as Chief Engineer in building the eastern part of the first transcontinental railroad.)

When construction was in progress near the edge of Lake Michigan in 1852, Chicago, then a town on the lake shore, wanted no part of it or any other railroad, believing that its future lay in Great Lakes shipping and the vast network of plank roads that stretched in every direction from the city. So great was the prosperity of merchants that they built a camp for teamsters at the foot of Randolph Street. While the gamblers, pickpockets, and thugs enjoyed good picking, Rahab's descendants plied their trade with red lanterns by night. It required nearly six months of political maneuvering to get a city ordinance passed permitting construction of the railroad along the lake front.

Despite political troubles in getting started and a dearth of labor during construction, the mainline was completed in December 1854. Only minor oper-

The 671 heads down the mainline with the Wabash's crack Banner Blue in the twenties. (Courtesy Wabash Railroad)

The Pacific engine 672, built in 1912, pulling out of Montpelier, Ohio, at 10:30 A.M., July 3, 1944, is on the head end of perhaps one of the most famous trains on this continent. Nearly everyman's railroad at one time or another had a train dubbed "The Cannonball" rolling over its lines—even Casey Jones was pulling a cannonball over the Illinois Central on his fateful run—but here we see the cannonball of them all—"The Wabash Cannonball." It is not known when the song was first crooned about "This train she runs to Quincy, Monroe, and Mexico,/She runs to Kansas City, and she's never running slow . . ." but the author has the words of it, written by his mother in her "Copy Book" in 1892. The Wabash Cannonball is running still—behind a diesel. (Photographed by and courtesy Richard J. Cook)

The last steam locomotive operated on the Wabash Railroad. It took its last trip on January 28, 1955, on the Blu... Keokuk branch. (Courtesy Wabash Railroad)

The man who built the charter lines, Roswell B. Mason. (Courtesy Illinois Central Railroad)

Good Illinois land was offered at bargain prices in the 1850's as an inducement for settlers along the Illinois Central. (Courtesy Illinois Central Railroad)

Chief Engineer Mason's gangs laying track. (Courtesy Illinois Central Railroad)

The charter lines of the Illinois Central, 705.5 miles in length, completed in 1856, made this the longest railroad in the world at that time. (Courtesy Illinois Central Railroad)

The foot of Madison Street and Michigan Avenue, Chicago,
showing the old Illinois Central station. (Courtesy Illinois
Central Railway)

Illinois Central skirts the lake and the skyline of Chicago
in 1865. (Courtesy Illinois Central Railroad)

Old Illinois Central Depot at Chicago—used from 1856 to 1893. (Courtesy Illinois Central Railroad)

Watering an engine was no easy task on the Illinois Central in the 1850's. (Courtesy Illinois Central Railroad)

Modus operandi of coaling and watering after the turn of the present century. (Courtesy Illinois Central Railroad)

ating troubles bobbed up in the next year or two, such as in November 1856 when it was reported: ". . . only a night or two ago two engines lay over at Kankakee for 24 hours while the engineers and firemen were off on a drunken spree." Another old report of the same year states: "On Saturday the northbound freight train, five miles north of Chebouse, encountered a drove of cattle, throwing engine #74 down the bank and nine cars with it. One bullock was killed and others injured."

The year 1856 must have been a particularly bad one for operations, for another report states: "Engine #72 went out on the trestle east of the roundhouse at Chicago and sank in the lake. It now lies like a stranded ship with the waves breaking over it." Perhaps the 72 was a "night crawler"

(engine with a leaking throttle), as no mention was made in the report of a crew being on her. To wind up the year it was reported: ". . . trains between Mendota and Dunleith have been at a standstill for ten days, on account of ice and snow. The twelve snowplows owned by the company have been of little use. Several engines are off the track."

Things went better for the road after the trying year of 1856. Through absorption of other lines and by expansion, the Illinois Central is now one of the best operated railroads in the country, with its rails stretching nearly ten thousand miles through Illinois, Tennessee, Alabama, Mississippi, and Georgia.

Crossing the Big Muddy

As yet, no train had crossed the Mississippi, but

No. 201 operated in Illinois Central suburban service hauling trains carrying commuters to and from Chicago's loop from the 1880's until it was retired in 1926. (Courtesy Illinois Central Railroad)

Taking it easy on the seatbox, the fireboy watches the drivers roll as his hog steps a through freight across Illinois prairies. (Courtesy Illinois Central Railroad)

Mr. Dey, Chief Engineer (later to hold same position in building Union Pacific). (Courtesy Rock Island Line)

Iowa City Station, as it looked about the turn of the present century. (Courtesy Rock Island Line)

Home of Antoine Le Claire was used as first depot west of Mississippi River, at Davenport, Iowa. (Courtesy Rock Island Line)

203

as early as 1845, citizens of the little town of Rock Island, Illinois, had the idea that one could. They even organized the Rock Island & LaSalle Railroad Company in 1847, but inability to finance it caused the project to die aborning. Undaunted, they reorganized in 1851, amending the charter to permit entry into Chicago, over 300 miles to the east. By the fall of 1852, these enterprisers had "a whitewashed depot 60 feet long illuminated by coal oil lamps" on 22nd Street in Chicago; on October 10th the first passenger train left the depot for Joliet (extent of the line at that time).

Folks across the river at Davenport, Iowa, wanted a bridge so that the railroad being built could cross over to their side. They wanted their own railroad and in February 1853 secured charter for the Mississippi & Missouri Railroad Company, to run a line from Davenport to Council Bluffs, over 300 miles west on the Missouri River. Being men of action, they made it possible for Antoine Le Clare, a half-breed Indian and a very prominent citizen of Iowa in that day, to stick his spade into the good soil in September—for the first railroad in Iowa.

Peter Dey and Grenville Dodge then took charge and by the last of October 1855 had laid the rails to Muscatine, a distance of 27 miles from Davenport. Dey and Dodge had sworn they would have the line to Iowa City before January 1st of the next year, but on December 31, 1855, they were nearly a quarter of a mile from the goal. With the thermometer registering 30 below, citizens worked side by side with the construction gang, and as each section of rail was spiked the locomotive *Le Clare* moved forward its length. By 11:00 P.M. they were within 100 feet of the goal but, alas! *Le Clare* had frozen up. The workers got it moving again by turning the wheels with pinch bars, and the first engine over rails in Iowa reached the little station as church bells tolled out the old and rang in the new year.

In the meantime the Illinois legislature had chartered the Railroad Bridge Company. Since there was a small island located about midway across the Big Muddy (for which the town Rock Island was named) this site had been chosen for the railroad bridge. While the bridge was under construction, the tracks of the RI&LS Railroad had been steadily creeping westward, and on July 5, 1854, the first train from Chicago arrived at Rock Island.

With the bridge completed, the locomotive *Des Moines* puffed over it on April 21, 1856, pulling the first train in history to cross the Mississippi. Steamboat operators took a dim view of the event, visualizing the eventual loss of their freight monopoly to the railroad. Two weeks later, the steam packet *Effie Afton* struck one of the piers, and a part of the new bridge was burned and destroyed, whether it was done through accident or intention will never be known. In the lawsuit which followed rivermen thought they had won, when in May 1858, an Iowa judge declared the bridge "a public nuisance" and ordered removal of that part of it which lay in Iowa. However, one of the shrewdest railroad attorneys in Illinois, Abraham Lincoln, appealed the case to the United States Supreme Court; he won it, and of course the bridge remained.

Thus did the first railroad bridge to span the Mississippi bring together the two roads that later joined their rails with others to bring into being the great Rock Island System with its nearly eight thousand miles of track stretching through fourteen states of the South and West.

Rails Go Down in the Bluegrass

When the incorporators received their charter from Kentucky on January 27, 1830, for the Lexington & Ohio Railroad, there was much glee in the Bluegrass State over the anticipated means of being able to travel by rail from Lexington across the state to Louisville—and eventually out into the neighboring state of Ohio. But the enthusiasm of the Lexington instigators soon dampened, for the Louisville people wanted no part of it; the Ohio River furnished all the commerce they wished.

Determined to have a railroad, the Lexington boys decided to go it alone, and a survey as far west as Frankfort was started. If Louisville didn't want a railroad they wouldn't take it to Louisville. By December 1833, strap-iron rails rested on longitudinal limestone sills all the way from Lexington to Frankfort, and several trips had been made over the line behind horses as motive power. Although the many curves in the meandering 24-mile-line were said by some to have been necessary to "respect property lines around barnyards" and at the same time "enable the engineer to keep the rear of his train in view," others advanced the thought that perhaps the surveyors might have overindulged in the excellent bourbon for which the area is noted.

First locomotive to roll over rails west of the Big Muddy, *Antoine Le Claire.* (Courtesy Rock Island Line)

First railroad bridge to span the Mississippi. (Courtesy Rock Island Line)

First train in history crosses Old Man River as crowds cheer the *Des Moines* as she puffs through the timbers. (Courtesy Rock Island Line)

Old No. 9, herself a lady of vintage, proudly reenacts the scene that took place a hundred years before. (Courtesy Rock Island Line)

A real engine in her day, the big Pacific 894 heads west for Los Angeles, pulling the first Golden State Limited on November 2, 1902. (Courtesy Rock Island Line)

Homesteaders await the opening of the famous Cherokee Strip at noon on Saturday, September 16, 1893. The old Choctaw Coal and Railway Company (later a part of the Rock Island System) brought thousands of home seekers from all over the United States to the border of the Cherokee Strip. Engineers of five trains, all loaded to capacity with even the tenders and car roofs crowded with seething masses of humanity, sat tensely at their throttles waiting for the signal which would send them into the "Promised Land." (Courtesy Rock Island Lines)

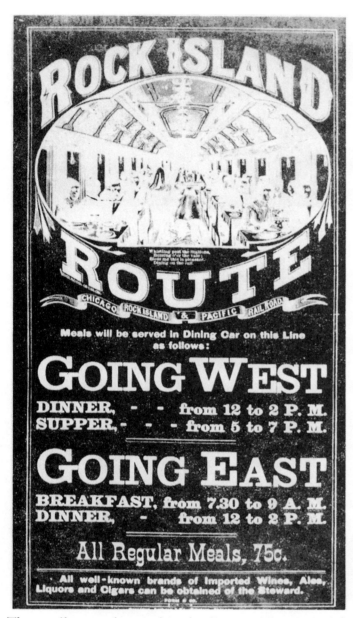

The excellent meals served in the diner on The Limited for only six bits, plus the "toddies" and imported wines to be had "most reasonably," inspired such ditty lines as:

"Whistling past the stations,
Buzzing o'er the vale;
Bless me this is pleasant,
Dining on the rail."
(Courtesy Rock Island Line)

Horse power was soon replaced by an "improved model engine" and when the line was opened for business on January 31, 1834, Lexington and Frankfort enthusiasts threw a real mint and bourbon party to celebrate their accomplishment. Although invited, nobody from Louisville showed up.

Perhaps offended by the impoliteness of the Louisvillians, the L&O apparently made no attempt to get closer to the Ohio River city, for in 1835 *The Lexington Observer* carried several articles relative to the enjoyment by the Lexington people of "the luxury of the cars" behind the little woodburners *Nottoway* and *Logan* running between Lexington and Frankfort. But there was difficulty sometimes, as evidenced by one news story which stated in part: "Able bodied men had to get out and push the passenger car [they only had one] and engine up the inclined plane [of less than one degree]; but after reaching the summit . . . in the deep cut, the engineer . . . having raised steam enough to carry passengers to the next slight ascension, cried out 'All Aboard' and away we went. 'All Out' was the engineer's next cry . . . [and] out we came . . . to help the little locomotive out of its terrible difficulty. Arriving at the top of the hill at Frankfort from a four to six hour's ride of twenty-four miles."

A short while after this description of a trip to Frankfort, the newspaper reported an accident on the line: "Some of the passengers on the two burthen cars attempted to jump; others . . . were thrown backwards and knocked off, those near the edge . . . under the wheels." Further investigation of the accident evidently convinced the editor of the paper that the train was overcrowded, for the next issue commented, "The number of passengers to go in each car should be limited. Huddling numbers on top is extremely hazardous." A further comment admonished, "Unless a wire sieve is fastened over the top of the chimney of the engine we shall soon have some dwelling house, barn or other outbuilding near the road burnt down or the cars themselves set on fire."

Financial difficulties struck the little road in 1842, and when it was sold for debt the state bought it, officially changed its name to Lexington & Frankfort Railroad, and continued its operation. Perhaps the state's operation of the 24-mile-line was in large measure responsible for the Louisvillians' change of mind about railroads. Determined that the Lexington boys should not have an exclusive on the "luxury

An exquisite illustration of a Brooks-built Atlantic type, probably built around 1900 for the Burlington, Cedar Rapids & Northern Railway (consolidated with Rock Island in 1885). (Courtesy Rock Island Line)

Beaver-topped and frock-coated station agent stands on platform of station at Indianola, Iowa, as passenger train stops in the fall of 1881. Attire of engine crew matched the keen-looking high-drivered 46, as attested by young derby-clad engineer. (Courtesy Rock Island Line)

Fireman Brown waves to photographer as Joe Kennedy opens the throttle and the 1889 moves across the trestle at Horton, Kansas, in 1904. Builder of engine is unknown; however, it well might be a John E. Wootten design, known as a "Wootten Boiler Engine," built in the 1880's. (Courtesy Rock Island Line)

Replica of *Nottoway,* "improved model engine," and one of the "Burthen cars" she pulled. (Courtesy Louisville & Nashville)

R. A. Shipp, Midway's last agent, looks up as he performs some final chores at his desk just before the official closing of the historic station. (Courtesy Louisville & Nashville)

Old Midway Station, about 13 miles west of Lexington, Kentucky, was a stop on the Lexington & Frankfort (later L&N). Two of the original longitudinal stone sills may be seen in right foreground. (Courtesy Louisville & Nashville)

Headed for far-away Nashville, the little woodburner
crosses Green River Bridge (just south of Munfordville,
Kentucky) on October 27, 1859. (Courtesy Louisville &
Nashville)

of the cars," a group of Louisville promoters obtained a charter for the Louisville & Frankfort Railroad in 1847, and by special act of the legislature took over the rights and privileges of the Lexington line west of Frankfort. By September 1851, a passenger could travel by rail from Lexington to Louisville.

Louisville had now become railroad conscious. Even before the two Frankfort lines got into joint operation a charter had been obtained on March 5, 1850, for the Louisville & Nashville Railroad. By September 1851, over a thousand shares of stock had been subscribed, but only $58 in subscriptions paid in; after paying an advertising bill of $22.55, the treasury held a net balance of $35.45 with which to commence operations.

This sickly condition of the treasury did not last long, however, for the city of Louisville had itself joined the railroad enthusiasts and to show its good faith subscribed to one-third of the authorized three million dollar capitalization. This, with other paid-in subscriptions, enabled the new road to get under construction in April 1853.

Getting the road built had its problems, for some of the terrain over which it was to pass was rugged, making tunnels and bridges necessary. In the early stages there was an epidemic of cholera which killed many laborers. As costs of construction mounted, the level of the treasury dropped; in fact, the finances were so low by the middle of 1854 that all work was suspended for almost a year. But by the summer of 1855, Lady Luck had smiled sufficiently on the project for rails to be laid for a distance of eight miles south from Louisville. This called for a celebration, and on August 25th an excursion train filled with "distinguished citizens, gentlemen of the press and hilarious folk in general, made the trip to the end of the line in 27 minutes. Warming to his task, the engineer made the return run in only 20 minutes."

Although the going was slow, persistence and determination of the backers never wavered, and October 27, 1859, was a gala day in Louisville: the new line opened for business. With flags flying and her whistle blowing, a little balloon-stacked woodburner pulled the slack out of the first train to roll over the five-foot-tracks and headed for the sparsely settled Nashville, Tennessee—187 miles away.

Sometime later, the Louisville & Nashville started

sprouting wing feathers which would eventually spread over 5000 miles and through thirteen states —taking over the two Frankfort lines and many others. A wing even spread to New Orleans, where in 1880 *Smoky Mary* ran under with the Pontchartrain.

Mr. Ogden Heads for the Mississippi

When William Butler Ogden arrived in Chicago from New York in 1835, he sensed the great possibilities of a railroad stretching west to the Mississippi. For over ten years he endeavored to rub his own rail enthusiasm into the vision of other business men, but their eyes took a dim view. The boys in the "Windy City" were smug with the ever-increasing commerce brought by the plank roads and lake shipping and wanted no part of a railroad.

With singleness of purpose, Ogden decided to go it alone and on his way learned that a railroad had been chartered in 1837 (during the internal improvement session of the legislature) but had slept quietly since. Reviving the charter of the Galena & Chicago Union Railroad, Ogden got in his buggy and visited every farmhouse in the vicinity for miles. Here he found fertile ground, and as railroad enthusiasm of the farmers rose, meetings were held in barns and schoolhouses until the day $250,-000 in stock had been subscribed. With sufficient funds for a start, Ogden lost no time, and construction got under way in late 1847. While the road was under construction, Ogden went in search of a locomotive and found the Michigan Central (which had managed to get as far west as Michigan City) agreeable to parting with one of their iron horses. The ten-ton *Alert* was loaded on a boat, taken across Lake Michigan, and unloaded at Chicago and pulled by team to the railhead of Mr. Ogden's road. The *Alert* was the 37th locomotive built by Baldwin in 1836 for the Utica & Schenectady; however, its original name was *Pioneer* (change of name having been made when the Michigan road acquired it about 1845). With some repairs, a coat of paint, and its original name, *Pioneer,* restored, the little engine was made ready to go into service pulling the few second-hand cars over second-hand rails which had been laid a distance of about seven miles.

On October 24, 1848 (so far as is known, without the fanfare usually accompanying such momentus occasions), Mr. Ogden and his board of

Typical scenes at the L&N station at Mobile, Ala., around the turn of the century. (Courtesy Louisville & Nashville)

With her throttle back, this big Pacific roars by WSM radio tower (just south of Nashville) at 5:39 P.M. August 15, 1933, heading the crack Pan American toward New Orleans. (Courtesy Louisville & Nashville)

The 1882 stops at Worthville, Kentucky, January 28, 1957, with local freight No. 86. Train and engine crew wave farewell, as this marks the last run of a steam locomotive on the head of a train over L&N lines. (Courtesy Louisville & Nashville)

First locomotive of the Galena & Chicago Union Railroad (predecessor of Chicago & North Western), *Pioneer*. Unfortunately, the cigar-smoking pilot cannot be identified, nor the gent by her tender. This picture was made after this great little engine had seen thirty years of service on Mr. Ogden's road. Taken at Turner Junction Roundhouse (West Chicago) about 1878. (Courtesy Chicago & North Western)

A class E 2 oil burner, the 2908, romps down the mainline, westbound across the prairies. (Courtesy Chicago & North Western)

Locomotive No. 248 bringing train No. 411 into Carpentersville, Illinois, in June 1908. This train operated between Chicago and Williams Bay over the West Chicago–Crystal Lake Division. (Courtesy Chicago & North Western)

The farsighted railroad pioneer and grand gentleman who started it all for the C&NW, Mr. William Butler Ogden. (Courtesy Chicago & North Western)

directors climbed into one of the little cars and the first locomotive to head west out of Chicago pulled out for Des Plaines. Returning late in the afternoon, the president and his board were hard pressed for space, since they shared it with the wheat that was loaded at Des Plaines.

Unlike so many of the pioneer roads, the Galena was a success from the very beginning and in its first year of operation had earned better than $2000 per month. Dividends were coming with regularity to the farmers along the line who had put their hard-earned savings into the stock of the road. Mr. Ogden had not only proved himself of excellent vision but a man of rare ability to run a railroad. By 1853 the rails had found their way to Freeport, and two years later the tracks stretched all the way to the banks of the Mississippi at Fulton.

Now determined to make a real railroad, Ogden got control of the Madison & Beloit and some other pioneer railroads in Wisconsin, consolidated them, and in 1864 merged the Galena with her sisters to become the Chicago & North Western. By 1867, Mr. Ogden's rails had reached Council Bluffs, Iowa, where they waited until after the Civil War as a connection east for the first transcontinental railroad.

With over ten thousand miles of mainline stretching through nine states of the Mississippi Valley, this great system actually stems from the little farmers' Galena & Chicago Union Railroad—first visualized by William Ogden.

4
The Bugle Blows

Charleston, South Carolina, had the honor of witnessing several firsts in the history of iron horses and railroads in America. We recall that it was from Charleston that the first American-built steam locomotive in regular, scheduled service pulled its first train on December 25, 1830. Legend has it, and in all probability is historically correct, that one of the passengers on this historic train (the bride, Mrs. Henry L. Pierson) became so enthused over rail travel that it was through her efforts that the New York & Erie Railroad got the boost that started it. It was also at Charleston that the first locomotive boiler explosion occurred, when *Best Friend* let go on June 17, 1832.

Now, just over thirty years after *Best Friend's* first run, Charleston was to witness her greatest first yet, when the 67-year-old Confederate, Edmund Ruffin, mounted the emplacement of a shore battery at 4:30 A.M. on April 12, 1861, got his range, and fired on the Federally occupied Fort Sumter in Charleston Harbor. This was the opening gun of a bloody conflict that has perhaps never had an equal.

In a sense, this first of modern wars was destined to be a curious admixture of both old and new methods of warfare. Old in that the troops, artillery, and horse-drawn supply wagons would move over roads, many of which were worse than those of the ancient Romans. New in that it would also be the first war in history in which much of it would be fought on rails.

Quite naturally, all of the railroads in the South, as well as some of the border roads, played their part. However, since Virginia was to be the chief battleground in this dramatic struggle, we shall for the most part confine our brief comments to Virginia railroads.

At the beginning of hostilities, Virginia could boast nearly fifteen hundred miles of track, with seventeen railroads operating within her borders. Five of these roads, Richmond & Danville (now Southern Railway System), South Side, Norfolk & Petersburg, Virginia & Tennessee (later to become a part of Norfolk & Western) and Roanoke Valley, operated generally in an East-West direction on a 5-foot-gauge. The remainder, Richmond & Petersburg, Petersburg (later a part of Atlantic Coast Line), Seaboard & Roanoke (later Seaboard Air Line), Orange & Alexandria, Mannasas Gap, Richmond & York River (later Southern Railway System), Winchester & Potomac (later B&O), Virginia Central (later Chesapeake & Ohio), and Richmond, Fredericksburg & Potomac, all operated in a generally North-South direction on standard gauge (4 ft. 8½ inches). Northern railroads operating in the state were Northwestern Virginia & Alexandria, Loudon & Hampshire (later B&O) and the Baltimore & Ohio, all operating on standard gauge and connecting the northeastern and northwestern part of Virginia with Washington and Baltimore.

Due to the conflict of gauges, connections at terminal points posed almost impossible bottlenecks, which were to delay desperately needed freight cars and their contents for sometimes weeks at a time. Roadbeds and tracks were fairly typical of the times, ties often being placed on bare ground, with iron "T" rail, weighing 50 to 65 pounds to the yard, laid on top. Some lines still used wooden stringers capped with strap-iron weighing not over 20 pounds

Roundhouse and depot at Alexandria of Orange & Alexandria (Southern Railway predecessor) in 1863. At this time and until end of hostilities practically the entire road was in the hands of Federal authorities. Motive power in view was typical of the war period. (Courtesy Southern Railway System)

The *Westward Ho* was one of the first locomotives owned by Louisa Railroad (Virginia Central in 1850) and is a good illustration of the type of engine in operation on Virginia railroads at the outbreak of the Civil War. Built about 1849, this little 4-4-0 woodburner did her part throughout the entire conflict. She must have been a good one, for the picture was made in 1875, when she was twenty-six years old. Incidentally, the man at the throttle is the author's grandfather, Andrew Jackson Phillips. ("Gramp" never stated the purpose of the big rope on her pilot; maybe she was a night crawler.) (Courtesy Chesapeake & Ohio)

Typical wooden passenger car of Civil War period. (Courtesy Pennsylvania Railroad)

Union Mills Station (now Clifton, Va.) on the Orange &
Alexandria Railroad during the Civil War. (Courtesy
Southern Railway System)

to the yard (47 miles of the R&D had this type roadbed).

At the beginning of the conflict, Virginia roads had in operation 180 engines, all woodburners and most of them American type, 4-4-0. The average length of a locomotive was 35 feet and weights varied from the 9-ton *Remulus* on the S&R to the 31-ton *Milborough* on the tracks of the Virginia Central. The R&P could boast ownership of the oldest locomotive, *Phoenix* (built by Bolton & Hicks in 1838), but the average age of the 180 engines was approximately seven years. Most of these locomotives had been built by Northern builders, such as Baldwin, Norris, Rogers, Boston Locomotive Works; however, 33 of them had been built in Richmond by Tredeger Iron Works. By contrast, just one state above the Mason-Dixon Line, Pennsylvania, had over 600 locomotives.

In April 1861 the rolling stock on Virginia railroads consisted of 158 passenger cars, 67 mail and express cars, and 1997 freight cars. Just two Northern roads owned more than three times the total of all Virginia roads—Pennsylvania 3700 and the B&O 3500 cars.

Almost at the very beginning of hostilities, Southern sympathizers prevailed upon Persident John Garrett of the B&O with such pressure that he reluctantly agreed to discontinue transporting Federal troops from Ohio and Pennsylvania over his lines. Doubtless Garrett soon realized his mistake, for when "Stonewall" Jackson observed train after train of loaded coal cars moving west over Mr. Garrett's line toward Baltimore, he concluded something should be done about it.

In a well laid trap at Harper's Ferry on May 22, 1861, the cunning Stonewall seized 50 locomotives and 350 cars belonging to Garrett's road. This was just the beginning of trouble for the B&O, as later in the contest this road was to receive preferred attention from Jackson and his subordinate officers. Since the industrial North had furnished the agricultural South with rails up to this time, and the supply source was now cut off, that part of Mr. Garrett's road in Virginia would furnish (unwillingly) Virginia lines with quite a bit of rail.

The war was hardly three months old when probably the first movement of troops to a battlefield by rail took place. On Thursday afternoon, July 18, 1861, three little woodburning locomotives, pulling three trains of assorted consists (flat, box, and passenger cars) moved Confederate troops from the little station of Piedmont, on the Manassas Gap Railroad, a distance of 34 miles to the battlefield at Manassas. Between July 18th and Sunday morning, the 21st, when the engagement started on Bull Run Battlefield, nearly ten thousand troops had been moved in; doubtless this first rail-transport of troops to a battlefield was responsible for the Confederate victory at First Manassas.

After the battle, it is almost certain that the first ambulance trains ever run took the wounded to hospitals in the rear of the lines. There were no ambulance cars then and mattresses were laid on straw-covered floors of freight cars. But the railroads were quick to grasp the need and one week after the battle the Wilmington & Weldon (later A.C.L.) had fitted up cars to handle about twenty patients, for use between Richmond and Wilmington, North Carolina. By October 1861, the Virginia Central had converted several of its 23 passenger cars, each with 22 single and 11 double berths which could accommodate 44 wounded soldiers. However, throughout the four-year conflict there were never enough ambulance cars and after an engagement any cars available were pressed into service. The railroads must be credited with saving many lives by transporting large numbers of wounded from battlefields to hospitals far behind the lines within a reasonably short time.

The first military railroad in history appeared in late 1861, when Joseph E. Johnston's Confederate Army of the Potomac (later Army of Northern Virginia) built a five-mile line from their base near Centerville to Manassas (junction of O&A and MG railroads). Incidentally, rails for the line were donated by the B&O (however, they were not a free-will offering).

Although the first military railroad was to serve only a few weeks, bringing in supplies, another first for the railroads came about through its disuse. On March 2, 1862, General Johnston ordered the evacuation of all military stores from Centerville to Gordonsville, 54 miles southwest over the O&A lines. This evacuation of a military supply base by rail, although successful, was not as successful as some previous firsts. A combination of bungling by both the war inexperienced railroad officials and the subsistence officers resulted in the employment of 32 locomotives and 300 cars—ten times the number needed. There were numerous wrecks over the single-

Destruction at Manassas Junction 1862 (where Manassas Gap and Orange & Alexandria's rails joined). (Courtesy Southern Railway System)

Rear view of mortar mounted on flat car; the gun is shielded by iron plates and heavy timbers. This was the forerunner of the giant rail artillery used in France in the First World War. (Courtesy Southern Railway System)

Destroyed Richmond, Fredericksburg & Potomac bridge
over the Rappahannock in 1862. Picture shows north end
of bridge at Falmouth, just across the river from Fredericksburg. (Archives Virginia State Library)

Wreckage like this was a frequent occurrence on the Orange
& Alexandria during the war years. Part of it operated by
Federal forces as the U.S. Military Railroad, part of it
operated by the Confederacy, it was a railroad divided.
(Courtesy Southern Railway System)

track line, costing over a million pounds of stores and the destruction of some 50 cars. Whereas it had been estimated that a train could make the run in five to six hours, pileups caused so much delay that many trains required up to 36 hours to get through.

By early June of 1862 the Confederates had come up with another first in railroad warfare. On June 29th, a 32-pound gun mounted on a flatcar appeared on the Richmond & York River line (now Southern Railway) and gave a good account of itself in the battle of Savage Station. This was the world's first railroad battery.

As the struggle intensified, with railroads and their equipment broken up, bridges burned, etc., the war on rails became more difficult for the South. Parts of some lines had "changed ownership" and were in the hands of the Federals; however, the roads were as difficult to operate by one side as the other. Perhaps one of the worst pileups occurred on the tracks of the O&A (then in Federal hands) near the little station of Bristoe on August 26, 1862. Hearing the rumble of an approaching train, Confederate soldiers spied a nearby pile of crossties and a woodpile and quickly "stacked the rails." In a few moments the flickering headlight of a little wood-burner made its appearance through the darkness and, unaware of what awaited him, the engineer plowed into the obstruction. Simultaneously volley after volley was fired at the engine, *Secretary,* but holding the rails she scattered lumber in all directions as her engineer pulled her open and the little locomotive and her train sped onward into the night.

Chagrined at their failure, the Confederates located a switch nearby and opening it waited like a cat at a mouse hole for any luckless train that might be following. They didn't have long to wait. The locomotive *President* hit the open switch point, climbed the rails, and carried half its long train down the steep embankment; volleys poured from the soldiers' muskets into the melee.

The terrific noise of the crash had hardly subsided when another unsuspecting train plowed into the rear of the *President's* cars that were left on the rails. Both wrecked trains were burned and the locomotives taken as prizes of war by the Confederates. The *President* was repaired, renamed *General Stuart,* sold to the Virginia Central for $25,000, and served as a freight engine on that road for the duration of the war. The second locomotive, *Red Bird,* was renamed *Mars* and sold to the Richmond &

Danville, on whose rails she served throughout the conflict. These engines, as well as many more, plus cars, carwheels, and rails, were unwilling donations of the B&O.

Wisely, the Federal government had early seen the necessity for coordination of railroads in the conflict, and in 1862 appointed Daniel Craig McCallum Superintendent of all roads outside of the Confederacy. McCallum was not only an able railroad man (he was formerly General Superintendent of the New York & Erie) but possessed rare executive ability.

In contrast, the South lacked this coordination of its railroads. Although Col. F. W. Sims, who headed the "Railroad Bureau" of the Confederacy, did his utmost, he was so handicapped by lack of authority due to political interference, petty jealousies, and bickering among the railroads themselves, that this bureau could accomplish little. As an illustration, the RF&P Railroad was pressing a suit against the O&A and Virginia Central for $160,000 in 1861, for infringement upon its (RF&P) exclusive right to transport passengers between Richmond and Washington. In 1862, the O&A brought suit against Virginia Central, charging that three of its passenger and a number of freight cars had been damaged and not returned to the road. In retrospect, this lack of authoritative coordination was second only to the inability of the railroads of the South to obtain the needed repair materials for their locomotives, rolling stock, and rails.

By late summer of 1862, the Confederacy had 825 miles of track open, with nearly 500 miles in the hands of the Federals. Deterioration of its locomotives, as well as rolling stock and roads in general, is well illustrated by the fact that prior to the existing "unpleasantness" Virginia Central was operating freight trains over the 72 miles between Richmond and Gordonsville in approximately eight hours. Now it was taking these trains 18 to 20 hours for the same run; for when the locomotive ahead had to stop for wood or water, all trains following were forced to halt.

Pressure was so great on some of the little railroads that in many instances the crews of engines and trains remained on duty for periods of a week at a time, catching naps as best they could in dirty and muddy boxcars. Out of food, the poor devils had to subsist on what could be rustled up wherever they happened to be. Such conditions were enough

Apparently this Danforth-built locomotive had just been received by the Federals at City Point, Virginia (Hopewell), and the boys had added potted flowers to her decorations to celebrate the occasion. (Courtesy Norfolk & Western Railway)

to drive any man to drink—and in some cases it did.

On June 23, 1862, several trains had reached the little station of Louisa, on the Virginia Central, when they were stopped. For 48 hours they waited, but, dutiful railroad men that they were, dared not leave their trains, other than to seek food. On one of the foraging expeditions one of the crews unexpectedly ran into a barrel of apple brandy; tired, hungry, and disgusted with the long delay, they decided to forget their troubles in the glow of applejack nectar. The boys were pretty well lubricated when orders came to proceed to Beaver Dam —20 miles east down line.

When leaving Gordonsville, the engineers had been warned that no bells should be rung or whistles blown, and that any crew responsible for a wreck would be punished by death. The night was dark and rain had started to fall when engineer John Whalley swayingly pulled himself up the gangway to the cab of his engine, *Monroe*. With difficulty he had found his seat on the box when conductor Carter Anderson (somewhat less inebriated than the engineer) suddenly appeared in the cab. All engineers considered the cabs of their engines sacrosanct from interference by anyone, and Whalley took a dim view of the whole situation. Knotting the whistlecord as he spoke, conductor Anderson called to the colored fireman, "Wesley, you apply those brakes if your engineer gets too much speed."

With the mellow applejack working, John Whalley was in no mood to be dictated to by a meddlesome conductor and, pulling the throttle open, he was soon highballing down the mainline toward Beaver Dam. Whalley was really rolling the *Monroe* down a grade when the urge came and he reached for his whistlecord. Anderson threatened the engineer with a stick of wood as the lurching train rounded a sharp curve near the little station of Frederick's Hall; at this gesture Whalley pulled his reverse bar back to stop, that he might settle the matter once and for all with the conductor. Suddenly, the dim red glow from an oil lamp on the rear of a caboose brought Whalley to sobriety and his senses, as he brought his train to a stop, just short of the one in front.

Difficulties of Southern railroad operation had become so great by 1863, that President Edmund Fontaine of the Virginia Central reported, "In some places the rails sag so on decayed ties that the ashpans of our engines press down the mud like a plasterer does his trowel." The faithful but necessarily neglected little woodburners on the Richmond & Danville had "reached such a state of health from wear and tear and lack of service" that they could hardly pull a train up a normal grade; it sometimes required two days to make a trip over the 140 miles of rails between Richmond and Danville. Railroads operated their own sawmills for producing ties and fuel, and in many instances the wood disappeared almost as fast as it was stacked along the lines. But in spite of the vicissitudes of war the game little railroads continued to do battle.

The Virginia railroads did get a slight break for approximately six weeks in 1863, when Lee's Army of Northern Virginia moved into "enemy territory" and on the northward march paid due respects to the B&O. Soon after crossing the Potomac on June 17th, the Confederate cavalry wrecked and burned an eastbound 17-car B&O train pulled by the Ross Winans-built locomotive #108 at Point of Rocks; the next day the same invaders wrecked the entire line between Cumberland and Martinsburg, burned all railroad bridges within three counties, and blew up an iron structure 400 feet long. As the rebels pressed northward the havoc wrought on the B&O became more intense, not only from the Confederates but also from the Federals. So extensive was the damage done to this road, from June 17th until Lee's retreat from Gettysburg in early July, that it required every available effort of the B&O from July 14th to August 10th to get through traffic moving again over the line.

The little breathing spell granted the Virginia roads was perhaps instrumental in bringing about one of the most outstanding operational feats performed by the railroads during the entire war. Barely two months after Gettysburg, on September 9, 1863, the first train, loaded with Confederate troops, pulled away from the encampment near Culpeper, Virginia, and headed toward Chattanooga, Tennessee, on its way to Georgia. When it was learned that Chattanooga had fallen into the hands of the Federals, the train was re-routed via tidewater railroads to Atlanta; thence to Ringgold (Georgia), arriving in the afternoon of the 19th, as the battle raged on the field at Chickamauga. Closely followed by other troop-trains, 15,000 men had been transported from Northern Virginia to the battlefield at Chickamauga within ten days. In this day, one hundred years later, such a feat would be

New rail stored by the U.S. Military Railroad at Alexandria. This was something that was in extremely short supply for the Confederates during the entire conflict. (Courtesy Southern Railway System)

The yards of the L&N, N&C, and N&NW at Nashville looked like this after a visit by "The Tiger in the Saddle," Confederate General Nathan Bedford Forrest. Incidentally, General Forrest became the first president of the Selma, Marion & Memphis Railroad in 1873 (Southern Railway predecessor)—a 280-mile line through the war-ravaged South. (Courtesy Louisville & Nashville Railroad)

View of roundhouse, Alexandria, Va., during the Civil
War. (Courtesy Southern Railway System)

After the bloody battle of Shiloh, when the hotel was jammed with wounded, awaiting trains to Memphis. (Courtesy Southern Railway System)

considered anything but spectacular; but when consideration is given to the then prevailing facts—motive power and rolling stock in dilapidated condition and moving over makeshift rail lines of various gauges—it must be considered one of the greatest feats ever accomplished by railroads.

Later the same month (September), the Federals accomplished an even larger movement, when 25,000 troops, 10 batteries of artillery with their horses, and over 100 baggage cars were transported by rail a distance of 1200 miles, from Northern Virginia to Bridgeport, Alabama, in eleven days. These two movements of troops certainly proved the excellence of railroad logistics during the Civil War.

As the railroad war raged, it was an almost everyday occurrence for roads to be torn up, first by one side and then by the other. Strap-rail on wooden stringers broke up like matchwood under the traffic. On December 8, 1864, Federals tore up the Petersburg Railroad (ACL) for a distance of approximately 40 miles to the Meherrin River (almost to the North Carolina border). Hundreds of men stacked their arms and literally turned whole sections of track upside down, knocking off the ties and piling them crosswise; the pile was fired and the heated rails corkscrewed around convenient trees and telegraph poles into "iron neckties."

On December 16th, other Union troops went to work in earnest on the Virginia & Tennessee (N&W), burning 15 trains, wrecking over 50 bridges and generally rendering the line unusable for a distance of 85 miles east of Bristol. For the duration—

Federal troops at Alexandria station, August 27, 1862, waiting to get aboard for transportation to the battlefield at Bull Run (second Manassas). Engine 162 had been captured from the O&A. (Courtesy Southern Railway System)

U.S. Military Train, somewhere along the tracks of O&A.
(Courtesy Chesapeake & Ohio Railway)

Bridge across Potomac Run (six miles north of Fredericksburg) built by Union forces in 1862. When President
Lincoln viewed the structure he described it as having
been built of beanpoles and cornstalks. (Courtesy Richmond, Fredericksburg & Potomac)

These rails will soon be "iron neckties." (National Archives)

United States military railroad yards at Alexandria, Va., in 1863. Note the various types of cars and locomotives and the hospital car. (Courtesy Southern Railway System)

Temporary railroad bridge built to replace one destroyed. (Library of Congress)

until the not-far-distant April 1865—the western portion of this road was out of the fight.

Ever tighter closed the net around the fighting hearts of the game little Confederate roads. General Sherman's armies gave their undivided attention to the Virginia Central and O&A railroads in early March 1865, and by the middle of the month, these roads and the RF&P were wrecked beyond repair and out of the fight. By March 29th the only remaining lines of rail communication in Virginia were the South Side and Richmond & Danville railroads. The two contesting armies were drawn up in battle lines around Petersburg and the long and bitter conflict was almost over. On April 2nd, a detachment of Grant's forces cut the South Side line, which left only the Richmond & Danville open.

Although preceding the formal surrender at Appomattox by a week, Sunday, April 2, 1865, actually marked the end of one of the fiercest struggles ever fought. In the Richmond yards of the Richmond & Danville was sufficient rolling stock and locomotives

to make up only eight trains. This meant that only a part of the archives and personnel of the doddering Confederate government could be transported to Danville (its last seat).

The streets of the capital in Richmond overflowed with ungovernable mobs that Sunday afternoon. In their haste to evacuate, the military authorities fired government warehouses; the holocaust quickly spread throughout an area three blocks wide and ten long. During the afternoon and throughout the night, panic-stricken mobs struggled to and in the area surrounding the Richmond & Danville depot, clamoring to get aboard the trains leaving for Danville.

President Davis and his official party had left the turmoil on the first train, early Sunday night; and following close behind, wheezing but game little woodburners pulled other trains loaded with archives, gold and silver bullion, and personnel of governmental departments, plus evacuees who managed to get aboard. As the last passenger train from the depot safely crossed, the long bridge spanning the James River was fired by a detachment of sailors. After completing their mission, the navymen quickly

234

This picture shows repairs being made to the Orange & Alexandria Railroad's bridge, which was destroyed by Confederate troops on August 27, 1862. The structure spanned Bull Run, just a short distance from the battlefield where the second bloody battle opened on August 28, 1862. (Courtesy Southern Railway System)

The little 4-4-0 that pulled President Davis's train out of Richmond on April 2, 1865. Built by Rogers Locomotive & Machine Works, her cab panel carried the name Charles Seddon when delivered to the Confederate Government in 1864. A short time after this trip the engine was purchased by the Richmond & Danville and numbered 24 (later changed to No. 14). This picture was made at the roundhouse in Manchester, after she had been converted from a wood burner to the use of coal. (Note pipe from sand dome in front of first pair of drivers, also elaborate scroll work on bellhanger.) (From Cook Collection, Valentine Museum)

Draped in black and accompanied by the military escort shown here, this car carried the body of President Abraham Lincoln from Washington to Springfield, Ill., in April 1865. Built at the United States Military Car Shops (which the Federal government had taken over from the Orange & Alexandria), the car was intended for the use of the President. He never rode in it during his lifetime, and its one official use was to carry his body to Springfield. (Courtesy Southern Railway System)

Remains of Richmond & Petersburg bridge after the fire. This picture was made at the north (Richmond) end of the bridge; across the stone piers in the background was the Manchester Yard. Piers and arch still stand under present A.C.L. bridge. (Courtesy Valentine Museum)

got aboard the little train waiting in the yards on the south side of the river and were under way toward Danville.

Because of the proximity of the raging fire to its depot, the Richmond & Petersburg moved a number of its trains South over its bridge to the yards in Manchester—then set fire to the bridge. Fanned by a southern breeze, the fire soon worked its way along the bridge to the depot in Richmond, spread to a government warehouse filled with ammunition, and added pyrotechnics to the holocaust of Richmond. Both the Virginia Central and RF&P depots, located on Broad Street, some distance from the big fire, escaped destruction.

Although the next Sunday, April 9, 1865, when General Lee accepted the magnanimous terms from General Grant at Appomattox, marked the end of the Confederate States of America as a government, it was a new beginning for the railroads of the South, their game little woodburning locomotives, and the gamer men who ran them during the conflict.

Unquestionably the railroads had been put through the acid test and had demonstrated their worth in time of war. At the beginning of the struggle, the railroads, in good condition, had served the armies and the South well; as they weakened, so did the strength of the land they served.

5

Rails Toward the Sunset

During the fever of the 1830's railroads had sprung up like mushrooms—all of them, however, east of Old Man River. When the big panic struck in 1837, there were approximately 200 railroads either in operation, being built, or in the planning stages. But even with the territory west of the Mississippi sparsely settled, visions of rails stretching to the Pacific had been caught as early as 1832. On February 6th an editor of *The Weekly Emigrant* of Ann Arbor, Michigan, advocated ". . . construction of a line from the Great Lakes to the Pacific Ocean."

There were other early advocates of a "Pacific Railroad" in the persons of Dr. Samuel B. Barlow of Massachusetts, and the Reverend Samuel Parker, a Presbyterian missionary who had travelled in the West and noted in his journal in 1838, ". . . there would be no difficulty . . . of constructing a railroad from the Atlantic to the Pacific Ocean." John Plumbe, who had just that year helped organize the Richmond & Petersburg Railroad in Virginia and moved to Dubuque, Iowa, held a public meeting in his home in 1836 to discuss "Organization of a Pacific Railroad."

Another who did yeoman's work in the endeavor was Asa Whitney, of North Groton, Massachusetts. Whitney immediately ran into conflict with Plumbe; he (Whitney) strongly advocated a northern route from Lake Michigan to Oregon, whereas Plumbe took a staunch and stubborn stand for a southern route. Although neither Plumbe nor Whitney were destined to get further than the talking stage, they did accomplish much by arousing the interest of prominent public men in such a project—two of these being Senator Benton of Missouri and Josiah

Perham, a railroad excursion promoter operating in Maine and Massachusetts. So much interest had been engendered by 1853 that Jefferson Davis, then Secretary of War, ordered a government survey of all proposed routes and sent out five different surveying parties to determine the most practical route.

All of the interest in a "Pacific Railroad" did not come from the East, however. At the invitation of C. L. Wilson of Sacramento, Theodore Dehone Judah, a brilliant young civil engineer who had already had some railroad experience, left Connecticut and arrived in California in 1854. Wilson and his associates wanted to build a railroad, and within a year after his arrival Judah had constructed the first railroad in California—The Sacramento Valley. Original intentions had been for a line from Sacramento to Mountain City, but by the time Folson had been reached, so had the bottom of the treasury, and the twenty-two-mile line of rails came to an end.

Ted Judah's brilliant and visionary engineering mind had become so impressed with railroad possibilities in California that 1856 found him in Washington, buttonholing congressmen for a land grant so that the Sacramento line could be carried all the way to San Francisco. Unsuccessful, he returned to California and with visions of even bigger things energetically went to work. "Crazy Judah," as some now called him, had created so much interest in railroads in California by 1859 that he arranged and staged his "Pacific Railroad Convention" in San Francisco. October 1859 found Judah again headed for Washington, this time to argue for "the construction of a railroad from the Atlantic to the Pacific." Again his mission failed, as the attention of Congress could

Theodore Dehone Judah, the dreamer and engineer with a consuming vision. (Courtesy Southern Pacific Company)

not be diverted from the disagreement raging between Northern and Southern legislators.

Undaunted and with singleness of purpose, Judah returned to California and spent his time seeking a suitable pass through the Sierra Nevadas; in late October 1860 he found it—at Dutch Flat. Immediately drawing up what he termed "The Articles of Association of The Central Pacific Railroad of California," Judah stumped the state from Sacramento to San Francisco to interest all and sundry. Listeners were interested in hearing what he said, but when it came to subscribe to stock they all kept their hands in their pockets. Finally, Leland Stanford, of Stanford Brothers Mercantile Company, lent a receptive ear and, liking what he heard, interested some of his Sacramento friends. Quickly, Mark Hopkins and Collis P. Huntington, partners in a hardware business, and Charles Crocker, a drygoods merchant, agreed to meet Judah and look at what he had in the bag. A conference with the young engineer was arranged by the "Big Four," who became so interested and enthused that the minimum amount of capital was pledged. On June 28, 1861, charter was obtained for "The Central Pacific Railroad Company of California" with a capitalization of eight and a half million dollars. Now that Judah had seen his vision come to life he immediately continued his surveys for the line until late fall, when he again journeyed to Washington.

Judah, whose vision, grit, and determination had

Ted Judah stands beside the tender of the *L. L. Robinson,* built by Holmes Hinkley, Boston, in 1855, first locomotive to puff over rails of California's first railroad, Sacramento Valley, February 22, 1856. (Courtesy Southern Pacific Company)

The bold Collis P. Huntington. "I never started anything I didn't finish." (Courtesy Southern Pacific Company)

Second floor of this building was headquarters where the Big Four met. (Courtesy Southern Pacific Company)

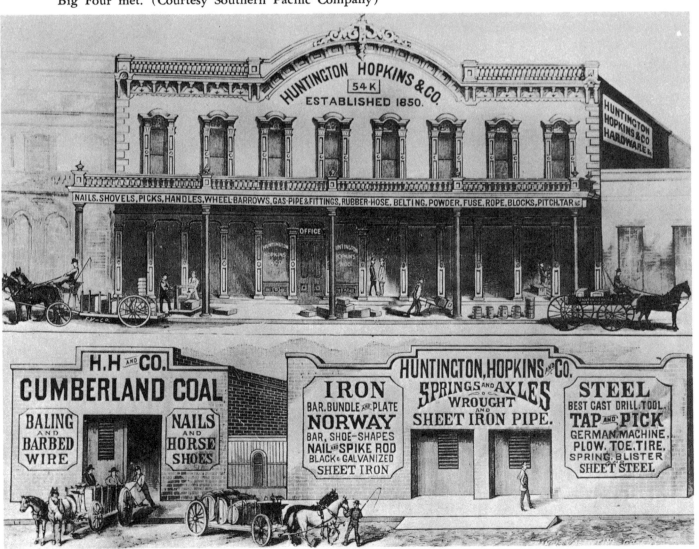

Thin, sad-faced Mark Hopkins, who loved dogs, horses, and bookkeeping, but was ill-at-ease with people. (Courtesy Southern Pacific Company)

Leland Stanford, first president Central Pacific, grocer-turned-governor. (Courtesy Southern Pacific Company)

Construction Chief, James Harvey Strobridge, the tee-totaler who drove his men with dedicated fury; known to the Chinese workmen as "One Eye Bossy Man" (he had lost the sight of his right eye in a blast of black powder in Bloomer Cut). (Courtesy Southern Pacific Company)

Sacramento Valley Railroad terminus at Sacramento. This
picture of California's first railroad terminus was made
about 1860. (Courtesy Southern Pacific Company)

certainly earned him the honor to be called "Father of the Central Pacific," if not father of the first transcontinental system, was in Washington when President Lincoln, himself a former railroad attorney, signed the Pacific Railroad Act on July 1, 1862. The ink on the signature had hardly dried when Judah, the man who had made and seen his dream come true, wired his associates in Sacramento, "We have drawn the elephant. Now let us see if we can harness him up."

Since the Central Pacific had already been chartered, the act specifically incorporated the name "Union Pacific Railroad Company." Under the act the CP was to construct a line from San Francisco to the eastern boundary of the state—and beyond if the UP had not reached that point—until the two roads met. The act also made provision for Federal land grants on both sides of the lines over the entire distance, government loans ranging from sixteen to forty eight thousand dollars per mile, and a telegraph line. (Judah had indeed drawn an elephant.)

On the murky and rainy January 8, 1863, after bales of hay had been laid on top of the knee-deep mud and a limited amount of "speechifying" had taken place, ground was broken at Sacramento and construction started on the Central Pacific.

Little progress had been made, however, before Judah, the dreamer and man who did things for the doing, crossed wires with those who held the purse strings. As Chief Engineer, he wished to construct a good road as rapidly as possible. On the other hand, Huntington and his associates insisted that the first 40 miles be built with all possible speed—regardless of construction (the huge government subsidies would not be available until the first 40 miles had been constructed). Arriving at an impasse, Judah withdrew, accepted the $100,000 proffered from the Big Four, and took ship (around the Horn) for New York. One week after his arrival, he was dead of yellow fever.

Perhaps the inauspicious weather at the ground breaking was a harbinger of what was to come during construction. The act had stipulated that only American-made rails and iron could be used and the Northern manufacturers, eager for the fast buck, promptly raised the price 80 per cent. The raging war in the East necessitated running Confederate blockades, with the result that eight to ten months were required for shipments by sea to come around the Horn to San Francisco. Freight charges advanced 275 per cent, boosting rates to over $50 and making the delivered cost of rails nearly $150 per ton. A shipment of 18 locomotives carried a freight bill of approximately $85,000.

The first shipload of material did not arrive until late October, and when the first rail was to be spiked down on October 26th, it was suggested to Huntington that the occasion be fittingly celebrated. But that gentleman was not a first-spike-celebrator and replied, "Any little nobody can drive the first spike . . . there are months of hard labor and unrest between the first and last spike. The last spike is the one we'll celebrate."

So right Huntington was. The prime necessity of any such venture was money, and it was hard to come by. The financiers of San Francisco wanted no part of it. The telegraph companies then in operation vigorously opposed the whole project, since a competitive line of wires was a part of the act. Steamship companies, stagelines, and toll roads joined in the opposition. Huntington had an office opened in San Francisco to sell stock, but in the thirty days of its life the promoter could interest only three investors, who subscribed to a total of 15 shares.

Charles Crocker, who had assumed the duties of General Superintendent, was racking his brains in an effort to solve his labor problem. No Californian with any inclination to work would put his energies to any labor other than "digging for gold"; and generally when such a man hired out with a construction gang his duration of employment lasted only until he had sufficient money to set out to some digging.

As Crocker kicked his problem around, the idea occurred that perhaps descendants of those who had built the Great Wall of China should be able to build a railroad, and to test his theory Crocker had fifty Chinese brought to the job. So satisfactory were these men that soon the state had been scoured clean and more were on the way from their homeland across the Pacific. When construction was under way full blast, over ten thousand Chinese were on the payroll.

Despite winter snows that sometimes accumulated to a depth of ten feet, avalanches that sometimes hurtled the camp, buildings, and men into some desolated canyon, difficulties of getting supplies to the job, and other obstacles, the pigtailed horde bored their way eastward and with black powder blasted through solid granite mountains. In June 1868 the tracks of the Central Pacific stretched from

244

Waterfront at Sacramento as it looked in 1864. (Courtesy Southern Pacific Company)

First freight engine on Central Pacific, built by William Mason in 1864. A 4-6-0, *Conness,* on the turntable at Newcastle railhead in 1864, had a total weight with her tender of about 120,000 pounds and the combination measured 52 feet in length. With a tractive effort of 15,350 pounds, she easily handled 18-car trains. (Courtesy Southern Pacific Company)

Snow was a problem from the beginning, and snow sheds were built for miles on end. Note tree trunks used as supports. Engineers said it "was like railroading in a barn." (Courtesy Southern Pacific Company)

Locomotive *C. P. Huntington.* (Courtesy Southern Pacific Company)

The men with pigtails pushing toward Dutch Flat and the summit at Donner Pass. (Courtesy Southern Pacific Company)

Chinese graders working the fill at Screwtown Trestle.
(Courtesy Southern Pacific Company)

The Central Pacific's first locomotive, *Governor Stanford*.
(Courtesy Southern Pacific Company)

The only honor Ted Judah ever received from his dream-road was his name given to the fourth locomotive of the CP. Note headlight and pilot on each end. (Courtesy Southern Pacific Company)

Sacramento to the line that separates California from the Nevada Desert.

Since October 19, 1865, Grenville Dodge had been pushing the Union Pacific west from Omaha. The wiry and tough Casement brothers, Dan and Jack, in charge of track-laying had rounded up more than a thousand men in their crews, consisting of ex-soldiers (both Confederate and Union), ex-convicts, several hundred Irishmen imported from the Boston area, and, to add zest and piquancy, a sufficient number of mountain men and mule skinners.

Construction had hardly gotten under way before gamblers and whiskey peddlers set up business at convenient locations. To complete and compete for the entertainment of these rough-and-ready boys, the painted dolls and calico cats, following that ancient profession Rahab conducted on the walls of Jericho, soon made their appearance. To the sufficiency of these attractions was soon added a more serious problem—Indians, and they were war parties of the Sioux of the Plains.

Survey parties, who had to work at considerable distances ahead of the construction gangs, all went armed, and military drills were a regular part of and in addition to the surveying activities. Military escorts of a dozen or more men regularly accompanied the survey parties, usually occupying some prominence near the activity. But in spite of this protection there were many occasions when members of the parties were killed and their stock driven off by the Indians.

As work progressed in earnest the construction force was increased by the importation of more Irishmen from the East, until finally nearly ten thousand of them were bulging their muscles to the task. Rail-laying became a science to these hardy men, and when an Easterner witnessed a track-laying scene he wrote: "We stood upon an embankment . . . about a thousand miles this side of sunset . . . with a feeling of profound respect. A light car, drawn by a horse, gallops up . . . with its load of rails. Two men seize the end of a rail and start forward, the rest . . . taking hold by twos, until it is clear of

253

Locomotive *Hercules* has just stopped with her work train at Cisco in November 1866 (rail head at that time, 92 miles east of Sacramento). (Courtesy Southern Pacific Company)

Known as "a hell on wheels town," Bear River City, on
White Sulphur Creek (965 miles west of Omaha), lived
up to its name in providing entertainment—gamblers, gals,
and the cup that cheered after a day's work of track-laying.
(Courtesy Union Pacific)

Come morning, those who were not too far gone from the night before were again heading the high iron West. (Courtesy Union Pacific)

Perpendicular walls of granite meant nothing to the survey parties, who scaled them like human flies. (Courtesy Union Pacific)

The gold and silver was good when they got it, but, with the ever-present whiskey peddlers, painted dolls, and "games of chance," it didn't stay with these hardy, fun-loving boys long. (Courtesy Union Pacific)

the car. At the word . . . the rail is dropped in its place. . . . The same process goes on at the other side of the car . . . Four rails go down to the minute . . . the moment the car is empty it is tipped over on the side of the track to let the next loaded car pass by, and then is tipped back again. . . . It is a sight to see it go flying back again for another load, propelled by a horse at full gallop . . . ridden by a young Jehu who drives furiously. Close behind . . . come the gaugers, spikers and bolters. . . . It is a grand anvil chorus . . . in triple time, three strokes to the spike. There are ten spikes to the rail, four hundred rails to the mile, eighteen hundred miles to San Francisco—21,000,000 times are those sledges . . . to come down

with their sharp punctuation before the great work of modern America is complete."

There was no law where these UP construction gangs pushed westward, except that very effective one enforced by the old six-gun, Winchester rifle, and a hemp rope. Once, when a bunch of roughnecks and gamblers took over a railhead, Casement was asked "to take a force and clean house." A short time later, Dodge went to the little shack-town (Julesburg, Colorado) to ascertain how proceedings had gone. More of a doer than a talker, Jack Casement escorted his chief to a slight rise where there was a new graveyard, saying, "The bad men all died with their boots on."

By November 1866, rails of the UP shined in the sun at North Platte, Nebraska, and by June of the following year had stretched their way to Julesburg,

258

One of the Casement construction trains "on location."
(Courtesy Union Pacific)

Rough and ready General Jack Casement—and he could and did use his mule-skinner on man as well as mule. (Courtesy Union Pacific)

Colorado. In November 1867 the western terminus was Cheyenne, Wyoming. On toward the sunset the sturdy crews pushed their line.

Snaking across Utah, the UP was nearing Great Salt Lake when there was a little altercation with Brigham Young, a stockholder, who wanted the line to pass through Salt Lake City. Young even denounced the UP in his tabernacle, but to no avail— the decision had been made on Ogden.

The race between the two roads was now on in earnest. What a pity Ted Judah, who had started it all, was not on hand to participate. The vision he had brought into reality had completed grading almost to Ogden, while the UP was on a grade just west of Humbolt Wells. It had been agreed that the meeting point would be Promontory Point, a little shack-town on the northern edge of Great Salt Lake.

The little yellow men had pushed so steadily eastward that for some distance their grade now paralleled that upon which the men from the land of the shamrock were carrying west. The Irishmen regarded themselves above, and looked down their noses at, the men from China, and in one recorded instance were a bit careless in setting off a blast, which killed several Chinese. Taking a dim and oriental view of this sort of reception, the Chinamen won lasting respect with a blast that buried many Irishmen in a common grave.

260

Sawmill camp at Cottonwood Canyon. (Courtesy Union Pacific)

Tunnel 3, east portal, Weber Canyon, Utah—and black powder blasted the hole. (Courtesy Union Pacific)

The Stanford Special at Monument Point, on the shore of Great Salt Lake, May 7, 1869. "Monument" and lake can be seen in left background, while wagon train of emigrants bound for California pass in foreground. (Courtesy Southern Pacific Company)

262

Devil's Gate Bridge, about 15 miles east of Ogden, Utah. Photo made in 1869, just before the UP and CP met at Promontory. (Courtesy Union Pacific)

Locomotive *Jupiter,* with steam up and ready to pull out
with Stanford Special for Promontory. (Courtesy Southern
Pacific Company)

Bovine motive power on wagon trains brings supplies to construction crews at Echo Canyon, Utah, in 1868. (Courtesy Union Pacific)

There were those who couldn t wait for rail transportation. With scouts on horseback ahead, a wagon train of emigrants on their way west passes construction trains at Archer, Wyoming (then end of track), in 1867. (Courtesy Union Pacific)

Snow played no favorites and the Union Pacific took it in stride. Many of the drifts were higher than the locomotives, and generally five engines were put behind a plow. (Courtesy Union Pacific)

Old 85 at the roundhouse after a bout with the snow. This type plow was approximately 11 feet high, 10 feet wide, and 25 feet long. (Courtesy Union Pacific)

The great day that all America awaited dawned and remained wet and blustery that May 10, 1869; however, the cup that cheers freely made the rounds to brighten the spirits of those hundreds gathered at Promontory for this auspicious occasion. After slipping the last tie beneath the adjoining rails, Construction Superintendents James Strobridge for Central Pacific and Sam Reed for the UP moved back a respectable distance as President Leland Stanford of the CP approached. Taking good aim, Stanford raised his sledge and let fly. Even though he missed the spikehead the resounding impact upon the laurel tie was telegraphed over America. With this part of the ceremony completed, the two locomotives moved slowly toward each other until their pilots touched; then each engineer left his cab and crashed a bottle of champagne against the other's engine. Up to this point East *was* East and West *was* West—but never again. The Twain *had* met and Theodore Dehone Judah's dream of a transcontinental railroad across America was a reality.

The party was on at Promontory. To the strains from the military band, which had accompanied the Twenty-first Infantry, men produced bottles from convenient pockets to fortify themselves against the weather and at the same time put proper spirit into such an auspicious occasion. As the telegraph carried the momentous news across the land, a hundred-gun salute was fired in New York. The Liberty Bell tolled in Philadelphia and thousands cheered in the nation's capitol. Gigantic parades lasted for two days in San Francisco, while at Omaha a one-hundred-gun salute set off a celebration that has not been duplicated in Nebraska since.

A few days later, when the first passenger train from Omaha crossed the spot in a swelter of singing steam, its dust flipped another page of history.

The last spike has gone down, Engineers George Booth on the *Jupiter* and Sam Bradford on the UP 119 have pulled toward each other until the pilots of the locomotives touched. (Courtesy Union Pacific Railroad)

The "Last Spike" ceremony at Promontory, Utah, May 10, 1869. This is the over-all view, with Central Pacific President Leland Stanford in the center of the picture with the spike mall on his shoulder (to the left of Mrs. J. H. Strobridge in the light dress). J. H. Strobridge, CP's construction boss, stands on the other side of his wife with the shovel in his hand. The Union Pacific officials are between Stanford and the table set up with the telegraph key—which transmitted the completion ceremony to the country. Central Pacific locomotive *Jupiter* is the diamond-stacked locomotive at left, and Union Pacific locomotive No. 119 is at the right. (Courtesy Southern Pacific Company)

The *General Sherman,* first locomotive on UP rails, was built in Paterson, New Jersey, loaded on a flat car, and sent by rail to St. Joe, Missouri, where it was put aboard a steamer and sent up the Missouri River to Omaha in the spring of 1865.

Fuel for these first locomotives of the UP was generally cottonwood, cut in six-foot lengths and piled on the tender. The firemen axed it into chunks to fit the firebox and many of them swore it was so green it sprouted after it was on the fire. (Courtesy Union Pacific)

THE RAILS FOLLOW AN OLD TRAIL

In 1806, Zebulon Pike had been sent on an exploration of part of the Louisiana Purchase by the United States Government. Following the Arkansas River into the foothills of the Rockies he had turned south toward the upper waters of the Rio Grande; arrested by the Spanish, he was taken to Santa Fe and held prisoner until the next year.

Upon his return to Missouri, Pike's fabulous news of Santa Fe set the blood of adventurers surging. In April 1812, Robert McKnight, operator of a trading post at Franklin, got a pack-mule train together, loaded up with trading merchandise, and set out for the Promised Land. The caravan made it, but on arrival at Santa Fe they had their mules and merchandise confiscated and they themselves were imprisoned until Mexico won her independence in 1821.

The real beginning of the Santa Fe Trail, as the white man knew it, was on September 1, 1821, when another trader at Franklin, William Becknell, got a party together and loaded their pack mules with merchandise to trade the Indians for horses. The season was late, and finding that the Indians had previously disposed of their stolen trading-stock, the party turned south at what is now LaJunta, Colorado, crossed Raton Pass, and shortly thereafter met a troop of Mexican soldiers. Expecting arrest, Becknell's group was surprised to learn of Mexico's independence; and further surprised at the invitation extended them to bring their merchandise to Santa Fe.

Arriving in Santa Fe on November 16th, Becknell quickly disposed of his merchandise at a fabulous profit and with one of his party loaded their silver into saddlebags and headed back toward Missouri. Trading possibilities at Santa Fe spread like fire in dry tinder before the wind, and on May 22, 1822, Becknell and twenty others crossed the Missouri and headed for Santa Fe. This was perhaps the most important caravan that ever moved over the Santa Fe Trail, for in addition to using pack animals, Becknell and two associates carried their merchandise in wagons—the first wheels to roll over the Santa Fe Trail.

Santa Fe not only built up a great trading center but a gambling center as well, for in 1831 an Eastern paper stated, "The Generals and the Colonels and

Engine No. 6, hot as a popcracker, at the head of a ten-car
passenger train coming through Fish Cut, near Green
River, Wyoming. (Courtesy Union Pacific)

Freight stopped at a siding in the Utah Desert along the
UP about 1900. (Courtesy Union Pacific)

272

Through freight highballing across the Nebraska plains near Gibbon in 1908. (Courtesy Union Pacific)

The *McQueen,* built by Schenectady Locomotive Works, was "spanking new" when this picture was made in 1866 at some little station in Nebraska. Fireman, at rest in shirt-sleeves, has apparently just finished chopping and loading his fuel and will probably be penalized for leaving two of his logs in foreground. Possibly telegraph wires come over the roof near chimney on station, just over the heads of the bystanders on platform. (Courtesy Union Pacific)

A little woodburner and a rotary plow opening the line in the high Sierras in 1889. (Courtesy Southern Pacific Company)

A big Pacific oil burner stepping high, wide, and handsome along the UP Trail in 1929. (Courtesy Union Pacific)

The crack Forty-Niner at Evanston, Wyoming, in 1937. On the head end is a big Pacific-type engine built in 1904 (class 7000). It was streamlined in 1937 when wheel arrangement was changed to 4-8-2, and was scrapped in 1941. (Courtesy Union Pacific)

Yard scene at Colfax in the 1860's. The big fellow with the whiskers evidently works the woodpile and has just refueled the engine. Note link and pin coupling and tow-cable on rear of tender and typical handcar of the period. (Courtesy Southern Pacific Company)

A diamond stack woodburner in Bloomer Cut, east of Newcastle, California. Black powder blasted out this 63-foot-deep, 800-foot-long cut. (Courtesy Southern Pacific Company)

Excellent illustration of the Southern Pacific diamond stack can be seen on the engine in foreground. Picture made at Tehachapi Loop in 1876. (The high pass is at Southern end of Sierras.) (Courtesy Southern Pacific Company)

Everybody looks, even the horses, as a passenger train on the SF&SJ rolls toward the trestle over San Francisquito Creek in 1864. Telegraph line skirts twin redwoods. (Courtesy Southern Pacific Company)

Passenger train stopped at Cisco in 1865, where waiting
Wells Fargo stagecoaches took over for the trip eastward.
(Courtesy Southern Pacific Company)

It is just possible that the nattily attired Beau Brummell standing at the pilot of the 149 is her engineer, reluctant to let his beautiful engine out of sight too long. Who can blame him? The 149 was as fast, dependable, and practical as she was beautiful—and proved it:

A train chartered by theatrical producers Jarrett and Palmer had rolled into Ogden from New York on the morning of June 3, 1876. With two engineers in the cab, Hank Small and Jim Wright, the 149 headed the Lightning Express west out of Ogden as their watches split the hair at 9:58 A.M. Stops for wood and water consumed a lot of time, but in spite of it the dependable engine skipped over the 879 miles to San Francisco in 23 hours and 45 minutes. When she stopped her "Special" at Oakland Wharf at 9:43 A.M., June 4th, she had hung up a record that would stand for the next thirty years. (Courtesy Southern Pacific Company)

The *Solano,* largest ferryboat in existence at the time, disgorging a passenger train at Port Costa in 1879. This ferry plied the Carquinez Strait (of San Francisco Bay) between Port Costa and Benicia. (Courtesy Southern Pacific Company)

The *El Gobernador,* the 14-wheeler freight engine built by Southern Pacific in its Sacramento shops was the giant of its day, and specifically built for service on the Tehachapi grade. It should have been a real workhorse but as often happens in design engineering her boiler was too small for the engine. Her firemen (she often used two at a time) said, "All hell couldn't keep her hot," and she was scrapped in 1894. (Courtesy Southern Pacific Company)

Derbies for the engine crews seemed to be in vogue on the CP, but the 4-4-0 passenger engines built in the shops at Sacramento "ran like hell" in spite of 'em. With 69-inch drivers getting their thrust from pistons sashaying in cylinders 17x26 inches, 75 miles an hour was old hat to them on the Peninsula Division. (Courtesy Southern Pacific Company)

Wood had a hot fire on this little diamond stack as she
gallops with her train near Oak Park (now Burlingame,
Cal.) in 1884. (Courtesy Southern Pacific Company)

These 4-6-4 woodburners dragged the freights in the 1880's. As with all CP engines then, the second rings of the diamond stacks exceeded the diameter of the boiler. (Courtesy Southern Pacific Company)

the Majors and the Captains gamble. The Judges and the Lawyers and the Doctors and the Priests gamble—and there are Gentlemen gamblers by profession."

In 1846, over 400 wagons carrying merchandise worth nearly two million dollars arrived in Santa Fe, and by 1849 a monthly stageline service was operating over the trail.

Spreading back over the East, the fabulous stories of the Santa Fe Trail reached the ears of a young attorney in Pennsylvania. In 1853, twenty-six-year-old Cyrus Kurtz Holliday had accepted as his fee for drawing the charter, stock in the Pittsburg & Erie Railroad. A few months after the line was completed, and sold to the Atlantic & Great Western, Holliday had sold his holdings for $20,000, and in 1854 was looking for new fields to conquer. Late 1854 found the young attorney at Papan's Ferry on the Kaw River. Believing that he saw great opportunity, Holliday joined with Enoch Chase, bought

up some cheap land, and proceeded to lay out a town. They named it Topeka, an Indian word meaning potato field or patch.

As the little settlement grew, thoughts of a railroad plagued the young man's mind. The more he thought, the better the idea seemed, and late in 1858 Holliday wrote by hand the charter, which was granted February 11, 1859, to the Atchison & Topeka Railroad. The line was to run from Atchison through Topeka "to such point on the southern and western boundary of Kansas Territory in the direction of Santa Fe as may be convenient and suitable and to any points on the southern boundary of Kansas Territory in the direction of the Gulf of Mexico."

But there were going to be delays before even a start could be made on Holliday's extensive dream. The worst drought ever known, before or since, struck soon after the road was chartered, and following close on its heels came the Civil War. Taking these setbacks in stride, Holliday talked about and perfected plans for his railroad, and on November 24, 1863, had its name changed to Atchison, Topeka & Santa Fe. The young lawyer must have rankled as

Scenes in San Francisco right after the earthquake and fire
April 18, 1906. (Courtesy Southern Pacific Company)

The first oil-burning locomotive placed in service on SP lines. Locomotive 1344 went into service for Southern Pacific in May 1895, to inaugurate new fueling operations for the railroad. Wood-burners had gradually given way to coal-burners although some of the former were still in use in the late 1890's. Shortly after the turn of the century, oil burning was successfully in general use. Although SP tried burning oil in an experimental way in a 4-4-0 type locomotive in 1879, No. 1344, converted from a coal-burner in 1895, was the first. Oil was used extensively in 1899 on SP's Los Angeles Division and coal was discontinued there in 1901. Locomotives on the Sacramento Division were converted from coal to oil in 1902, and on the Salt Lake Division in 1912. (Courtesy Southern Pacific Company)

Emergency lunch room of the SP at the Ferry Building operated by the railroad in connection with its relief activities at the time of the 1906 San Francisco earthquake and fire. E. H. Harriman, president of SP, is the man in the business suit seated at the table on the left. (Courtesy Southern Pacific Company)

A high-saddled passenger engine heads one of the first trains to cross Great Salt Lake over the causeway on the Lucin Cutoff in 1904. Historic Promontory Point had now been bypassed with a saving of many miles along the old route. The new causeway rested on 20 miles of rock fill and 12 miles of trestle. During its construction, Camp 20 had been set up midway across the great inland lake and it was at this spot that the single track fanned out into three on a platform 120 feet wide by 240 feet long. A telegraph station was set up with three women operators and they, together with some 25 other SP employees, made their homes in houses resting on piling for 41 years until 1945, when Midlake became a ghost town. (Courtesy Southern Pacific Company)

Overland Limited train No. 1 at Reno in 1908. The Overland a short time before had received $2 million in new equipment and this premier, first-class-only train operating between San Francisco and Chicago was also advertised as being "electric lighted." (Courtesy Southern Pacific Company)

The Sunset Limited stopped at Santa Barbara, California, about 1910. (Courtesy Southern Pacific Company)

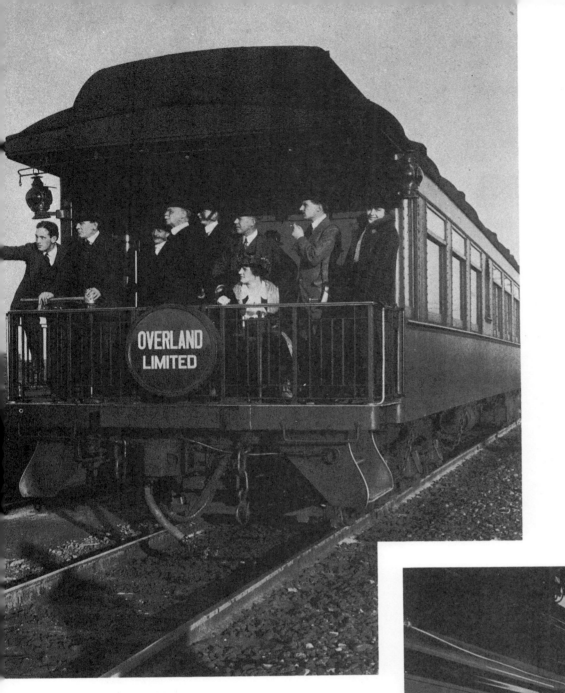

Inside and outside view of observation car of the de luxe Overland Limited, extra-fare train on a 65-hour schedule between San Francisco and Chicago in 1915. (The author had the never-to-be-forgotten privilege of being a passenger on this ultra-ultra varnish job the same year, and needless to say the picture brings back fond memories of the long ago.) (Courtesy Southern Pacific Company)

A 2-8-8-4 cab-ahead, built by Baldwin about 1941 for freight service, rolling through a southern California town in 1943. (Courtesy Southern Pacific Company)

A familiar scene in an all-important dispatcher's office. (Courtesy Southern Pacific Company)

A time freight highballs at the speed of a passenger train over a valley trestle along the scenic Southern Pacific. (Courtesy Southern Pacific Company)

Ruts made by the old caravans are still visible in the foreground of this old picture of the Santa Fe Trail. Roadbed of the Santa Fe, on a slight fill in left background, can be seen as it parallels the old trail. (Courtesy Santa Fe Railway)

A powerful 4-8-4 swings a Daylight streamliner on a curve through the scenic Santa Lucia Mountains. On a 9¾ hour schedule over the 470 miles between Los Angeles and San Francisco, pulling 600-ton trains, these streamlined engines "had what it took." (Courtesy Southern Pacific Company)

Mr. Holliday, who started it all. (Courtesy Santa Fe Railway)

the war dragged on, delaying his plans. Traffic over the old trail was ever-increasing with freight aboard wagons behind bulls and mules; passengers were shelling out $250 for fare between Independence, Missouri, and Santa Fe on Barlow & Sanderson stages.

Finally the great day dawned—and with a bang. October 30, 1868, was cold and blustery as ex-senator Ross made a flowery speech and introduced "The father of the Santa Fe Railroad." With great enthusiasm Holliday told his listeners that this new road would reach "from Topeka to Santa Fe, far into Mexico and meet the Pacific on the Gulf of California, thence on into the Rocky Mountains." Stepping from the improvised platform, Holliday and Ross each turned a spade of earth. Thomas Peter, in charge of construction, probably turned the atmosphere blue with the profanity for which he was noted, as the twenty or thirty laborers he had been able to get together dug in and headed the Santa Fe Railroad west.

In late March 1869, Tom Peter had completed the new bridge over the Kaw, and on the 31st the first locomotive to roll over Santa Fe tracks backed

Hays City Stagecoach stopped at station along the old trail.
(Courtesy Missouri Historical Society)

"Concord Model" stagecoach was the mode of travel over the Santa Fe trail from 1848 to 1872. It was only a month's journey from Independence, Missouri, to Santa Fe, New Mexico. (Courtesy Santa Fe Railway)

294

Where the traveller had a choice of conveyance to his or her hotel from the station. The Santa Fe even shuttled a "bus," seen in left background. (Courtesy Santa Fe Railway)

over the bridge to North Topeka. The *C. K. Holliday* had four 60-inch driving wheels and had been built by Niles Machine Works, at Cincinatti, some years before for the Ohio & Mississippi Railroad.

Now that they had some tracks and a good second-hand engine, all that was needed was rolling stock. From the Indianapolis & Cincinatti Railroad a second-hand day coach was purchased and proudly lettered. From Barney & Smith, over at Dayton, Ohio, the budding Santa Fe bought twelve flatcars; and with a handcar purchased in Chicago, the new road was ready to commence operations.

No sooner was the equipment gotten together than a train had to be made up and a run made. On April 26, 1869, Brit Craft had a hot fire and the popvalve humming, Bill Bartling was at his brakes, and as the last passenger climbed aboard conductor W. W. Fagan gave the highball. George Beach pulled the throttle open on Mr. Holliday's namesake and the "Picnic Special" pulled out of Topeka for Wakarusa Creek—seven miles away. The run was made in

good time, 30 minutes, but as the creek had not yet been bridged, the crew and passengers disembarked and boarded wagons for the stretch over the roadbed to Wakarusa Grove, five miles south. After the picnic, the celebrants climbed back in the wagons and returned to the waiting train at the creek, which was backed into Topeka.

At Carbondale were some shallow coal mines, which in addition to supplying fuel for the motive power also produced much needed revenue for the railroad's treasury. So well was the road prospering that in July 1869 another locomotive, *General A. E. Burnside,* was purchased, along with 12 boxcars, another passenger coach, and a baggage car.

Southbound out of Topeka, the engine would stop at Wakarusa Creek. A grade ran from the creek up to the top of the flatland, so after taking on water the train was backed almost a mile—to run for the hill.

By September 1869, 26 miles of railroad had been laid to Burlingame, where it hit the Santa Fe Trail, and two passenger trains were in daily service on a schedule of 2 hours and 35 minutes. There was no telegraph line and, as James Marshall has so well

Newton Station and yard office in 1871. Grass covered the streets of Newton when this picture was made and just south of the railroad tracks were the honky tonks. Saloons, with nude paintings lining the walls, were the first attractions for the trail drivers, and after slaking their thirst the boys moved on to the attraction of the dance halls, gambling joints, and painted dolls. When the cowboys had been cleaned out, they headed back down the trail to bring another herd in. (Courtesy Santa Fe Railway)

296

A trail herd on the move toward the high corral at Newton, Kansas, in the 1870's. (Library of Congress)

Perhaps to dress the windows for this early picture, the *C. K. Holliday* was coupled to all the rolling stock owned by the Santa Fe in 1869. (Courtesy Santa Fe Railway)

Millions of longhorns coming north from Texas put their hoof prints on the old Chisholm Trail, named for the old Cherokee trader Jesse Chisholm. Many herds went to Abilene and other Kansas railheads to be loaded in cars for the trip to eastern markets over rails. (Courtesy Oklahoma Historical Society)

put it, "trains ran by smoke and headlight, which was all right except that at night trainmen often couldn't see the smoke and the headlight rarely shone more than a [city] block ahead."

By 1870, Mr. Holliday's road had followed the old trail 30 miles, to Council Grove, and was steadily pushing west. When the rollicking population of Newton, Kansas, heard that the rails were coming it had trebled and when the Santa Fe reached there in 1871 it had reached nearly 6000. The old Santa Fe Trail was crossed near Newton by another famous trail, the Chisolm, named for its founder, Jesse Chisolm, whose outfits had driven millions of long-

horns from Texas north to Abilene, Kansas. Later the Santa Fe Railroad would follow the Chisolm Trail across the plains south to the Gulf of Mexico.

By the middle of 1872, trains were rolling East out of Hutchinson, Kansas, over rails of the Santa Fe. On September 19, 1872, the line had reached Dodge City (originally Buffalo City), where passengers shot buffalo out of car windows; in 1874, half a million hides and over 800 tons of buffalo meat left Dodge City by rail for the East. Bone collectors added to the railroad revenue, selling buffalo bones at $8 a ton (100 skeletons to the ton). By 1875, freight revenue was so good that the Santa Fe took over the Kansas Midland, a line from Topeka to Kansas City. Following the Arkansas, Mr. Holliday's line passed Granada, Colorado, in 1873, and through Las Animas to Pueblo in 1875 (over 600 miles from Topeka), lifting itself almost a mile.

Bone picker arrives with another load to go on the pile.
Buffalo bones offered good revenue to Santa Fe. (Courtesy
Santa Fe Railway)

A Dodge City street in the "business section" in the 1860's,
before the Santa Fe arrived. (Courtesy Santa Fe Railway)

William Barstow Strong. Coming to the Santa Fe as its general manager on November 1, 1877, Mr. Strong really lived up to his name. A shy, unassuming man by nature, he had no regular hours and might show up any night in a yard, roundhouse or office, shaking hands of switchmen, train and engine crews, and dispatchers. When he joined the road it operated over 786 miles of track, but by 1889 this mileage had expanded to over 7000. His rare ability as a gifted railroader had been recognized when on August 1, 1881, he became the president. (Courtesy Santa Fe Railway)

Chief Engineer Albert Alonzo Robinson came to the Santa
Fe as it was ready to get under way, made surveys under
Tom Peter, worked his way to Chief Engineer and later
Vice President and General Manager. In 22 years he had
supervised the building of over 5000 miles of this railroad
empire. (Courtesy Santa Fe Railway)

"Uncle Dick" Wootton, with whom Strong and Robinson maneuvered the deal for the tunnel at Raton Pass. (Courtesy Santa Fe Railway)

This sign on a hill outside of Arkansas City, Kansas, along the Santa Fe right-of-way, was built by Fred Horton, who worked as a dispatcher for the Santa Fe for 38 years. He worked on his sign in his spare time and on his days off. (Courtesy Santa Fe Railway)

Fred Harvey Hotel, Wallace, Kansas, about 1880. Fred Harvey arrived in New York from Liverpool in 1850 and found a job as dishwasher in Smith and McNeil's restaurant at two dollars a week plus meals. Restless feet soon carried the fifteen-year-old boy in search of opportunity, and five years later he was working in mail cars on the Hannibal & St. Joe. The dirty eating houses serving terrible food along the line soon revived his memory of his first job in New York, and in 1876, he and Charlie Moss had raised a few dollars between them, sold an idea, and had a restaurant going in the Santa Fe depot at Topeka. So successful was this venture that on May 28, 1893, Harvey consummated a deal with the railroad to control and operate all hotels and restaurants on the system. By 1901, Harvey was operating 15 hotels, 47 restaurants, and 30 dining cars.

The "Harvey Girls" were "young women of good character, attractive and between the ages of 18 and 30." The girls were employed with the understanding that they would not marry for a year (but when some couldn't make the year, Harvey relented and put on a big wedding party for the newlyweds). Standard uniforms for the ladies consisted of black or dark dress, white collar with black bow tie, a white hair ribbon, and black shoes and stockings; salary was $17.50 per month plus room, board, and tips. (Fred furnished thousands of brides for engineers, conductors, and station agents as well as travelling gentry.

In those pioneer days, a brakeman would go through the train "announcing," and when he knew the number of passengers desiring breakfast, lunch, or dinner, wire ahead from the next telegraph stop. When the train neared the meal stop and the engineer pulled his long blast for the station, food started to the tables, and when the train stopped all was ready for a leisurely meal of the best food, and the tab was four bits. Menus were varied daily to prevent monotony, for Fred Harvey didn't want some passenger who might read the 8th verse of the 13th chapter of Hebrews to think the passage referred to his meals.

All men were required to wear coats (provided by Harvey if they were coatless) except at Santa Fe, where the caballero tradition prevailed along with the informal spirit of the artists and writers, who were always about. Any child who sat in a high chair got his meal at half price. In a Harvey House no passenger ever felt hurried, left hungry, or missed a train. (Courtesy Santa Fe Railway)

304

THE **Super CHIEF**

- DINNER -

ROMANOFF FRESH MALOSSOL CAVIAR 1.75

ANTIPASTO 75   HEARTS OF CALIFORNIA ARTICHOKES 35

Hearts of Celery 30   Salted Almonds 30   Colossal Ripe Olives 25

NEPTUNE COCKTAIL 50   AVOCADO 40

GRAPEFRUIT, ORANGE AND RAISINS 40

CHICKEN OKRA, LOUISIANNAISE IN CUP 20; TUREEN 30

Consomme, Hot or Jellied 25   Clam Broth 20

SWORDFISH STEAK SAUTE, MEUNIERE WITH CAPERS 75
POACHED TRANCHE OF SALMON, AU VIN BLANC 70

FRESH MUSHROOMS SAUTE, AU FINES HERBES, AND BACON 75
OLD FASHIONED BONELESS CHICKEN PIE, AMERICAINE 85
POACHED EGGS ON FRIED FRESH TOMATO, SAUCE HOLLANDAISE 65
SPAGHETTI WITH JULIENNE OF VIRGINIA HAM, MADAME GALLI 65
ROAST LARDED TENDERLOIN OF BEEF, SAUCE MADERE 95

Small Sirloin Steak a la Minute 1.25

Sirloin Steak for one 1.60   Sirloin Steak for two 2.75

Calf's Liver and Bacon 70   Lamb Chop, Extra Thick (1) 80

(to order—20 minutes)

Bacon 65; Half Portion 40   Ham 70; Half Portion 40

Bacon and Eggs 70   Ham and Eggs 70

FRESH ASPARAGUS, DRAWN BUTTER 30

NEW CORN ON COB 25   NEW LIMA BEANS 20

NEW POTATOES, PERSILLADE 15   MASHED 15   COTTAGE FRIED 25

COLD

ASSORTED MEATS, POTATO SALAD 90   BRISKET OF CORNED BEEF 70
TOMATO STUFFED WITH LOBSTER SALAD 60
CHEF'S SPECIAL COMBINATION SALAD, PLATE 30
ROMAINE, COTTAGE CHEESE AND RAISIN SALAD, PLATE 30

Lettuce Salad 35   Potato 25   Chicken (White Meat) 80

Rye Bread and Dinner Rolls with Butter, per person 10   Dry or Buttered Toast 15

Melba Toast 15   Milk Toast 30   Boston Brown, Raisin or Whole Wheat 10; Toasted 15

OLD FASHIONED FRESH STRAWBERRY SHORTCAKE WITH WHIPPED CREAM 30

CANTALOUPE 20   RAISIN PIE 20   APRICOT PARFAIT 35

VANILLA ICE CREAM 25; WITH ASSORTED CAKE 35
ENGLISH CHESHIRE CHEESE WITH PRESERVED GUAVA 50

Roquefort 35   Petit Gruyere 35

Coffee, per Pot 25   Demi Tasse 15   Kaffee Hag Coffee, per Pot 25

Cocoa or Chocolate, Whipped Cream, per Pot 20   Tea, per Pot 20

PRICES SHOWN ON THIS MENU ARE SUBJECT TO VARIOUS STATE SALES TAXES

Guests will please call for checks before paying and compare amounts charged
An extra charge of twenty-five cents each will be made for all meals served outside of Dining Car

SANTA FE DINING CAR SERVICE
Fred Harvey

The engine 54 heading for and within a short distance
of Los Angeles on November 27, 1892, pulling behind her
the first California Limited. This was a de luxe, extra-fare
train from its beginning and made its last run on February
14, 1915. She was a dilly in her day and, incidentally,
"Death Valley Scotty" and his party rode this flyer on their
return trip to Los Angeles. (Courtesy Santa Fe Railway)

306

Hauling livestock has always been a big part of Santa Fe freight service and here a long drag, solid with live freight, pulls into the Argentine yards in Kansas. (Courtesy Santa Fe Railway)

Two old Timers J.P. McMurray 1877 ... Stitt Uncle Dick 1878 ...

Just eight years after George Beach pulled the throttle out on the *C. K. Holliday* for the first run over Santa Fe rails, the road put an order in with Baldwin to "build the most powerful locomotive ever built." Named for Mr. Wootten, the "Uncle Dick" arrived in 1877 with a thousand-gallon saddle tank slung across her boiler, resting on eight 42-inch driving wheels which got their thrust from pistons working in cylinders 20 by 26 inches. With her 65 tons of weight, the 140 pounds of steam pressure gave her a tractive effort of 23,200 pounds for the work she was assigned on the New Mexico–Southern Pacific Section.

Given to rail-climbing, she was later rebuilt as a conventional consolidation type as she appears in the picture and was used as a pusher at Raton (which the old hoggers invariably pronounced Rat-toon) Pass. She frequently pulled a passenger train between Trinidad and Las Vegas and on many occasions headed the De Luxe Express (a 3-car-train consisting of combination coach, baggage, and express car and a dilly of a varnish job purchased second-hand in Canada, lined with hardwood and equipped with red plush-upholstered chairs) between LaJunta and Santa Fe (298-mile run). *Uncle Dick* was a real workhorse and as rugged as her namesake—she wasn't scrapped until 1921. (Courtesy Santa Fe Railway)

Locomotive No. 2414, consolidation class 2-8-0 type, is the oldest on the Santa Fe system, having been built by and purchased from the Baldwin Locomotive Works in 1880. After sixty years of service, it was retired in 1939. (Courtesy Santa Fe Railway)

Discontinued on February 14, 1915, one of the last of the
great California Limiteds crosses the old bridge, spanning
the 222-feet-deep Diablo Canyon for a distance of 531 feet.
Construction for new bridge is seen in left foreground.
(Courtesy Santa Fe Railway)

November 1, 1877, was a great and lucky day for the Santa Fe. Forty-year-old William Barstow Strong had arrived to take over as General Manager. The road was now operating over 600 miles of its own track plus 168 miles leased. Now, headed for New Mexico, Strong saw the best route for his railroad through Raton Pass. In 1852, Richens Lacy Wootton, former scout for Fremont and friend of Kit Carson, had driven 9000 sheep from Taos to the Sacramento Valley in California in 107 days and sold them all to the hungry seekers after gold for $50,000 worth of their precious diggings. Ready to take life easier, he had secured franchises from the Territorial Legislatures of Colorado and New Mexico, blasted out and built a 27-mile-road from Trinidad, Colorado, to Red River in the south, swung a chain across his road near the summit at Raton Pass, and collected toll. Fortunately for the Santa Fe, unpleasant brushes with the narrow gauge Denver & Rio Grande had made Uncle Dick Wootton an enemy of that line. Now Uncle Dick "j'ined up" with Strong, and in July 1879 the Chief Engineer had his tunnel through the pass.

Snaking along southwest, rails went down at Santa Fe early in 1880, and on February 9th there was a big celebration. Led by the Ninth Cavalry Band, the parade marched to the depot, where General Lew Wallace (of *Ben Hur* fame) sent a silver spike home into an oak tie, and whistles blasted from the *A. G. Greely* and *Marion* as the doubleheader pulled its train up to the station and stopped.

The rails of the Santa Fe now stretched over 800 miles from Westport Landing (now called Kansas City) to Santa Fe. The old trail, over which in its peak year oxen and mules had struggled with 5000 wagons, was gone forever; never again would the Barlow & Sanderson stages sway and roll over the Santa Fe Trail.

On through the Southwest pushed Mr. Holliday's dream road; Arizona was crossed in 1881 and California the next year. And in years to follow its lines spread as it built an empire of rails stretching from Chicago, on Lake Michigan, to Denver, in the heart of the Rockies; down the old Santa Fe Trail, on its way to the Gulf of California, and on the Pacific; down the old trail that Jesse Chisolm blazed into the great Southwest, to Galveston and El Paso on the Gulf of Mexico.

6
Innovations and Developments

Although the trial-and-error method is a costly one, the pioneer railroads were forced to use it. They had no guide or pattern to follow and through necessity had to learn everything the hard way. It was soon realized that roadbeds and rails must be improved if the railroad itself was to progress.

The roadbed from the beginning had presented quite a problem. Experience with the early granite sills and wooden stringers convinced railroad men that something better had to be devised. As time went on, the bed was sloped slightly from the center to provide proper drainage, then ballasted with broken stone to form a firm yet elastic foundation. On this ballast, ties (generally creosoted oak) were placed about two feet apart; the two ties at each railjoint were placed slightly closer together to give additional support to this weakest point in a line of rails. Rails were then aligned and steel tieplates were placed between the rail base and tie; spikes were driven through the square holes in the plate to prevent lateral spreading of the rails. A splicebar was bolted on each side of the joint where the rail-ends abutted.

By 1840, the T rail, brought about by Robert Stevens, was being used more and more. Its weight had gradually increased to approximately 36 pounds to the yard. As more was learned, steel took the place of iron and rail weight gradually increased to approximately 75 pounds by the close of the nineteenth century. Today it is upward of 150 pounds to the yard.

When Robert Stephenson had built the *Rocket* for the Liverpool & Manchester in 1829, his ingenuity had put the first practical steam locomotive on rails. This is true because he had combined in the same unit such basic elements as outside cylinders directly connected to driving wheel crankpins, a horizontal tubular boiler, and exhaust steam utilized for forced draft on the fire. Previously, there had been many cumbersome levers and gearing attached to cranked driving-axles.

To further clarify locomotive descriptions, we should state that F. M. Whyte originated an identification system of wheel arrangements on locomotives about the turn of the present century. Shortly after the birth of the locomotive, two wheels of small diameter were placed under the front end to give support. These were known as leading or pony trucks. A little later, four wheels were sometimes used on the leading truck. Next to and behind the ponies came the driving wheels, of much larger diameter. As wheel arrangements were experimented with, a truck of two or four wheels, frequently of larger diameter than the leading truck-wheels and generally spoken of as trailers, was placed in the rear of the drivers to give increased support to the rear of the engine. These three groups of wheels became the Whyte system of identification. Assuming that a locomotive carried no leading wheels, four drivers, and no trailers, Whyte's system would classify the arrangement as 0-4-0. The earliest pioneer locomotives and many engines used in switching and yard service a hundred years later, carried this wheel arrangement. To go a step further, a locomotive with two leading wheels, four drivers and two trailer wheels, would be classified as a 2-4-2. Whyte's system greatly simplified identification by wheel arrangement.

Original strap iron used by RF&P in 1836 compared with their "T" rail of 1941 (heavier welded steel rail is presently used). (Courtesy Richmond, Fredericksburg & Potomac Railroad)

Left: Wooden stringer and strap rail (1830); center: 67-pound Bessemer Rail (1874); right; 140-pound rail (1948). (Courtesy Baltimore & Ohio Railroad)

Special machinery now takes the place of gandy dancers, whose melodious songs were attuned to whatever track work they might be engaged in. In the foreground are the power cribbers, followed by the power adzers, Dunrite gauger, track laying machinery, crane—all followed by the power tampers. (Courtesy Chicago & North Western Railway)

Rail train pulling out of Chicago yard of Illinois Central. This continuous welded rail is in sections 1360 to nearly 1500 feet and will weigh from 140 to 152 pounds per yard. As more and more of this rail is laid the "clickety-clack" is fast disappearing. (Courtesy Illinois Central Railroad)

The heart of any railroad, the locomotive, improved steadily but by slow degrees. Baldwin had built a 2-2-0 for his first locomotive (*Old Ironsides*) in 1831, but because of poor riding, or rather tracking, characteristics, it was not satisfactory and shortly thereafter this type of wheel arrangement was discontinued. Arrangements of 2-4-0 were tried, but soon discarded because of too much rigidity and stiffness. Then came the 4-2-0 (Baldwin's second engine, *E.L. Miller,* and Rogers' first, *Sandusky*), which was immediately accepted as standard wheel arrangement. Although these were high speed types and in use until about 1860, their adhesive qualities were limited.

It should be said here that the *Sandusky,* built by Tom Rogers (Rogers Locomotive & Machine Works, Paterson, New Jersey) in 1837, carried the first counterbalances ever put on locomotive driving wheels. This proved to be a great forward step, as it distributed the hammerblow caused by the thrust of the piston and mainrods.

Many wheel arrangements were tried, but by 1840 the 4-4-0 had come into its own. Designed to provide more adhesion on the drivers than the 4-2-0 and give better riding stability than the 0-4-0, it had all the desirable features for an engine that had to operate over the uneven roadbeds with sharp curves and heavy grades prevalent at the time. Because of their balance and stability on the rails at

GRAPHIC HISTORY OF THE LOCOMOTIVE.

(Courtesy Association of American Railroads)

GRAPHIC HISTORY OF THE LOCOMOTIVE.

high speeds, 4-4-0's were used extensively. With underhung driving springs providing easy riding by allowing the engine to roll on its springs at high speeds, this light, flexible, and easily handled locomotive wheel arrangement was a favorite for both passenger and freight use throughout the nineteenth and into the present century. A beautiful example of this class was the famous 999 of the New York Central.

In 1850, the 4-6-0 came on the scene. It was an excellent general purpose locomotive for both freight and passenger service, and over 17,000 of this type were built between 1850 and 1935.

around steam domes, sand boxes, wheel covers, steam chests, and cylinders. Smokestacks and wheels were painted all shades of red, with vermilion predominating. Hundreds of dollars were spent in painting portraits and picturesque scenes on headlights, cab panels, and tenders. The locomotive had really become an overdressed woman.

Engineers spent their own money in "keeping up appearances" of their charges and the time spent by them and their firemen in decorating and polishing was truly a labor of love. Deer antlers were a favorite to mount atop the headlights, or fix to the smokebox. Not infrequently, a shining brass eagle,

First locomotive used on Louisville & Frankfort. Mason would later make a name for himself with the beautiful and well engineered locomotives built from 1853 to 1890. (Courtesy Louisville & Nashville Railroad)

About 1860, the "Mogul," a 2-6-0 type, put in its appearance as a freight locomotive. Giving more adhesion to the rails than the 4-4-0, it was also a flexible, good riding engine below speeds of 50 miles an hour. With drivers not exceeding 63 inches in diameter, it was seldom used on fast passenger runs, but it did an excellent job pulling freights up to about 1915.

Cabs did not come into use until about 1847, although sometime before this unsatisfactory attempts at stretching canvas over frames had been made. Until about 1850 the locomotive had been developed and built for strictly utilitarian use; however, about this time, and continuing for the next twenty-five years, builders vied with each other in decorating the iron horse. Brass bands were worked

with wings spread, rode the headlight, but more often his perch was atop the sanddome.

When an engine was assigned to him, the engineer regarded it as his own. In most instances the headlight did belong to him, and with some it was removed after a run and placed in a locker in the roundhouse or sometimes taken home. As a youngster, this writer frequently assisted his father in taking his headlight to some plating shop to have the reflector "done over"—of course at his own expense.

The highly decorative stage commenced to wither in the 1870's and with few exceptions the locomotive had returned to its utilitarian appearance by about 1880. As engineering knowledge grew, so did the locomotive. Improvements came about steadily, and with them came increase in power, size, and weight.

Because of its prevalence, wood was generally used as locomotive fuel until about 1870, when bituminous coal came into general use. Whereas

318

4-4-0's as they looked in the early 1880's. (Courtesy Seaboard Air Line Railroad)

A 4-6-0 built in 1890. (Courtesy Seaboard Air Line Railroad)

Old No. 1 of the Illinois Central. (Courtesy Illinois Central
Railroad)

320

Excellent illustration of a highly dressed lady in the decorative period. The *Seminole*, built by Rogers Locomotive & Machine Company, Paterson, New Jersey, in April 1867 for the Union Pacific (Eastern District) was decorated her whole 50-foot length, including a highly varnished walnut cab and an engineer's seat of ash. With two cords of wood and two thousand gallons of water in her tender, her over-all weight was 115,000 pounds. (Courtesy Union Pacific Railroad)

Forerunner of the popular Atlantic type (4-4-2) locomotive was the Columbia type (2-4-2) built by Baldwin in 1893. This locomotive was exhibited at the 1893 World's Fair in Chicago. (Courtesy Association of American Railroads)

anthracite burned more slowly and with little smoke, it was not nearly so widely distributed geographically; then, too, it required a thinner fire, which necessitated a grate area of about two and a half times that for bituminous. Roads traversing territory where it was obtainable economically were using oil by the latter part of the nineteenth century.

BRAKES

From the time the first steam locomotive had pulled a train in America, nearly all of its development had been in the forward direction, of starting and pulling trains. Through forty years, power, size, and speed had ever been on the increase, bringing with it the need for ability to control and to stop the engine and its train in the least possible distance. Engineering minds had been aware of this serious drawback and various means of accomplishing the desired end had been tried.

In the earliest days, the engineer would signal his approach to a station by raising the safety valve. Upon hearing the hiss of escaping steam, gangs of men would rush toward the approaching train. As the engineer yanked his reverse bar back, the men on the ground would endeavor to grab the engine and retard momentum by brute force. Needless to say, this method of braking failed completely. About the same time or a bit later, heavy timbers were shoved between the spokes of the car wheels; this, too, came to nought. Still later, brake shoes were fitted to the car wheels and from a wheel atop the cars brakemen used the leverage of heavy sticks to windup mechanically; this was an improvement over former methods but left much to be desired.

As early as 1843, Robert Stephenson, son of old George, father of the locomotive, had devised a steam brake which pressed two wooden blocks against the treads of the locomotive's driving wheels; but he was ahead of his time. It was not until about 1850 that the engine's driving wheels were equipped with brake shoes operated by a steam power cylinder.

In America, experiments continued; chains, which when wound up on the rotating axles of cars would pull the brakes on, steam brakes, and vacuum brakes. But any problem remains a problem until the right man grasps and solves it. Convinced that any effective braking system must be continuous, with every wheel of the train braking simultaneously, and must be controlled by one man from one point, George Westinghouse set his great inventive mind to the task. In 1869 he secured a patent and by 1872 had perfected his air brake to such a point that a fast-moving train could be controlled and stopped by the action of one man's hand on a lever—the engineer's in the locomotive cab. This, perhaps, was the greatest forward step made in the operation of a train since the advent of the steam locomotive.

By the beginning of the present century, the working pressure of the locomotive boiler had increased from the 40 to 50 pounds of steam pressure of the pioneer locomotives to 200 pounds; the horsepower from less than half a hundred to over fifteen hundred. The steam locomotive had now reached the maximum size that could be fired by hand (a fireman was unable to handle more than the approximately two and a half tons of coal per hour required to keep a head of steam). The mechanical stoker was on the way by 1905 but it was to be nearly twenty years before it was put into general use. After the stoker was adopted, about 1925, engines grew in size and power until at the last of steam, in 1950, some engines rated as much as 8000 horsepower.

Another very important improvement came into use about 1908—the superheater. Condensation of steam in the cylinders of the locomotive had not only brought about a loss of heat but with it the problem of water collecting between piston and cylinder head. It was well known that at a pressure of 200 psi and a temperature of 387° the steam was saturated; with any reduction in temperature, condensation would take place; with any temperature rise, the steam would behave more like a gas. The advent of the superheater eventually made possible and practical a steam temperature of from 600 to 700 degrees. By this means, the power output of the locomotive was increased better than 25 per cent, on the same amount of fuel that formerly produced saturated steam.

The reverse lever (used to regulate valve travel and to reverse the engine), generally known as the "Johnson bar," had been in use since the early days of the locomotive, and as the iron horse grew in size and power this manually operated lever became increasingly difficult to handle. It generally required both hands and all the strength that could be mustered, and there were instances where the engineer had received serious injury in its manipulation.

322

George Westinghouse.

In this excellent photo, showing the inside of a cab, we see the power reverse lever (the lever furthest to the right) just forward of the engineer's seatbox. The old Johnson Bar was formerly placed right beside the seatbox and because of the leverage required for manual operation extended vertically a distance of about four feet from the deck floor of the cab. (Courtesy Pennsylvania Railroad Company)

Incidentally, the Johnson bar was, of necessity, so placed that for many years the engineer was forced to sit in a most awkward position, generally with his legs straddling the bar. After much experimentation, the pneumatically operated power reverse gear was put in general use about 1913.

As improvements came about and were adopted by the railroads, the steam locomotive continued in its development. From the first little low-pressure boilers carrying perhaps 25 to 30 psi, the locomotive had progressed until, before 1950, some locomotive boilers were operating at a pressure of 500 psi. Water capacity of tenders in 1870 was about 2000 gallons; by 1900, six thousand; 1920 saw double this capacity; and in 1940, twenty-five thousand gallons of water were carried. Some roads had constructed water scoops alongside the tracks as early as 1875.

ROLLING STOCK

In 1830, a Baltimore newspaper carried an advertisement of the B&O Railroad, which stated in part, "A brigade of cars will leave the depot on Pratt Street at 6 and 10 o'clock A.M. . . . Positive orders have been issued . . . to receive no passengers into any of the cars without tickets." A short time later a passenger on this road described the car he occupied as "a little clapboard cabin on wheels, for all the world like one of those North Carolina mountain huts."

These little boxes on wheels were about as uncomfortable as can be imagined. Smoke, dust, cinders, and sparks choked the passengers by day in summer, and at night there was the added discomfort from tallow candles dripping upon them and their clothes. Winter travel brought even more discomfort; there was no ventilation; a wood-burning stove in one end of the car roasted the passengers near it while those at the other end froze, and at the same time filled the atmosphere with smoke.

Trains moved so slowly in those early days that the need for a sleeping car soon became apparent. In 1836, the Cumberland Valley Railroad decided to do something about it and employed Embry & Dash, in Philadelphia, to do the job. The Philadelphia car builders lit into the job with gusto, proceeding to divide an old day coach into four compartments, placing bunks against the sides. As the car was to have every luxury and convenience, a wash basin was fixed to a little stand in the rear. Christened the *Chambersburg,* the innovation was gaily painted and put into service between Harrisburg and Chambersburg, Pennsylvania. No bedclothing, other than a mattress, was provided, and on this the weary traveller lay, fully dressed, as the first sleeping car bumped along over the uneven roadbed. After some complaints and prodding, the railroad did add a small closet in the rear, stocked with sheets and blankets. As bedclothing was washed irregularly, there was quite a skirmish among the passengers to get to the closet first to obtain the cleanest sheets and blankets with which to make their bunks for the night.

Competition was now becoming keen, and hearing of the successful operation of the bunk cars in Pennsylvania, the Erie decided to show them up. In 1843, Erie had the Stephenson Car Works, in Harlem, build two sleepers, the *Erie* and *Ontario.* Eleazor Lord still had Great Lakes ideas, although at the time his road had stopped for one of its rests at Goshen (less than forty miles from its starting point at Piermont in 1835). The new cars were called "Diamond Cars," since to comply with the sidewall construction it had been necessary to cut the windows in the shape of a diamond.

Since the Erie's gauge was 6 feet, the cars had a width of 11 feet. Six seats, back to back, were placed on each side; a bed could be made by sliding a bar from under one seat and fastening it to the frame of the opposite one, and then putting cushions on the bar. Incidentally, the principle was not unlike that put in later use by Pullman. One of the cars, the *Ontario,* was put in the consist of the *Thunder and Lightning Milk Train,* running between Piermont and Otisville.

So successful was the operation of these supersleepers of their day that Erie ordered several more through the years. In the early 1850's a more or less regular passenger to occupy a berth between Buffalo and Westfield (approximately 50 miles apart) was a young contractor named George Mortimer Pullman. Impressed with the miseries of the Diamond Car while being tossed about in his bunk one night, young Pullman formulated some ideas of his own for a car in which a passenger might really sleep.

The year 1858 found Pullman elevating some sunken streets and raising buildings in the overgrown country town of Chicago (population then 100,-

George Mortimer Pullman. (Courtesy The Pullman Company)

Old No. 9, Pullman's first sleeper. (Courtesy The Pullman Company)

Interior of No. 9. (Courtesy The Pullman Company)

000). He had not forgotten the Diamond Cars and took his ideas to the Chicago & Alton, who were interested. Taking two of their day coaches (numbers 9 and 10), each 44 feet long, with flat roofs just over six feet from the floor and with fourteen 12-inch windows on each side, Pullman set to work.

There were no plans, and details were worked out as they came up in the remodeling of the two old cars. When Pullman completed operations, each car was finished inside in cherry, upholstered in plush, lighted by oil lamps, heated by a boxstove at each end, and 4-wheel-trucks were substituted for the conventional two. There were ten sleeping sections, a linen closet, and two wash rooms. Since there were no porters yet, the brakeman substituted by making the beds.

J. L. Barnes, the first Pullman conductor, stood near the entrance of his car at Bloomington the night of September 1, 1859, as his passengers climbed aboard. In recollection, Captain Barnes reflected: "All the passengers were from Bloomington and there were no women on the car that night. . . . The car moved away in solitary grandeur. . . . I had to compel the passengers to take their boots off before they got into the berths. They wanted to keep them on. . . . After I made a few trips it was decided it did not pay to employ a Pullman conductor and the car was placed in charge of the passenger conductor of the train. . . . I was out of a job."

Since George Pullman was a perfectionist, he was not satisfied with the results of his first sleeping car and continued to experiment. In 1864, when Pullman went to work on his dream car, which was to cost an estimated $20,000, officials of the Chicago & Alton, as well as other railroad men, were not sure he had not suffered brain damage. To them, it seemed impossible to make a profit out of such extravagance; but men of vision and ability are never thwarted in an adventure, and in 1865 the first real Pullman car was completed.

The *Pioneer* was longer, wider, higher, and larger than any passenger car of its day. Those who had called it "Pullman's Folly" predicted it would be too big to get under bridges and past protruding platforms and made other disparaging remarks. Some disagreed, however, and an article in the *Daily Illinois State Register* of May 26, 1865, stated: "This carriage . . . we found to be most comfortable and complete in all its appurtenances,

and decidedly superior . . . to any similar carriage we have ever seen. It is 54 feet in length by ten in width. . . . Besides the berths, sufficient in number to accommodate upwards of a hundred passengers, there are four state rooms formed by folding doors. . . . When the car is not used for sleeping purposes . . . every appearance of a berth or bed is concealed, and in their stead appear the most comfortable seats. . . . A daily change of linen is made in the berths . . . rendering the car much more attractive than are similar carriages where this is neglected."

Pullman himself must have been somewhat concerned about his fortune, for he had gambled all-or-nothing on this one car, but fate or luck or whatever such coincidence may be termed often takes a hand at such times. Death was the coincidence to take the hand this time. After the assassination of President Lincoln, the government engaged the *Pioneer* (at the insistence of his widow, who had seen the car) to be put in the funeral train between Chicago and Springfield. This of course forced the Chicago & Alton to add two feet additional clearance to all bridges, platforms, and other installations along the line to be traveled. Later, Grant used the car for a trip from Detroit to Galena, Illinois, and the Chicago & North Western found it necessary to adapt itself likewise.

Now assured of success, Pullman organized the Pullman Palace Car Company in 1867, and the same year brought out another innovation in de luxe rail-travel, by introducing the *President*. Put into service on the Great Western Railroad of Canada, this combination dining and sleeping car met with such good reception that in 1868 Pullman built the first dining car, known then as a "Hotel Car."

The *Delmonico* was also put into service on the Chicago & Alton, on which sumptuous meals were prepared and served for one dollar. This event brought about the great change in comfort and luxury in passenger cars. At the time the first dining car was introduced, passengers had to pass over the open vestibules or platforms between cars on their way to and from the diner. Various attempts had been made to enclose these passageways with canvas but this had proved impractical. One of Pullman's employees, H. H. Sessions, solved the problem by the use of flat steel frames held against each other by stout springs, the whole being substantially cov-

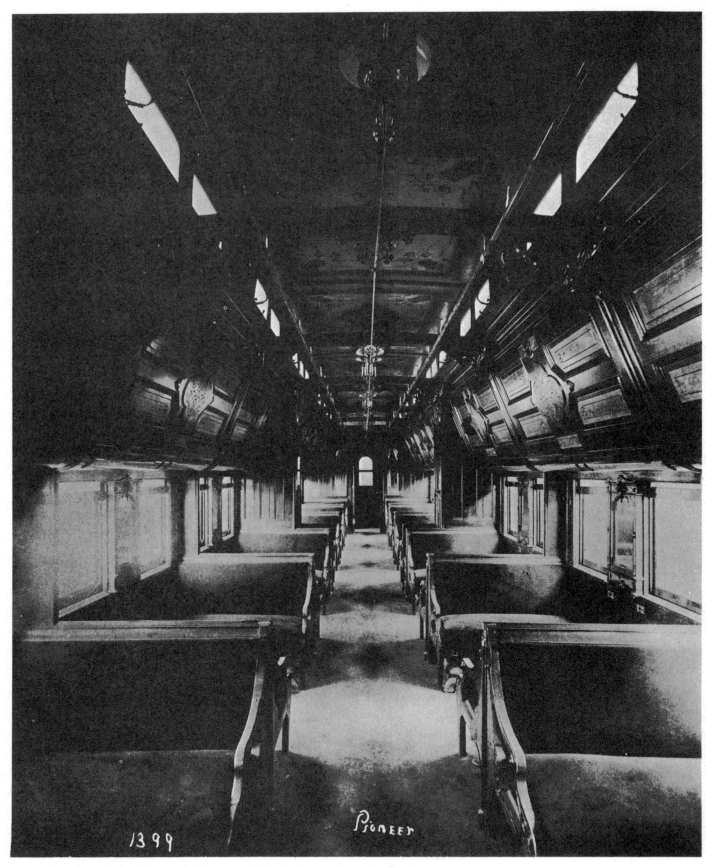

Interior of the *Pioneer*. (Courtesy The Pullman Company)

"Pullman's Folly." (Courtesy The Pullman Company)

Interior of *President*. (Courtesy The Pullman Company)

Pullman's Private Car Was Known the World Over

OLD STYLE ORNAMENTATION PREVAILED

THE saga of many a noted Pullman car has been sung in these pages, such as old *No. 9*, George M. Pullman's first experimental sleeper; *Pioneer*, the 1865 forerunner of the endless string of all-Pullman built vehicles for the comfort of railway travelers; the first vestibuled train, etc. But hardly a word—and certainly not a picture—has been printed about Mr. Pullman's p r i v a t e car, *P. P. C.*

Celebrities Among Its Guests

Which is hardly just since this was without doubt the best known private car of all time in America. It probably enjoyed the longest life of any—44 years—and in this time it had carried a notable array of celebrities: Americans and foreigners; statesmen and royalty, and so on. Moreover, it was a honeymoon car, transporting Miss Florence Pullman, eldest daughter of its owner, on her bridal tour as Mrs. Frank O. Lowden. Principally, though, it was the home awheel of the Pullman family, and a year after the death of the great car builder's widow the *P. P. C.* was destroyed at Calumet Shops, Chicago.

The *P. P. C.* was built at the Detroit Shops of Pullman's P a l a c e Car Company in 1877, or four years before the construction of Pullman Car Works at Chicago had begun. According to the recollection of old timers who worked on this car the cost was about $50,000, and Mr. Pullman made weekly trips from Chicago to note progress and supervise the work personally. It was a wood car, of course, and vermilion and satinwood were extensively used in the interior which, was, as the picture shows, decidedly opulent, as the taste then was. Fifteen wood carvers produced designs to entrance the eye and, it is to be feared, to attract the dust. *P. P. C.* stood for "President's Private Car" or "Pullman's Palace Car," according to varying recollections.

In 1892 the *P. P. C.* was remodeled to some ex-

$50,000 Was the Original Cost

DINING AND LOUNGING ROOM

tent at Calumet Shops, being lengthened, for one thing. The exterior picture shows it in its later stages, including the gold scroll work that was an ornamental feature on all Pullman cars during the '90s. At the exact center of the skirt of the car was the monogram, P. P. C. In its final state the car was 66 feet, 10 inches in length, exclusive of the platforms.

It may be of interest to know how the *P. P. C.* was arranged since it differs considerably f r o m other private cars in this respect, as well as in length. Entering from the observation platform (shown at the left of the picture) the curious would find themselves in the observation room, 7 feet, 11 inches in depth, which contained chairs and a large double sofa. Passing

Much Gold on the Exterior

Self-explanatory Page from *The Pullman News*. (Courtesy The Pullman Company)

Modern luxury in present-day Pullman cars. (Courtesy The Pullman Company)

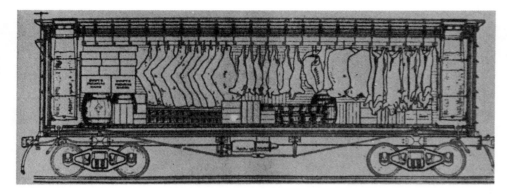

Diagram of Swift's early day refrigerator car. (Courtesy Swift & Company)

Early-day Tiffany refrigerator car. (Courtesy Swift & Company)

A Santa Fe refrigerator. (Courtesy Santa Fe Railway System)

ered. Not only did this covering shut out cinders, dust, and drafts, but added considerably to the safety of the passenger. In this writer's opinion, George Pullman, more than any other individual, carried the torch and led the way in the development of the passenger car.

Freight cars had to be developed, too, for from the movement of freight was to come the bread and meat revenue of the railroads. Perhaps the most outstanding improvement came in 1875 with the development of a special type—the refrigerator car. The loss in weight of cattle while in transit, together with the additional freight cost of shipping on the hoof, led G. F. Swift of Chicago to the idea of slaughtering first, then shipping only the dressed meat to eastern markets. A boxcar of special construction was equipped with roof ventilators and end compartments for salt and ice. With the dressed meat hanging from the ceiling, a constant low temperature was kept by the chilled air flowing downward to the floor. This was the beginning of another new era in freight handling, resulting in thousands of such cars being put into use by the large meat packers.

7
More Innovations

In what has gone before, we have had a brief look at the development of the roadbed, the locomotive (heart of any railroad operation), rolling stock, etc. Unlike a jigsaw puzzle, the many pieces necessary to form the composite whole of a railroad were not parts already available. All of the many parts that must work together to "run a railroad," had to be discovered through need, developed by trial and error, and finally put together as a railroad.

From the very beginning the necessity for various signals was recognized. On the first railroad, the Stockton & Darlington, George Stephenson sent a man on horseback ahead with a flag to warn of the approaching train. A bit later the horn used by the stagecoach guard was used. Although the early locomotive was noisy enough to warn of its approach, the need of a whistle soon became apparent.

According to legend, more than probably true, the Liverpool & Manchester Railroad in England offered a prize for "a device operated by steam that would make a *satisfactory noise.*" A musician along the line entered the contest and in collaboration with George Stephenson produced a rather crude device which they called a whistle. Continuing to toy with the idea, the experimenters came up with a tube to which steam could be admitted by the use of a valve. Although the wailing screech produced probably made ghosts dance around in their bones, and had no resemblance to the beautiful mellow tones associated with the steam locomotive, builders everywhere latched on to the idea and equipped their creations with a whistle. In America, the first known whistle was placed on the locomotive *Samp-son,* built by Rogers, Ketchum & Grosvener of Paterson, New Jersey, in 1835. This engine went to the Mad River & Lake Erie, Ohio's first railroad.

In the early days of the whistle, most roads equipped their freight engines with a single-toned, stubby affair that produced either a high-pitched screech or a toned-down raucus sound. But the passenger engineer would have none of this; he learned to "quill" while pulling freights, but when he got his exalted seat on the right-hand side of his passenger engine, he wanted all and sundry to know who held the throttle on his high-heeled lady.

At their own expense, many passenger engineers would experiment with different lengths and diameters of bronze tubes until the desired tone was obtained. Occasionally these fellows would have some machinist band together four or more slender tubes of varying length, to produce the early chime whistle. Some of the more fastidious would place steel balls below the cup-plates at the bottom of the whistle, getting the desired effect by having the balls bounce as the steam entered. These were the artists with the whistlecord, who were known from one end of their division to the other, and far beyond, by their fancy whistle calls. Not until 1883 did the Cincinatti, Hamilton & Dayton Railroad introduce to America what was commonly known as the chime whistle.

Occupying a most important place in railroad operation, the locomotive whistle is an audible signalling device and is used to transmit certain messages between the train crew, railroad employees, and others on the ground. All of us are familiar with the warning signal of two long and two short whistle blasts as a train approaches a grade

A TRAIN IS COMING -

IN THE EARLY DAYS, SOME LOCALITIES REQUIRED A SIGNALMAN ON HORSEBACK TO PRECEDE A TRAIN WAVING A FLAG AND SHOUTING "A TRAIN IS COMING", TO WARN THE WATCHING AND SOMETIMES SKEPTICAL POPULACE AWAY FROM THE TRACKS.

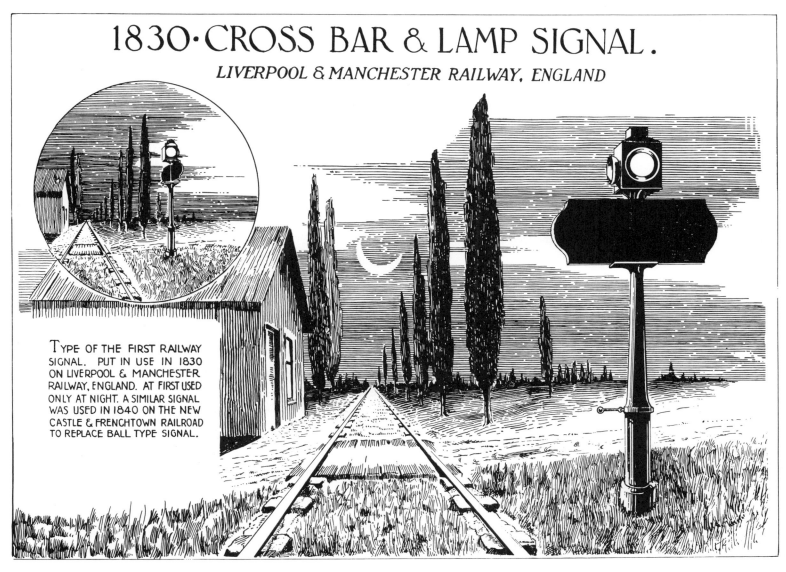

1830·CROSS BAR & LAMP SIGNAL.

LIVERPOOL & MANCHESTER RAILWAY, ENGLAND

TYPE OF THE FIRST RAILWAY SIGNAL. PUT IN USE IN 1830 ON LIVERPOOL & MANCHESTER RAILWAY, ENGLAND. AT FIRST USED ONLY AT NIGHT. A SIMILAR SIGNAL WAS USED IN 1840 ON THE NEW CASTLE & FRENCHTOWN RAILROAD TO REPLACE BALL TYPE SIGNAL.

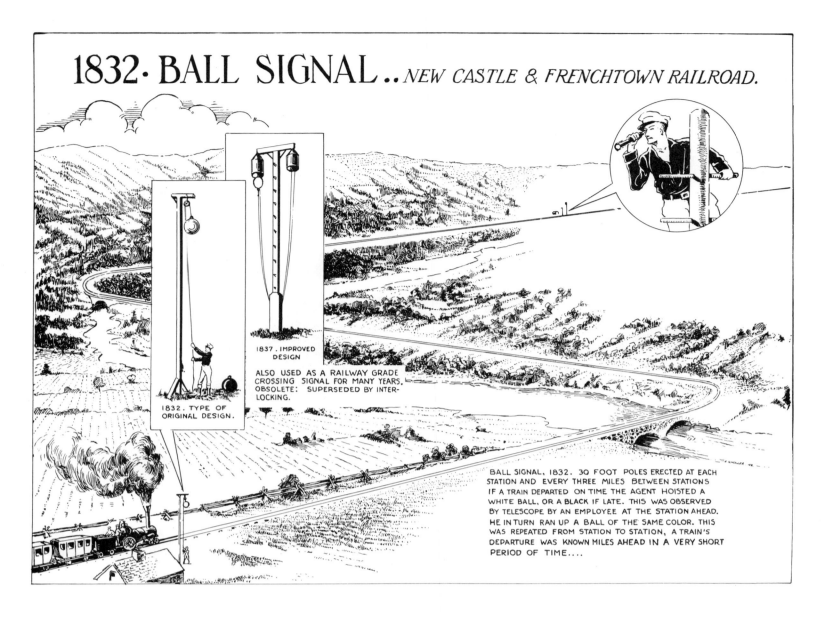

1832· BALL SIGNAL .. *NEW CASTLE & FRENCHTOWN RAILROAD.*

1837. IMPROVED DESIGN

ALSO USED AS A RAILWAY GRADE CROSSING SIGNAL FOR MANY YEARS, OBSOLETE: SUPERSEDED BY INTERLOCKING.

1832. TYPE OF ORIGINAL DESIGN.

BALL SIGNAL, 1832. 30 FOOT POLES ERECTED AT EACH STATION AND EVERY THREE MILES BETWEEN STATIONS IF A TRAIN DEPARTED ON TIME THE AGENT HOISTED A WHITE BALL, OR A BLACK IF LATE. THIS WAS OBSERVED BY TELESCOPE BY AN EMPLOYEE AT THE STATION AHEAD. HE IN TURN RAN UP A BALL OF THE SAME COLOR. THIS WAS REPEATED FROM STATION TO STATION, A TRAIN'S DEPARTURE WAS KNOWN MILES AHEAD IN A VERY SHORT PERIOD OF TIME....

1841 .. SEMAPHORE SIGNAL

INTRODUCED ON RAILWAYS OF ENGLAND BY C.H. GREGORY IN 1841 AND SOON BECAME THE STANDARD SIGNAL ON ENGLISH AND AMERICAN RAILROADS.

MECHANICAL INTERLOCKING
FIRST INSTALLATION IN ENGLAND, BRICKLAYER'S ARMS JUNCTION 1843.

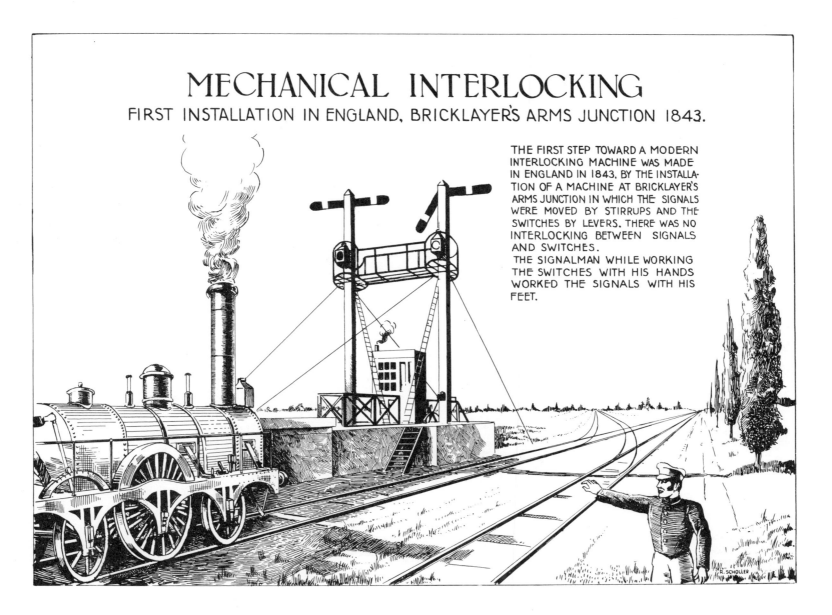

THE FIRST STEP TOWARD A MODERN INTERLOCKING MACHINE WAS MADE IN ENGLAND IN 1843, BY THE INSTALLATION OF A MACHINE AT BRICKLAYER'S ARMS JUNCTION IN WHICH THE SIGNALS WERE MOVED BY STIRRUPS AND THE SWITCHES BY LEVERS. THERE WAS NO INTERLOCKING BETWEEN SIGNALS AND SWITCHES.
THE SIGNALMAN WHILE WORKING THE SWITCHES WITH HIS HANDS WORKED THE SIGNALS WITH HIS FEET.

1857 · TILTING CROSSBAR SIGNAL

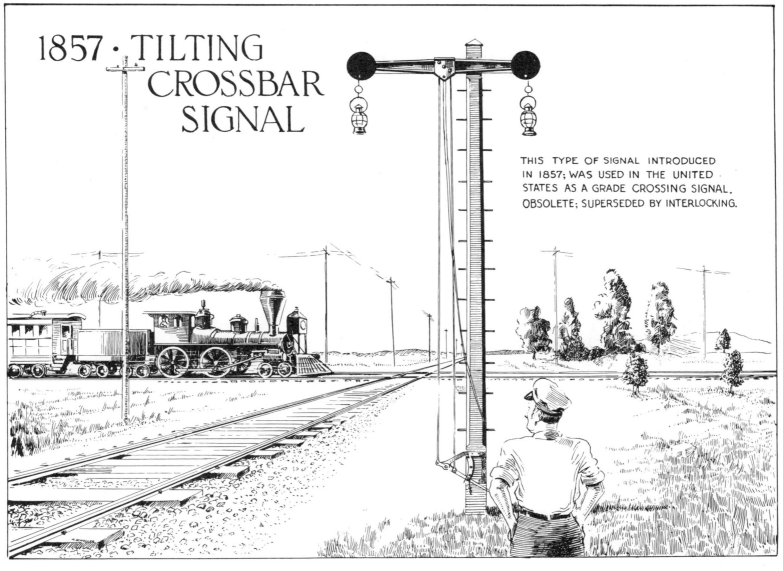

THIS TYPE OF SIGNAL INTRODUCED IN 1857; WAS USED IN THE UNITED STATES AS A GRADE CROSSING SIGNAL. OBSOLETE; SUPERSEDED BY INTERLOCKING.

1860 · GATE SIGNAL

THIS TYPE OF SIGNAL USED FOR MANY YEARS IN THE UNITED STATES AS A RAILROAD GRADE CROSSING SIGNAL. THIS GATE SIGNAL, WHEN PLACED ACROSS THE TRACK, MEANT STOP.

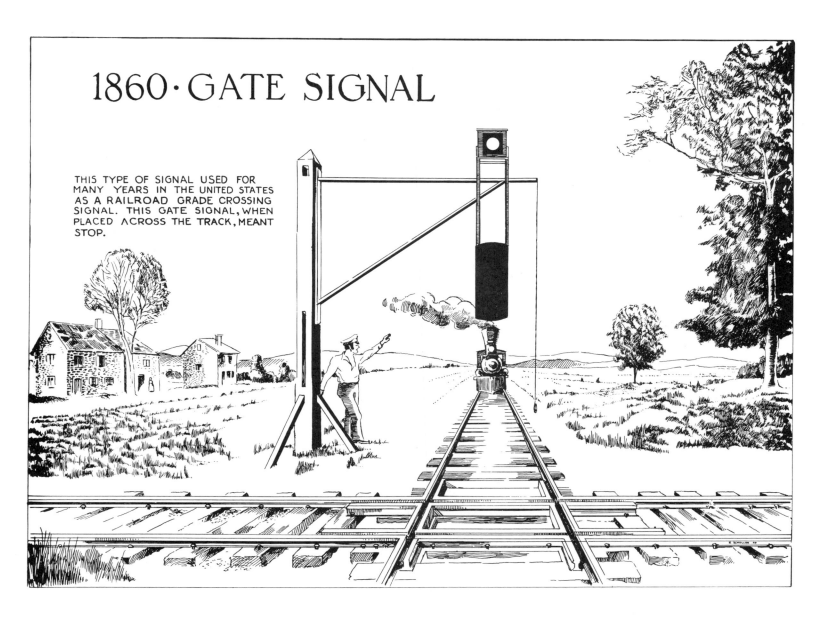

1863 BANNER SIGNAL

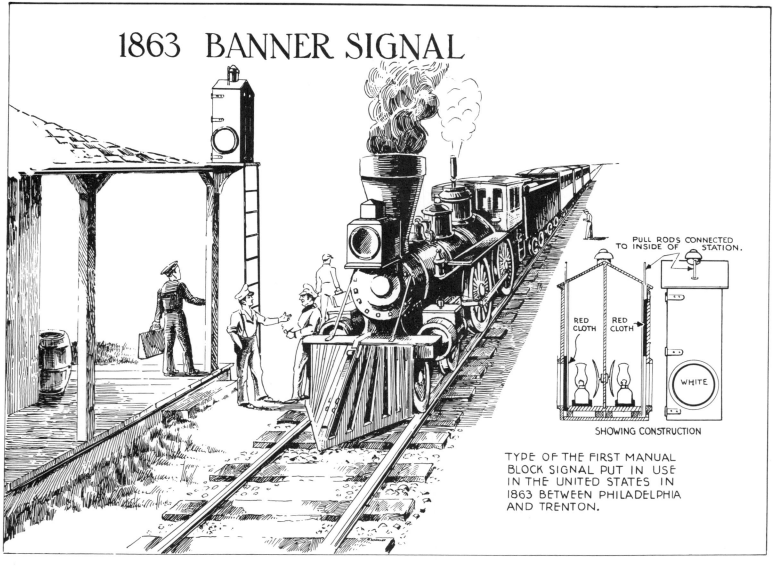

PULL RODS CONNECTED TO INSIDE OF STATION.

RED CLOTH   RED CLOTH

WHITE

SHOWING CONSTRUCTION

TYPE OF THE FIRST MANUAL BLOCK SIGNAL PUT IN USE IN THE UNITED STATES IN 1863 BETWEEN PHILADELPHIA AND TRENTON.

1868·· SMASHBOARD DRAWBRIDGE SIGNAL

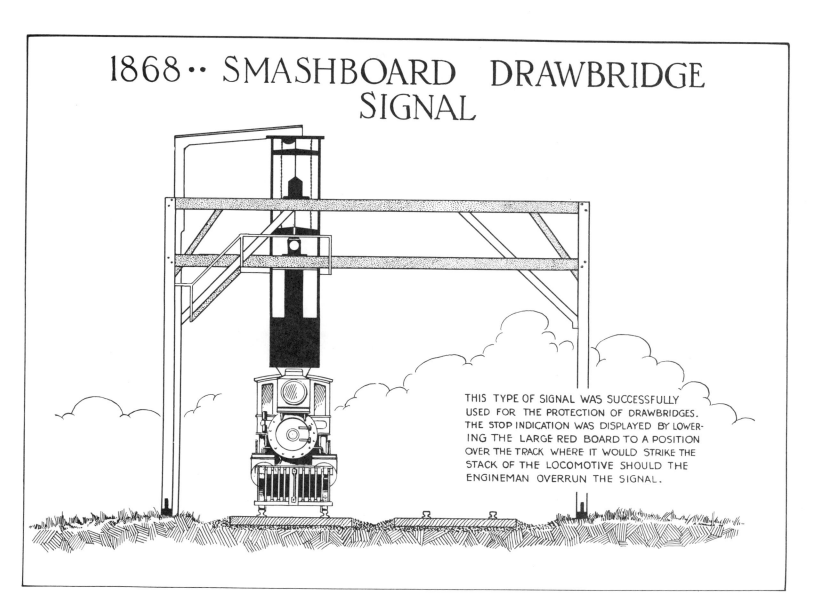

THIS TYPE OF SIGNAL WAS SUCCESSFULLY USED FOR THE PROTECTION OF DRAWBRIDGES. THE STOP INDICATION WAS DISPLAYED BY LOWERING THE LARGE RED BOARD TO A POSITION OVER THE TRACK WHERE IT WOULD STRIKE THE STACK OF THE LOCOMOTIVE SHOULD THE ENGINEMAN OVERRUN THE SIGNAL.

1871... BANJO SIGNAL

TYPE (ENCLOSED DISC, OPERATED BY ELECTRICITY) OF THE FIRST AUTOMATIC BLOCK SIGNAL INTRODUCED ON RAILWAYS OF THE UNITED STATES BY THOS. S. HALL IN 1871.

1872 . DISC SIGNAL

TYPE (ENCLOSED DISC OPERATED BY ELECTRICITY) OF AUTOMATIC BLOCK SIGNAL INSTALLED AT IRVINETON, PA. BY DR. WILLIAM ROBINSON. THE FIRST AUTOMATIC BLOCK SIGNAL TO BE CONTROLLED BY THE CLOSED TRACK CIRCUIT. THIS INSTALLATION MARKED THE BEGINNING OF AUTOMATIC BLOCK SIGNALING NOW IN GENERAL USE ON THE LEADING RAILWAYS OF THE WORLD.

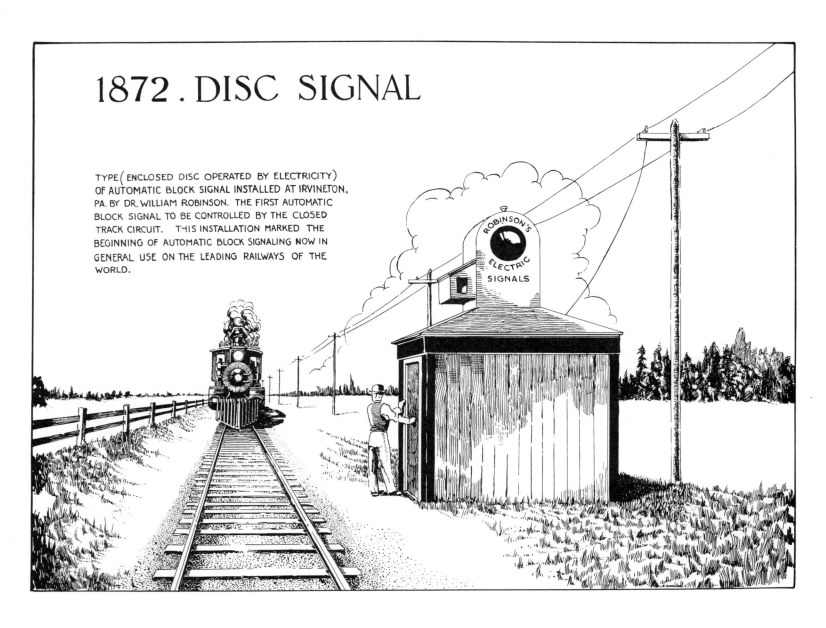

1879 ·· CLOCKWORK SIGNAL ..

TYPE (EXPOSED DISC, OPERATED BY WEIGHT-DRIVEN CLOCKWORK) OF AUTOMATIC BLOCK SIGNAL FIRST INSTALLED ON RAILWAYS OF THE UNITED STATES IN 1879. THIS TYPE NOW OBSOLETE.

1881· SEMAPHORE SIGNAL..

TYPE (ELECTRO-PNEUMATIC OPERATION) OF FIRST AUTOMATIC SEMAPHORE BLOCK SIGNAL. OPERATED BY AIR PRESSURE CONTROLLED BY ELECTRICITY INTRODUCED ON RAILWAYS OF THE UNITED STATES IN 1881. USED ALSO AS AN INTERLOCKING SIGNAL.

1893· SEMAPHORE SIGNAL

TYPE (ELECTRIC OPERATION) OF FIRST AUTOMATIC SEMAPHORE BLOCK SIGNAL OPERATED AND CONTROLLED BY ELECTRICITY. INTRODUCED ON RAILWAYS OF THE UNITED STATES IN 1893. USED ALSO AS AN INTERLOCKING SIGNAL.

This multiple-toned chime whistle was made in the shops at Waycross, Georgia, and was presented to the author's father in 1906, when he was assigned his regular passenger run. Shell measures 6 by 12 inches and the six 1 by 2-inch wells have a respective depth of 6, 7½, 9, 10½, 12 and 4 inches. It was tuned to the old song "Sweet By and By," and when he was in the mood "Uncle Frank" would open up with, "O-h-h-h-h Lord . . . O-h-h-h-h Lord" and after a slight pause continue with some interpretations that were his and his alone. Mute upon my hearth since his death in 1922, this beautifully toned whistle was known to untold thousands along the Atlantic Coast Line.

TRAIN DISPATCHING PRIOR TO THE USE OF THE ELECTRIC TELEGRAPH

THE New Castle and Frenchtown Railroad, one of America's pioneer roads, ran from New Castle, Delaware, on the Delaware River, to Frenchtown, Maryland, near Chesapeake Bay, a distance of seventeen miles. It was the connecting link for the steamboat line from Philadelphia to New Castle and from Frenchtown to Baltimore.

In 1832 when its motive power was changed from horses to the locomotive, a system of visual signals was put into use for sending information from terminal to terminal as to the movement of the train. This was twelve years before the invention in 1844 of the electric telegraph. These visual signals, located about three miles apart, were ball signals hoisted on poles about thirty feet high.

When the train started, the flagman at the terminal hoisted a white ball to the top of the pole. The flagman at the second station, observing the position of the signal through a telescope, hoisted the white signal ball at his station to a few feet from the top of the pole. The flagmen at the other stations repeated this signal so that at New Castle, it was known that the train had started from Frenchtown within a few minutes after it had left there. If the train was delayed, a black ball was hoisted in place of the white ball.

This primitive method of signaling the movement of the train by visual signals, used prior to the invention of the electric telegraph, was an early effort in train dispatching but was limited to dispatching or sending out of the trains as no means were then available for quickly reaching the trains with instructions for directing their movements.

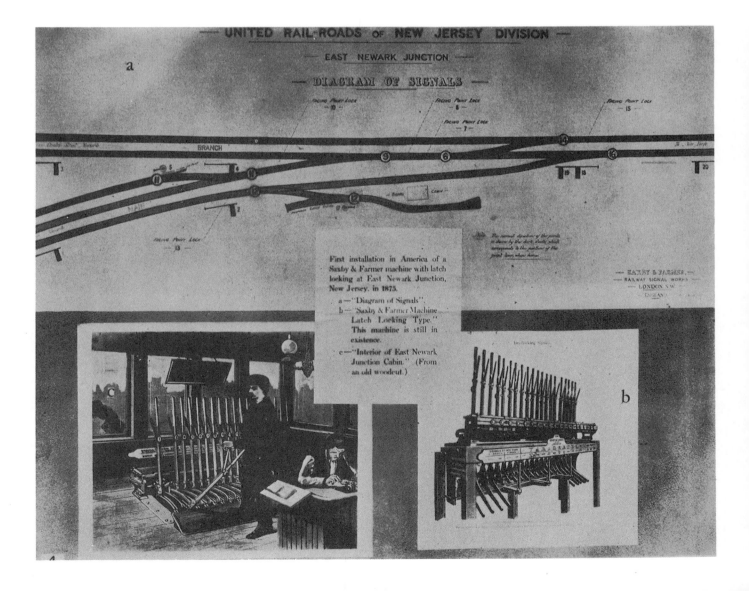

First installation in America of a Saxby & Farmer machine with latch locking at East Newark Junction, New Jersey, in 1875.

a — "Diagram of Signals".
b — "Saxby & Farmer Machine Latch Locking Type." This machine is still in existence.
c — "Interior of East Newark Junction Cabin." (From an old woodcut.)

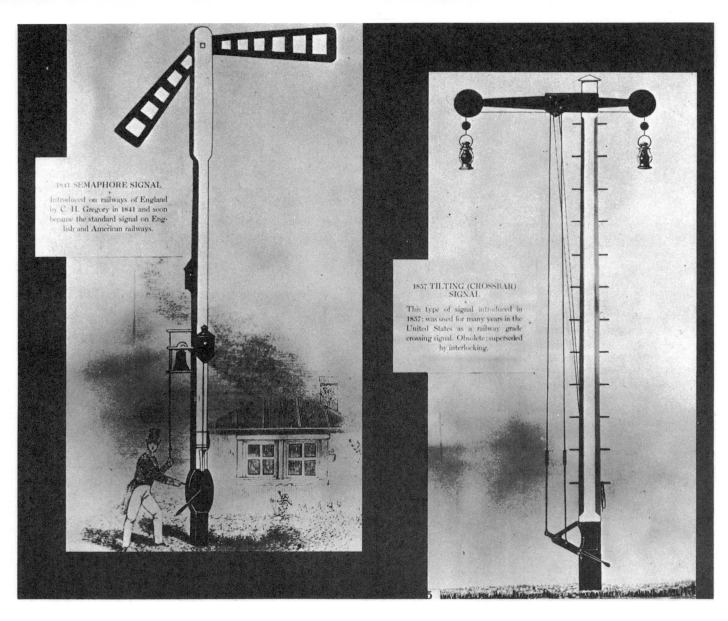

1841 SEMAPHORE SIGNAL

Introduced on railways of England by C. H. Gregory in 1841 and soon became the standard signal on English and American railways.

1857 TILTING (CROSSBAR) SIGNAL

This type of signal introduced in 1857; was used for many years in the United States as a railway grade crossing signal. Obsolete; superseded by interlocking.

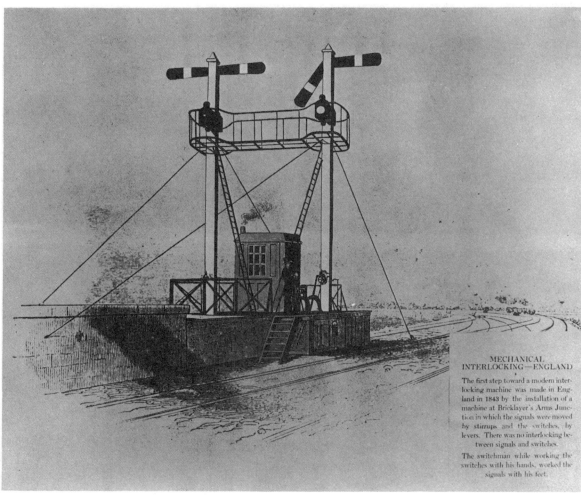

MECHANICAL INTERLOCKING—ENGLAND

The first step toward a modern interlocking machine was made in England in 1843 by the installation of a machine at Bricklayer's Arms Junction in which the signals were moved by stirrups and the switches by levers. There was no interlocking between signals and switches.

The switchman while working the switches with his hands, worked the signals with his feet.

344

MANUAL BLOCK SYSTEM

THE first block system in America was put in use in 1863-64 on the line between Kensington (Philadelphia), Pa. and Trenton, N. J., following a disastrous rear collision at night of eastbound trains carrying soldiers from the seat of war to New York and New England.

This block system provided for maintaining a *space* interval between trains. The earliest authentic record of the block regulations that has been found, is dated November 12, 1869. These regulations issued by F. Wolcott Jackson, General Superintendent of the New Jersey Railroad (Jersey City, New Brunswick), gave the rules under which the space interval was to be maintained.

The block signal at each station consisted of a box mounted on a post with two red flannel banners, one for each direction, which were dropped in front of a white surface or a white light for the "stop" indication. (See illustration under Fixed Signals, "Banner Box Signal of 1863".)

The banner box signal was superseded by the semaphore signal. One of the early types was a station block signal with the arms for controlling train movements in both directions both mounted on the same post. (See illustration.) The two arm semaphore signal used in the manual block system on the Baltimore and Ohio Railroad represents the present day type of manual block signal. (See illustration under Manual Block System "Baltimore and Ohio Railroad".)

The block stations were provided with telegraphic apparatus and an independent wire extended from block station to block station. The operator at a block station was required to make a record of every train that passed his station, the exact time that the train passed and the time that notice was received from the next station that the train had passed it.

The maintenance of a space interval between trains which was made the basis in 1863 of the first American block system, is the basis of all present day block signaling as the safety of train operation depends upon maintaining a space interval between trains.

Today the manual block system is extensively in use on railroads in this country and abroad.

crossing. Many are also familiar with the two short blasts, indicating that the engineer who pulled them understands some signal given him; and the four short whistle blasts, given for a red board when the engineer can see no reason why his path through an interlocking plant should be blocked. Another familiar whistle call is that long blast to notify the train crew that a station is being approached.

Another audible signalling device is the locomotive bell; bells, however, were in use long before the locomotive was born. The locomotive bell, small at first, grew in size as the engine itself grew and developed its own distinctive shape. In this writer's opinion, it is the most graceful of any bell made. Various alloys of copper, silicon, and tin were combined to give the steam locomotive bell the pleasing tone that sets it apart from all others. In the early days silver was added to the alloy, which enhanced its musical ring; however, few if any of these silver-toned bells now exist. The bell-founders lowered or raised the pitch by increasing or decreasing the diameter for the desired distinctive tone. Before the days of automatic bellringers, some firemen became artists with the bellchord, as much so as engineers with the whistle. Used primarily as a warning signal, the bell also had its place.

In passing, we would be unjust to those early foundry workers if we failed to mention their beautiful artwork on some of the bell-hangers of yesteryear. The bell frames came in for the most intricate designs, such as acorns, spheres of brass, and replicas of birds, particularly eagles, adorning the tops of yokes.

Other fundamental signals had to be devised, such as hand signals given by flag or lantern, torpedoes, fuses, rear-end train markers, etc. Before intercom by voice was available, the language of the railroads was spoken to a large extent through signalling.

The signals briefly discussed up to this point, however, are not those known in railroad parlance as "fixed" signals. Fixed signals are those which keep the engineer informed as to the conduct of his train from some fixed point along the right-of-way. These include semaphore, low or dwarf signals, switch targets, slow and stop signs, station signals, whistling posts, and other signals having a fixed location and intended to control the movement of trains over the road.

The Union Switch and Signal Company of Pitts-

burg has very graciously supplied illustrations and commentary which so fully, clearly, and chronologically show the development of fixed signalling systems that textual comment would be superfluous. Therefore we shall allow these illustrations to tell their own story.

BIRTH OF THE TELEGRAPH

To be sure, it was necessary that signals and a signalling system put in their appearance early in railroading, else there could have been no progress. But even with the great boost from audible, fixed, and other signals available and in use, there was a void that had to be filled before real progress could continue.

In spite of the signals in use in the early days, there were breakdowns and unexpected stops to replenish wood for fuel and water for the boilers of the little teakettles. And for other reasons trains got lost on the road. This problem of lost trains became so acute on the Eastern Railroad (later a part of the Boston & Maine) that it became necessary to work out some system of finding them. This road's *Instructions for Conductors and Enginemen* contained the statement: "When anything shall happen to a train to render assistance necessary a brakeman must be dispatched on horseback." The instructions failed to reveal from whence the horse might be procured. In the same rule book, the Master Of The Depot was instructed: "If at any time a train should not arrive at either depot, in one hour from the time of its starting from the other, he shall immediately start on horseback to learn the cause of the delay." Evidently the two depots referred to were East Boston and Salem, approximately twelve miles apart from each end of the road, and we must conclude that the Master Of The Depot kept his horse saddled and tied nearby.

Such were conditions on that January day in 1838 when two young men near Morristown, New Jersey, were in high glee over what they had accomplished. Samuel F.B. Morse and his associate, Alfred Vail, were in a barn-like building over which had been looped some three miles of copper wire, and Vail had tapped out to his partner in Morse code: "A patient waiter is no loser." The first message by telegraph had been sent and received.

But there was much wandering through sloughs, created by lack of finances and interest, before

Long since removed from her place atop the boilershell.

347

An exceptionally beautiful stretch, showing well ballasted and drained roadbed along the Boston & Maine at Rollinsford. However, of much more interest is the old ball system of signals, shown on right. Time Table #1, as late as April 24, 1928, contained the following, with regard to the movement of trains at Rollinsford:

One ball, or one red light; trains may pass in either direction on main line. Two balls, or two red lights; trains from Somersworth Branch may come onto main line and proceed towards Dover, and also eastward trains may pass on main line, but stops all trains approaching Rollinsford from the east. Three balls, or three red lights; eastward trains may cross main line to Somersworth Branch, but stops all other trains.

The movement of trains or engines over the Somersworth Branch to the eastward main line must be protected by flagman as per rule 99.

All Somersworth Branch trains to or from the main line will make full stop within one hundred feet of nearest connecting switch before entering or crossing the same. (Courtesy Union Switch & Signal Division)

There were periods on every man's railroad when business was slack in the 1850's, and it was at such a time when this Master of the Depot relaxed between trains. Apparently well fed, he contents himself on the platform near the station door as he listens to the dots and dashes coming over Sam Morse's "new fangled machine." His duties even then were multitudinous—telegraphing, selling tickets, and otherwise generally supervising the activities of a well run railroad station. (Courtesy Cook Collection, Valentine Museum)

Artist Edward L. Henry captured more with his brush when he made this painting in 1839 than any commentary could explain. The pioneer train was stopped at a station between Harrisburg and Lancaster, Pennsylvania. (Archives Virginia State Library)

Congress passed an appropriation bill on February 23, 1843, making $30,000 available to further the much-ridiculed project. Another year was to pass before May 24, 1844, when Annie Elsworth, in the Supreme Courtroom at the Capitol, handed Morse the message to be transmitted to Alfred Vail in Baltimore. When back from Vail came the message he had received, "What Hath God Wrought," another page of history had turned—the telegraph was here.

This innovation, ridiculed at first, was to play a large and important part in the development of the railroads. Aside from its many other important uses, it made possible one of the greatest steps forward yet taken by the pioneer railroads in the operation of trains.

In 1847, Ezra Cornell, later to found the great university at Ithaca bearing his name, had constructed a commercial telegraph line along the Erie Railroad's right-of-way from its eastern terminus through the counties of the Southern Tier to Fredonia, New York. The wireline was of course independent of the railroad, but for many years it was the practice of commercial telegraph companies to construct their lines next to the tracks of railroads. To reciprocate, the telegraph companies would set aside certain wires for the exclusive use by the railroads for dispatching trains and other railroad message work. (Later, about the turn of this century, the railroads started constructing and operating their own wirelines.)

As was quite natural, telegraph operators (one of the most famous, Thomas A. Edison) spent their idle time in back-and-forth chitchat about politics, the weather, etc. since the wireline was adjacent to the railroad, much of the idle gossip had to do with the movement of trains over a given line. Like all innovations, this new means of communication, which was to play such an important role in train operation, was not immediately adopted by the railroads.

In the early fall of 1851, engineer Isaac Lewis was pulling his westbound train over the Erie lines when he took the siding at Turner's (Now Harriman, N.Y.) to await the passing of an eastbound express. The express was late and under the existing rules Lewis's train was to wait one hour before proceeding.

One of the passengers on the stopped train was Charles Minot, superintendent of the road and a gifted railroad man. Irked by the delay, Minot stepped to the nearby telegraph office and wired the operator at Goshen, 14 miles west, as to whether the eastbound express had passed that station. Advised that it had not, Superintendent Minot telegraphed: TO AGENT AND OPERATOR AT GOSHEN. HOLD THE TRAIN FOR FURTHER ORDERS. CHARLES MINOT, SUPERINTENDENT.

Minot then wrote an order addressed to the conductor and engineer of the stopped train: "Run to Goshen regardless of opposing train," and handed it to conductor W. H. Stewart. Erie's historian, Edward Harold Mott, states that conductor Stewart, relating the incident, said, "I took the order, showing it to the engineer, Isaac Lewis, and told him to go ahead. The surprised engineer read the order, and handing it back to me exclaimed:

" 'Do you take me for a damned fool? I won't run by that thing!'

"I reported to the Superintendent, who went forward and used his verbal authority on the engineer, but without effect. Minot then climbed on the engine and took charge of it himself. Engineer Lewis jumped off and got in a rear seat of the rear car. The Superintendent ran the train to Goshen. The eastbound train had not yet reached that station. He telegraphed to Middletown. The train had not arrived there. The westbound train was run on a similar order to Middletown, and from there to Port Jervis, where it entered the yard from the East as the other train came into it from the West."

So far as this writer has been able to ascertain, this is the first time a train was moved by telegraphic order over an American railroad. The brilliant railroader, Charles Minot, soon worked out a system of dispatches, a code of signs designating stations, such as "PO" for Port Jervis, "XN" for Lackawaxen, etc., and the operation of trains by telegraphic messages was a reality.

In spite of the fact that many engineers, accustomed to being on the loose with their trains, looked on the telegraph with disdain, this great forward step toward safety in train operation played a major role until superseded when the block system of train control came into use about 1880.

THE AUTOMATIC COUPLER MAKES
ITS APPEARANCE

In the beginning, the carriages making up the

Other young geniuses started their careers on railroads, but none ever held the light for this one. This picture of Tom Edison was made when he was fifteen and working trains on the Grand Trunk Railroad as newsbutcher. Just a few years later he handled his trick as railroad telegrapher. (Courtesy Association of American Railroads)

train were coupled together with links of chain. Understandably such coupling had many drawbacks, to say the least, and early in those days of trial and error the link and pin coupling came into use. For the most part, this device did a fair job of holding cars together. However, it was responsible for more dead and injured railroad employees than any other single cause. To make up a train it was necessary for the brakeman to stand between the cars as they were being coupled, guide the link into the socket, then drop the pin that would hold the two together. As was to be expected, such a dangerous operation was responsible for the loss of many lives and countless fingers and hands. It has been said that in the link and pin days when transients would appear in the yards looking for jobs as brakemen, the yardmaster would ask for a show of hands rather than references, and when hands appeared with missing fingers the yardmaster knew they were experienced.

Recognizing the need for a coupler, minus the human injury and death feature, many minds tackled the problem. The beginning of the avalanche of patents on the idea started in 1848, when A.G. Heckrotte made his filing; his device, however, was

Coupling in the link and pin days. (Courtesy Louisville & Nashville)

The Miller Hook. (Courtesy National Castings Company)

Top: Janney's first automatic coupler, 1868. Bottom: Improved model, 1873. (Courtesy National Castings Company)

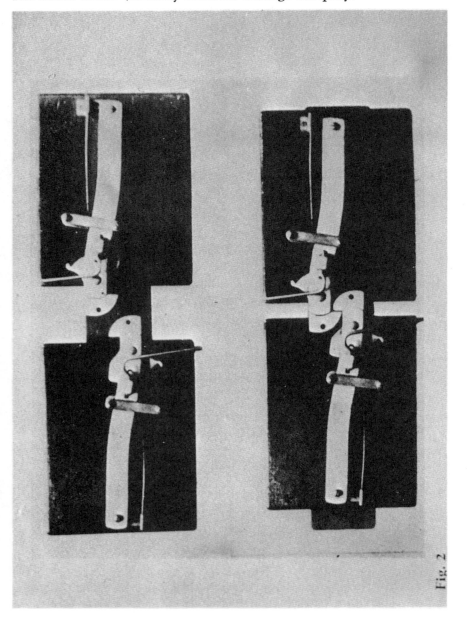

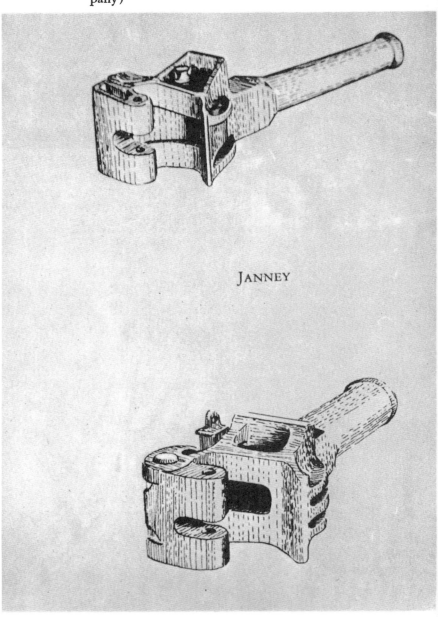

Top: Janney's first automatic coupler, 1868. Bottom: Improved model, 1873. (Courtesy National Castings Company)

JANNEY

not accepted by the railroads. Twelve years later, D. A. Hopkins, of Elmira, New York, patented a device that was tried for a short time by the Erie but abandoned as unsatisfactory. In 1863, Ezra Miller came up with what was called the "Miller Hook." This was hailed as the answer and many roads tried it out, but it, too, had its defects.

About this time an ex-Civil War Confederate, Major Eli Hamilton Janney, of Fredericksburg, Virginia, had put his mind to the task, and in 1868 patented his automatic coupler. By 1873, Janney's coupler had been perfected to such a point that it is recognized as the ancestor of all present-day couplers.

Janney must have thought he "had it made" when the Pennsylvania Railroad agreed to test his invention and in 1877 adopted it as standard equipment, but he was due for some disappointment when the majority of the roads showed little interest. After exhaustive tests, the Master Car Builders Association adopted the automatic coupler in 1882, and the fortunes of Janney's company, which manufactured his patent, began to improve.

George Westinghouse's great invention of air brakes and Janney's automatic coupler came almost on each others heels. As with any other innovation they filled a distinct need, and on first arrival were not perfected; however, improvements in both were made as rapidly as inventive minds could bring them about. Since railroads then were not as safety conscious as they would later become, neither of these great forward steps were immediately taken by the railroads. There were exceptions, where a road here and another there did adopt these great inventions as soon as they were available, but this was not generally the case. According to Alfred W. Bruce, only 62 per cent of the 29,000 locomotives in use in America in 1889 were fitted with train air-brake connections. Up into the last decade of the nineteenth century, many freight trains moved over the road with only a few cars in the consist equipped with air brakes, and on some roads the link and pin coupling was still in use.

Whatever the reasons for the tardiness of the railroads in the general adoption of these two great safety devices, a zealot who would not let them rest certainly played his part. In 1874, Lorenzo Coffin, a farmer near Fort Dodge, Iowa, was a passenger on a freight train when it stopped at a station to pick up a car. In coupling, a brakeman lost the last two fingers on his right hand (the other three having been lost the year before in a similar accident). The accident Coffin had witnessed, plus what he learned from other members of the crew, acted as a catalyst and made the man a fanatic on the subject of safety in railroad operation. Taking for his text the air brake and automatic coupler, he set out to preach his gospel to the officialdom of railroads. When railroad officials would no longer listen, Coffin turned to the press (religious, family and farm periodicals; the dailies would not print what he wrote).

A man fired with the zeal of fanaticism on any subject recognizes no barriers; his entire attention is on his goal. In 1883, Coffin was made the first railroad commissioner of Iowa. Inviting himself to railroad conventions, this unwelcome guest proceeded to dose the officials with his preachments. At other times he preached his text of safety through the adoption of air brakes and automatic couplers to the Master Car Builders Association until this body finally agreed to a test run on a long freight train.

The first test, in 1886, was disappointing, but in 1887, at the famed Burlington Trials, both the inventor, George Westinghouse, and the fanatic, Lorenzo Coffin, watched perhaps the most satisfying event they had ever witnessed. At a given signal, a long freight train rolling down a grade at 40 miles an hour over the tracks of the Chicago, Burlington & Quincy Railroad, came to a halt within 500 feet.

8
With the Throttle Back

CHARLIE HOGAN SETS THE PACE

Now, with good engines and rolling stock, power to start and power to stop, real railroading was just around the corner. A far cry from the little weak teakettles at the beginning, pulling their brigades over wooden longitudinal rails capped with light strap-iron, the iron horse had come of age—and in the process had revolutionized America.

By 1890, most of the larger railroads had become speed conscious and competition between them was real and furious. Record speeds between terminals was a strong invitation to new business, and among the early prizes to be captured by speed was a contract to carry mail.

One of the first and most notable speed events occurred in upstate New York. William Buchannan, Superintendent of Motive Power, had turned out some handsome and high stepping engines for the New York Central & Hudson River Railroad, and goaded by the company's public relations man, George H. Daniels, he had built an engine that pulled a train between New York City and Buffalo at an average speed of 61.4 miles an hour, on September 14, 1891. This run received great publicity, but Daniels wasn't satisfied and shortly thereafter approached Buchannan for a real speed queen to pull the Empire State Express.

Given a free rein, the Superintendent of Motive Power pulled out all the stops; he wanted to build something that would overshadow any engine ever built. Design engineers had learned that the diameter of the driving wheels in inches roughly indicated the safe speed of the engine in miles per hour. And

when the 999 rolled out of the West Albany shops in April 1893, with her barrel resting on four 86-inch drivers, her very looks epitomized speed. Perhaps following the same rule-of-thumb, both the engine and tender trucks had been increased from the conventional diameter of 33 inches to 40.

Coming out of her preliminary tests with flying colors, Buchannan proudly reported her performance to his superiors. The mainline track between Syracuse and Buffalo had been selected for the official run of this high-heeled lady, and every precaution was taken to see that the roadbed was in condition to take the great speed anticipated in this special run. Three of the road's "brag engineers" had been called into President Webb's office, but when it was explained that a speed of 100 miles an hour or better was expected, two of them gracefully declined the honors. The third, Charles H. Hogan, said quietly, "I'll do it."

May 18, 1893, was a balmy day and the sun glistened on her rising rods as Charlie Hogan backed the 999 up and coupled to the Empire State Express at Syracuse. Alf Elliott had his fire right, with the needle on the steam gauge hovering just under the 180-pound hair. No one knows what was running through Hogan's mind as he waited the highball to start the Central's finest four-wooden-coach train on that record run; perhaps the "Drive her, boy, drive her" that has beat the eardrums of more than one good engineer might have reverberated against his own in unending repetition.

There was much speculation and excitement among the time-keepers, officials, and other VIP's who rode the cushions as Hogan eased out of

354

Syracuse. Straightening out, Hogan's steady hand loosed the power of his 180-pound steam pressure, and, slowing a bit for curves, he reached a speed of 80 miles an hour before going into Batavia.

Thirty-six miles of almost straight and level track stretched westward from Batavia, and this was where Charlie Hogan was going to make his move and also history. Giving prompt response to the throttle, this queen of the high iron increased speed steadily. Finally, the lever was all the way out, and with the reverse bar back almost to the center of the arc, the exhausts drowned each other in a continual roar; and to this rhythm shuttling mainrods played until the driver treads seemed strips of steel wed to the rails.

speed of 112½ miles an hour. In the hands of a great engineer, William Buchannan's creation had done what she was designed and built to do.

Riding the crest of the wave, publicity man Daniels headed Hogan and Elliott for the World's Fair at Chicago, with their famous engine and train. After being admired and marvelled at by thousands, the famous locomotive returned to passenger service on the Syracuse division, where she served until major repairs became necessary.

In 1899, the 86-inch drivers were replaced by those of 70-inch diameter and her 40-inch trucks by wheels of 30-inch diameter, and she was put in local passenger service on the Rome, Watertown & Ogdensburg Division. In May 1905 she was further

This old picture shows the famous Speed Queen stopped on the tracks of the New York Central in 1893, when the line ran down the middle of of the main drag of Syracuse.

Like a coyote in a hurry, with its ears pinned back, William Buchannan's masterpiece and Charlie Hogan's charge increased her speed. The time-recorders perhaps wondered if they would live to report their findings, of the fastest speed ever made over rails. But in the cab of that lurching engine, Alf Elliott was too busy passing coal to a roaring fire to be much concerned, and the man at the throttle through long experience had bred a confidence that paid no mind to speed—under circumstances where speed was proper and controlled.

As this record-shattering speed queen approached Buffalo, her master's hand closed the throttle as she drifted in and came to a hissing stop at the station. For the first time in history, man had ridden at a

desecrated with a boiler of modified design; but the crowning insult to this originally graceful and high-heeled queen came in 1913, when her distinguished number was changed to 1086.

Ten years later someone must have realized that a mistake had been made, and to partly atone for it, what little was left of the original (only the main frames) was "done over" and the number 999 restored. There was slight resemblance of what was exhibited at the New York World's Fair in 1940, as the 999, to the original artistic, graceful, and historic performing creation of William Buchannan.

ALBERT LODGE CARRIES THE MAIL

Nearly eight years after the historic speed record set by the 999, another speed event took place, this

This picture, made in 1913, bears little resemblance to the creation William Buchanan built in 1893. (Courtesy New York Central System)

Here we see the famous engine churning those 86-inch drivers at the head of the Empire State Express. It is not known what crew was in the cab when this picture was made at Palatine Bridge, New York, in 1894, just about one year after her historic run, but it certainly lets us see plenty. Incidentally, the spray from beneath her tender rushes from her open scoop as she takes water on the fly. (Courtesy New York Central System)

time far to the south, between Savannah, Georgia, and Jacksonville, Florida. The prize for the winner was a United States postal contract, brought about to give faster mail service between the Nation's capitol and the West Indies.

Both the Atlantic Coast Line and Seaboard Air Line had bid on the contract, but the government took the stand that "seeing was believing" and allowed the two rival roads to prove which could deliver the mail first. In March 1901, eight cars of mail were hauled from Washington over the Richmond, Fredericksburg & Potomac to Richmond, and from there to Savannah by the Atlantic Coast Line. At Savannah, the train was split and four cars each given to the Seaboard and Savannah, Florida & Western (then operated in the Plant System, to become a part of the 'Coast Line in 1902). The crew of each rival train was briefed on what it was all about, with instructions to get to Jacksonville *first*.

Lovers of the iron horse, its romance and accomplishments, are indeed fortunate in getting this story first hand, since one of the old-time dispatchers on the A.C.L., D. S. McClellan, just happened to hitch a ride on the engine that made history on this run. He left the following account of the trip:

My recollection of the famous run in March 1901 was that the Seaboard Air Line changed their schedule between Savannah and Jacksonville for the purpose of getting their train into Jacksonville ahead of our train No. 23 in order to secure the handling of the Havana mail. For us to compete it was necessary to operate the mail cars special from Savannah to Jacksonville.

The crew handling this train with engine 111 was Conductor Lindsey Kirkland, Engineer Albert Lodge, Flagman Knight, Fireman Charlie Johnson; also a colored coal passer and a colored train porter whose names I do not recall. Travelling Engineer "Uncle Jimmie" Ambrose and myself were riding the engine. "Uncle Jimmie" having started with the train out of Savannah, and I caught it at Jesup and rode it to Jacksonville.

All trains on the road had "31" train orders requiring them to clear this special 30 minutes at an open telegraph office, with instructions that conductors and engineers must personally examine switches to see that they were set and securely locked to the main track.

This train consisted of three mail cars and either a baggage or combination car. It left Savannah with engine 107 (Engineer Ned Leake) on it ahead of train No. 23, engine 111 (Engineer Lodge). Engine 107 developed a hot driving box at Burroughs, sustaining a delay of one hour at that point and between Burroughs and Fleming. Upon reaching Fleming, engine 107 was

still running hot and instructions were issued to exchange engines with train No. 23, placing engine 111 (Engineer Lodge) on the special. When this was done, the special was was over an hour late on the special schedule.

The train arrived at Jesup about daylight; remained there three minutes taking water and oiling. We passed Screven between 5:10 and 5:15 A.M. When within a few miles of Screven, "Uncle Jimmie" said to me, "This train is going awful fast." He and I took out our watches to time him from Screven, as I realized that we were running at a remarkable rate of speed and I knew that there was a downhill stretch after passing Screven.

The time consumed from Screven to 74 milepost siding (which is now known as Satilla) was two minutes and thirty seconds—a distance of five miles (120 m.p.h.). The run was made from Jesup to Waycross in 27 or 28 minutes (a distance of almost 40 miles) and from Waycross to Folkston in 24 or 25 minutes (34 miles). The total time from Waycross to Jacksonville was 59 minutes.

I shall never forget the things that passed through my mind, as this train reached the top of a little hill just south of Screven and started down the fill for Satilla River. There is a little curve just after passing over the river and I wondered if the engine was going to take that curve at its speed or if it was going to take to the woods.

Another moment fresh in my mind is when we went around the curve at 120 milepost between Race Pond and Uptonville. When we were about a hundred or so yards from this curve, the Negro coal passer yelled to the fireman, "Charlie, don't you spose he is gwying to shut off?" Charlie's answer was, "No, he's jest gwying good now." About the time Charlie answered, Engineer Lodge closed up the throttle about three notches and immediately changed his mind and pulled it out again five notches. Then we hit the curve. "Uncle Jimmie" grabbed me and I grabbed the hot iron pipes on the front of the boiler head, which felt rather cool, and when the engine settled down after getting around the curve there was quite a relief.

When the train stopped at Jacksonville, "Uncle Jimmie" and I got down off the engine. He pulled his little cap off, reached for his handkerchief to wipe off some of the coal dust, and said to me, "I've been running an engine a long time, but have never ridden that fast before and never expect to again."

The Seaboard Air Line competing train had passed our special at Burroughs where their line crosses ours. After our train had been in Jacksonville for some time, the Seaboard train pulled in. I was in the telegraph office when their conductor came in to register. He asked the operator when they expected the Plant System special, that he had passed at Burroughs with an old broken-down engine pulling it, to get in. I told him that we had more than one engine, and we had been in Jacksonville an hour and the mail that we handled was over half way to Cuba.

Needless to say, the Coast Line got the contract.

As far as known, no picture of the 111 exists; however, she was identical to her sister, 110, shown in this picture. Built by Rhode Island Locomotive Works (later ALCO) about 1900, or just before, this fleet 4-6-0 with 9½ tons of coal and 5000 gallons of water in her tender weighed 252,900 pounds, and with 180 psi going into her 19x28-inch cylinders made a tractive effort of 21,240 pounds. It is thought that her drivers were 76 inches in diameter, but they could have been 80. In any event, they were high enough to really let her roll. (Courtesy Atlantic Coast Line Railroad Company)

A COWBOY IN A HURRY

Because Walter Scott, perhaps better known as Death Valley Scotty, loved the limelight, he was responsible for one of the greatest high-speed train movements ever made over a long distance. Born at Covington, Kentucky, he gravitated to Nevada in his teens, punched cattle, and at one time served as a water boy for a government survey party in Death Valley. Having a flair for showmanship he toured the country for twelve years with Buffalo Bill's outfit. Somewhere in his travels he became acquainted and formed a fast friendship with Arthur Johnson, millionaire insurance executive in Chicago, who established the fantastic Scott in Grape Vine Canyon, above Death Valley.

Ever loving the spectacular and having a mania for speed, the high-heelbooted Scotty with his flaming red tie had come to the right place when just before noon on Saturday, July 8, 1905, he walked into the office of J. J. Byrne, General Passenger Agent of the Sante Fe in Los Angeles. Pitching his Stetson into a corner and throwing his cheap blue serge coat on a settee, Scotty dropped into a chair as he quietly said, "Mr. Byrne, I've been thinking about taking a train over your road to Chicago. I want you to put me in there in forty-six hours. Kin you do it?" At that point Scotty pulled a roll from his pocket and began to peel off thousand dollar bills. He continued, "I'm willing to pay any old figure, but I want to make the time. Kin you or can't you? Let's talk business!"

Mr. Byrne figured as he talked, and when his computation was completed, put $5,500 in his safe; the train had been bought and paid for. Turning, Byrne said, "Young man, the Sante Fe will put you in Chicago in 46 hours, if steam and steel will hold together. We've got the roadbed, the equipment, and the men; don't forget that. But let me tell you that you'll be riding faster than a white man ever rode before!"

"Pardner," Scott drawled simply, "I like your talk. It sounds good. Line 'em up along the way and tell 'em we're comin'."

The following day, Sunday, Engineer John Finlay had just backed the Baldwin 10-wheeler, 442, up to the three-car train of baggage car 210, diner #1407, and the Pullman observation car, *Muskegon*, when promptly at 12:47 P.M. Scott and his wife alighted from a big automobile and fought their way through a throng of people to the train. Mrs. Scott headed for the Pullman, where Frank Holman, a Sante Fe representative, restlessly walked and Charles E. Van Loan had already started to type the story for his newspaper. Scotty made his way to the engine, climbed into the cab, and gave a warm handshake to the engineer and fireman. Such a cheer came from the crowd on the ground that the spectacular cowboy climbed over the coal pile and made a speech from the rear of the tender.

Promptly at 1:00 P.M., Conductor George Simpson gave the highball and within sixty seconds John Finlay had the eastbound "Coyote Special" out of sight of the cheering crowd. The train had made about thirty-five miles when a sudden shock came as air-driven brake shoes took hold. Returning inside from the platform, from which he had swung out to see what went on, Conductor Simpson reported, "Too bad! A tank box has gone hot on us! The fireman's playing his hose on it."

At San Bernadino a helper engine was coupled on for the run over Cajon Pass. Near the summit, a brakeman climbed over and uncoupled the helper, which then ran ahead into a siding. As its tender cleared the mainline the switch was thrown back and the Coyote Special roared past.

With his delays behind him and over the summit, Finlay let her drop and was clocked between mileposts 44 and 43 in thirty-nine seconds (96 miles an hour). When the 442 stopped at Barstow, John Finlay had his train 26 minutes ahead of the schedule laid out for him.

Within two minutes the 442 had been uncoupled and a ready engine had the special moving eastward toward the desert, and at 7:17 P.M. the cowboy's train came to a grinding halt in the yards at Needles —308 miles in 6 hours, 17 minutes.

In exactly 80 seconds after the stop, Fred Jackson's hand was opening the throttle on the high-wheeled Prairie engine 1010. One hundred and forty-nine miles of mountain railroad lay ahead on Jackson's division, and determined to hold his part of the schedule, Fred Jackson really let her roll. With a mighty roar the *Prairie Queen* slammed her train across the muddy Colorado and into Arizona, at a speed of better than 65 miles an hour. Three hours after leaving Needles, Jackson had covered the 150 miles of his winding division and in the process had lifted his train a mile. As he stopped at Seligman,

Arizona, Division Superintendent Gibson came aboard the Pullman and jokingly asked, "What detained you?"

Under twinkling stars of the great Southwest, the flying Coyote sped through the desert night as Scotty revelled in the speed and Van Loan punched out the story of the run on his typewriter. As the train stopped at Albuquerque, Superintendent Gibson bid the party good-bye with "I've brought you over the Albuquerque Division thirty-four minutes faster than any train ever went over it before."

Gibson had hardly bid adieu when Ed Sears pulled the throttle open on his big Pacific engine, 1211, and dropping the train down grades like an elevator with a broken cable, headed for Raton. A helper engine coupled on at Lamy for the ten-mile climb, 158 feet to the mile, to Glorietta (altitude 7421 feet). With the helper cut loose, Ed Sears now showed his passengers some real mountain railroading as he dropped down grade from the summit and into reverse curves at the bottom at a speed of better than a mile a minute.

Back in the lurching Pullman, Van Loan's typewriter carriage swapped sides with amazing speed and a bang as Scotty smiled nervously and the other passengers hung on to their seats. When Sears brought his train to a stop at Las Vegas ahead of schedule he had shown his passengers how mountain railroading was done on a tight schedule. More winding curves and then the climb to Raton, where within two minutes Hud Gardner had the Special rolling behind his Baldwin Pacific, 1215. Roaring out of the tunnel, Gardner's brake-hand steadied the lurching train on the descent toward Trinidad, but he made his run to La Junta with his train way ahead of schedule.

Between La Junta, Colorado, and Newton, 355 miles of fairly straight and level track stretched eastward across the plains of Kansas. This was the Santa Fe's race track, where a train could really make time. Four engineers, Oliver Halsey, Dave Lesher, Ed Norton, and H. G. Simmons alternated in the cabs of their 79-inch-drivered Atlantic engines.

Leaving his Pullman at La Junta, Scotty rode the engines over the two divisions to Dodge City, where he sent a telegram to President Theodore Roosevelt: "An American cowboy is coming east on a special train faster than any cowpuncher ever rode before; how much shall I break transcontinental record?"

Through that Monday night the headlights of the

The high-wheeled Prairie engine and exact replica of the train that Fred Jackson rocked and rolled over his winding division between Needles and Seligman the night of July 9, 1905. (Courtesy Santa Fe Railway)

360

The fireman must have been dosing his firebox as Harry Rehder widens out with the 478 just west of Grants, New Mexico, heading for Albuquerque. (Courtesy Santa Fe Railway)

Ed Sears showed his passengers how mountain railroading was done with this big Pacific. (Courtesy Santa Fe Railway)

high-drivered Atlantics cut through the darkness at speeds up to 90 miles an hour, with an average for 300 miles of a mile every fifty seconds.

The Special had already set a speed record but the final burst was to come on the home stretch. When the train stopped at Fort Madison, Iowa (Shopton), the ready engine had been coupled and was rolling east within three minutes. Charlie Losee was no daredevil, just a modest man, but he was an engineer with nerves to match the steel of his engine. Pulling the throttle out on the 510, a Baldwin Atlantic balanced compound, he soon had his train stretched out across the level prairies of Illinois. With his reverse bar back almost to the center of the arc and his throttle wide, Losee carried his train over the 2.8-mile stretch between Cameron and Surrey in just 95 seconds—a speed of 106 miles an hour. He made the 105 miles from Fort Madison to Chillicothe in 101 minutes.

Five minutes were lost at Chillicothe and four more at South Joliet, but the run from Shopton to Dearborn Station, Chicago, 239 miles away, was made in 239 minutes. At 11:54 A.M. on July 11th, the Coyote Special had made a record run of 2267 miles in 44 hours and 54 minutes. Nineteen engine crews and 19 engines had given their best to prove the speed over rails two-thirds of the way across the continent. Nine of the locomotives were of the Atlantic type, four Prairies, three Pacifics, and one ten-wheeler—all built by Baldwin. Two were ten-wheelers built by the Rhode Island Locomotive Works.

It should be borne in mind that at the time of the record-shattering long-distance run over rails the Santa Fe was a single track road and half the distance was over four mountain ranges. There were slow-downs coming through big yards, compliance with speed ordinances of towns through which the train passed, a couple of hot boxes, and the necessary stops for fuel and water; but with it all, a 50.4-mph average speed over such a distance was a feat never to be forgotten. Such an accomplishment could never have been brought about without the know-how and teamwork of the able and dedicated men of a great railroad.

SPEED RECORDS THAT ENDED IN DISASTER

Speed under control and used with good judgment plays an important and necessary part in railroading.

Danger, to greater or lesser degree, constantly surrounds any moving object, and with such a heavy mass as a train, moving frequently at great speeds, wrecks were and are to be expected. It is a great credit to American Railroads that these mishaps have been held to such a minimum.

Since the man at the throttle is always more closely associated with a wreck than anyone else, the brave engineer has been eulogized in song and story —if he lost his life when the crash came; if he survived, the odds are long that he got time off, whether blameless or not.

"HE TOOK HIS FAREWELL TRAIN TO THE PROMISED LAND"

Perhaps number one of the famous wrecks occurred on April 30, 1900. John Luther Jones, more familiarly known as Casey Jones, had started his railroad career as an apprentice telegraph operator on the Mobile & Ohio in 1879, when he was fifteen. But engines were in his blood, and at eighteen he was firing one. Six years later, Casey was still firing, but now on the Illinois Central, and in 1890, he passed his examination and realized his boyhood ambition—to run an engine.

It was in the fall of 1893 that he was assigned the 2-8-0 engine, 638, which had been exhibited at the World's Columbian Exhibition in Chicago, and this locomotive was to rate second only to his wife in his affection until the end of 1899. It was during this period, pulling freights, that Casey fashioned his noted six-tone whistle and his art with the whistle-cord made him and his whippoorwill call from the 638 known by all from one end of his division to the other (Jackson, Tennessee, to Water Valley, Mississippi).

Not unlike that of most engine crews, Casey's climb from firing to the right-hand side of the cab had been slow (eight years); then he had pulled freights for ten years as an engineer. But, as always, the door finally opens to those who wait, and in December 1899 Casey "stood for" and was offered a regular passenger run. He perhaps had misgivings about giving up his love, the 638, and moving to Memphis, but the privilege of piloting the Illinois Central's fastest Chicago-New Orleans passenger train, popularly known as the "Cannonball," was too tempting for the 36-year-old engineer to turn down.

On January 1, 1900, Casey reported for his assignment and, in order that he might learn the road before taking his passenger run, was temporarily assigned to freight runs. Within a few weeks he had learned the road by heart and had memorized his time card, and the high-drivered 4-6-0 Rogers-built engine, 382, had been assigned the engineer for his first passenger run. Fond memories of the 638 probably faded into oblivion as Casey and his fireman, Simm Webb, rolled the Cannonball back and forth over the 190 miles of his division, between Memphis, Tennessee, and Canton, Mississippi.

Pride in keeping his train on time is an inherent part of a good engineer, and Casey had brought the northbound Cannonball into Memphis on time April 29th. The engineer scheduled to take it south that night was off because of illness and the train had gotten off schedule north of Memphis. Instead of leaving at the appointed time, 11:15 P.M., it was 12:50 A.M. when Casey pulled out of Poplar Street Station. It was a foggy night and clouds hung low along the Mississippi as the train moved over the Beale Street trestle to Central Station, where a stop of five minutes was made. As he headed out into the foggy night, Casey called across the cab to Sim, "We're going to have a tough time going into Canton on time, but I believe we can do it—barring accidents."

One hundred miles of fairly straight and level track stretched southward from Memphis to Grenada, and as the 382 skipped over the rails Casey must have been in fine fettle, as evidenced by his famous whistle calls piercing the murky night. The regular scheduled running time between the two points was two hours, forty-five minutes, but at 2:35 A.M., one hundred minutes after pulling out of Central Station at Memphis, Casey had made his scheduled stop and was pulling out of Grenada.

Casey had his train almost back on schedule when he stopped at Durant, 53 miles further down the line. It was here that the engineer was given orders to meet the northbound cannonball at Goodman and "saw through" two side-tracked freights at Vaughan (Vaughan was 22 miles south of Durant). After passing the northbound train at Goodman, Casey was apparently intent on going to Canton on time and pulled the throttle wide as he headed for Vaughan at an estimated speed of better than 70 miles an hour.

But things do not always work out as scheduled, even on a railroad. The side track east of the main-

line at Vaughan was 3148 feet long, bypassing the station. There was a shorter siding on the west side of the mainline. Two freights, one northbound, the other southbound, had crawled into the long siding to allow passenger traffic to pass over the mainline, but because the two trains were too long to completely clear the mainline, it was necessary for them to "saw" in each direction to allow passage over the mainline. The sawing operation was a common occurrence, particularly on single-track roads where a train was too long to get in a siding and clear the mainline. Under such circumstances it would pull in a sufficient distance to clear that end of a siding toward which the passing train was moving, and as the last car of the passing train cleared that switch the train doing the sawing would move out on the mainline just cleared in order that the passing train could clear the other end.

The northbound cannonball Casey had passed at Goodman had made the saw at Vaughan and of course had left the two freights in the south saw when it cleared the north switch. Doubtless the freights would have held their position for Casey's arrival had it not been that two sections of northbound passenger train No. 26 arrived. Sawing north to allow the newly arrived passenger trains to take the short siding and thereby be out of the way of Casey's southbound cannonball, an air hose burst near the rear of freight No. 72 (northbound), leaving a caboose and three cars of the southbound freight, No. 83, out on the mainline at the north switch. Faced with this dilemma, and aware that the southbound cannonball was roaring toward them, a flagman named Newberry started to run northward, clamped a torpedo on the rail, and was over half a mile north of the blocked switch when he saw the headlight of the approaching train.

Casey's speed, as he roared by Newberry's waving lantern, will never be known, but was probably 70 to 75 miles an hour. Newberry stated later that he heard the explosion of the torpedo as the 382 rolled over it. Sim Webb stated that when the torpedo popped, Casey immediately applied his brakes and he (Webb) looked out of his side into the darkness. As the engine roared into the curve (on the fireman's side) Webb saw the marker lights on the caboose ahead, yelled to his engineer, "Look out! We're going to hit something," swung down the gangway as low as possible, and jumped.

Casey stayed with his engine and, although his

The engine that carried Casey to "The Promised Land."
(Courtesy Illinois Central Railroad)

split-second actions at this juncture will never be known, probably rode the 382 into the rear end of the standing freight, and to his death, with his brakes set and both hands yanking the reverse bar back. According to eyewitnesses, Casey's speed had been considerably reduced within the approximate half mile from where the 382 exploded the torpedo to the point of impact, but not enough to stop before plowing through the caboose and two other cars of the standing freight.

The circumstances surrounding this wreck were to be a subject of discussion among railroaders for a long time. It was a known fact that there was speed, and plenty of it, yet it was in the hands of an able and experienced engineer who must have certainly known the road over which he was running, even though the night was a murky one. From the orders he received at Durant, Casey was bound to have been aware that he must saw through Vaughan (22 miles south), and yet eyewitnesses estimated his speed at around 70 miles an hour when the 382 roared by Newberry's frantically waved lantern (approximately 3200 feet north of the north switch at Vaughan), to which the engineer apparently paid no attention. The questions raised, however, were never answered, for the only man who could have given the answers carried them with him into death.

Casey Jones was the only fatality in the wreck. Fireman Simm Webb recovered from the injuries received when he jumped, and within a few months was back firing the same run for Casey's successor, Harry Norton.

Wallace Saunders, a Negro engine-wiper in the Illinois Central's shops at Canton, Mississippi, perhaps deserves the lion's share for Casey's undying fame. When Saunders learned of the death of his colorful friend, he began a chant about "Casey Jones —Casey Jones." The chant was picked up and carried on by others until a professional songwriter heard and polished it up and put it to music in one of the most famous ballads of American folklore.

"HE WAS GOIN' DOWN GRADE MAKIN' 90 MILES AN HOUR"

Certainly occupying second place among railroad wrecks carried to fame in song was that which occurred near Danville, Virginia, soon after the turn of this century. The fast mail and express train, No. 97, had been placed in service on the Southern Railway System between Washington and Atlanta (via Monroe, Lynchburg, and Danville) in December 1902 (and, incidentally, was taken out of service on January 6, 1907). Although the advertised departure was 8:00 A.M., it cannot be established whether the train left Washington late or lost time on the 163 mile run to Monroe, Virginia. In any event, it pulled into Monroe, the end of a division, approximately an hour late on Sunday, September 27, 1903.

Joseph A. Broady (dubbed by his friends "Steve," after Steve Brodie who had supposedly jumped from the Brooklyn Bridge to win a bet), formerly an engineer on the Pocahontas Division of the Norfolk & Western, had recently come to the Southern and this was his first trip pulling the fast mail train from Monroe to Spencer, North Carolina. Good engineers have ever taken pride in keeping their trains on time and when one picks up a run that is off schedule it is only natural for him to do what he safely can to make up the lost time.

Broady probably swung up the gangway with a song in his heart as he anticipated what he could do with his practically new Baldwin-built 4-6-0 engine, particularly happy that he had two men to keep her hot—his regular fireman, A. G. Clapp, and a learner by the name of Dodge. Sometime between 1:25 and 1:40 P.M. the engineer had the 1102 moving south out of Monroe.

The roadbed between Monroe and Danville wound through foothill country with naturally some grades, but the real one was across White Oak Mountain, approximately five miles south of Chatham and eight miles north of Danville, near what is known as Dry Fork. As mountains go, White Oak might more aptly be called a big hill, with a grade on either side which would make an old Jack's exhausts bark loud going up and swallow each other rolling down the other side.

As far as is known, there was no event of consequence as the big ten-wheeler ate up grades and swung around curves on the "mighty rough road from Lynchburg to Danville," trying to make up that lost hour. And as she came down the grade off White Oak Mountain old 97 must have been rolling high, wide, and handsome on that eight-mile-stretch to Danville.

But eight miles may hold anything in waiting for an engineer trying to put a fast train back on schedule. In a report of what happened just outside of Danville, a morning paper of September 28, 1903,

Old 97's engine, 1102, and the remains of the train in Stillhouse Hollow after the wreck (Courtesy Southern Railway System)

The Richmond Times Dispatch, stated that at 2:30 P.M., Sunday, September 27th, the train had taken the curve just north of Stillhouse Ravine and was approximately 100 feet from the trestle when it climbed the rails and ran along the cross ties. As it was about to pass onto the trestle the engine careened, striking the wooden supports of the bridge structure. Four 13-foot-long supports gave way under the weight of the engine which fell through the opening and was partly buried in the mud of Cherrystone Creek, 75 feet below, with the twisted debris of the cars on top of it.

Mailbags, letters, and parcels flew in all directions and almost immediately the wreckage caught fire from the locomotive's firebox. "Steve" wasn't "found in the wreck with his hand on the throttle" but his and both firemen's bodies lay in the mud beside the engine, while those of Conductor Thomas J. Blair, Flagman J. S. Moody, and four mail clerks lay scattered among the wreckage.

To add weirdness to the horror and tragedy, a large shipment of canary birds, freed from their cages as the express car crashed, warbled from their perches on low branches of nearby trees as the rescuers went about their grim task. The report further stated, "Two boys were under the trestle when 97 came through and one has been insane ever since. He has flighty spells and imagines he can see trains flying through the air."

The next day Vice-President Finley was quoted as having made the official statement, "The train con-

Close to base.

It isn't often that we see a highway blocked by an old hog lying across it. This one split a switch about two miles west of Williamson, West Virginia, in the early 1950's and rolled down the embankment onto the highway. Bill Alley just happened to run up on this scene and fortunately had his camera along. In this picture, cable had just been placed.

Almost.

On the plate again.

367

Engineer Blanchard had his big Mallet "right on the paper" with her time freight that night in 1950 as he slugged eatward along Tug River in West Virginia. As he rounded a curve he suddenly made out a stopped westbound with three of its derailed empties blocking his line ahead. A situation of this kind calls for split-second action. Calling to his fireman, "Look out, we're going into a wreck," Blanchard set his brakes and the two men jumped into Tug River. After the impact, the big engine left the rails, rolled down a steep embankment and came to rest with her nose in the river. After giving all they had for over eight hours, four industrial wreckers were able to move the engine only about six feet. Finally, the locomotive was dismantled and moved in three pieces, loaded on flat cars, to the shops, where it was rebuilt and of course put back into service. The big fellow is the engineer—and to this day is known as "Tug River Blanchard." (Photographed by and courtesy of William L. Alley, Jr.)

In an effort to put a crack train back on schedule, an engineer will sometimes stretch his luck too far. This one did, when he went into a 35 mph curve on a mountain division with too much speed in the early hours before dawn. His lack of caution cost him his life, and serious injury to his fireman and a number of passengers.

In old Hollywood Cemetery, Richmond, Virginia, this shaft was erected to the memory of 32-year-old James E. Valentine, who died at the throttle of his 4-4-0 wood-burner on December 20, 1874, in a wreck on the New Orleans, St. Louis & Chicago (long since a part of Illinois Central). Exposed to the elements for ninety years, parts of the inscription are just barely legible:

> Until the brakes are turned on time,
>   Life's throttle valve shut down,
> He wakes to pilot in the crew
>   That wears the martyr's crown.
> On schedule time on upper grade
>   Along the homeward section,
> He lands his train at God's roundhouse
>   The morn of resurrection.
> His time all full, no wages docked,
>   His name on God's payroll,
> And transportation through to Heaven
>   A free pass for his soul.

(Photo by Lance Phillips)

370

sisted of two postal cars, one express and one baggage car for the storage of mail. . . . Eyewitnesses said the train was approaching the trestle at a speed of 30 to 35 miles an hour." In spite of the speed estimated by "eyewitnesses," Joe Broady had rolled and rocked the 1102 over the 70 miles of "mighty rough road" between Monroe and Stillhouse trestle in approximately one hour, which was really railroading over the existing roadbed he travelled.

It has been said that Broady might have pulled the bridle off 1102 at the wrong place; had he waited to get out of Danville, where the road was more level and curves less severe, the chances are he could have "put her in Spencer on time."

Among those engaged in the rescue work was David Graves George, jack-of-all-trades, including brakeman and telegraph operator. Like so many natives of the hill country, George liked to sing, and, perhaps inspired by the warbling canaries, composed the words of the famous ballad known by all as "The Wreck of Old 97." With the words sung to the tune of the old song, "The Ship That Never Returned," it immediately caught on and was soon being rendered by railroaders, seafaring men on the deep, lonely cowboys riding night herd, ballad lovers in general, and even singers under the lights on Broadway.

9
Lure and Lore

THE MAN AT THE THROTTLE

From its very beginning, the glamour and romance of railroading has held a fascination for men in spite of the fact that the work was hard and dangerous. The sound of the steam locomotive whistle made the blood pumped by adventurous and youthful hearts course faster through the veins, and when the engine with its train roared into sight, resolves were made then and there to become a railroader.

It was only natural that the overalled master silhouetted in the cab window, whose hand held the throttle and controlled this hissing monster of steel, was the chief attraction to the youth in search of adventure. It was only human that thoughts, if there were any, of the hard work of firing through long years to finally reach the coveted seat on the right-hand side of the cab were quickly forgotten, or totally lost in the romance of it all. It was perhaps because of these attractions that railroad management was literally able to hand pick its men for future service as locomotive engineers.

When a young man applied for a place as fireman he was generally given an oral test by the Road Foreman of Engines, an engineer himself who was directly over the other engineers. During this question and discussion period the youngster was pretty well sized up by the foreman and if it appeared that the candidate might someday make an engineer, he was employed, subject to passing a rigid physical examination. He then worked on his own with other firemen for the necessary period, usually a week or two, to fire a run.

Generally a fireman would serve four years "pass-

ing coal to a jack" and at the same time learning all he could about the operation of the locomotive. During this time various engineers for whom he fired would allow him short periods on the right-hand side, running the engine. At the end of his apprenticeship, if engineers for whom he had fired recommended him, the fireman would be eligible to take the examination "for running"; however, passing the examination did not mean that the man would abruptly make the changeover from firing to running an engine. It did mean that he would get his name on the "extra board" as an engineer, but in most instances those extra calls were few and far between and he still earned his bread and meat shoveling coal. As business of the road picked up, or if for other reasons additional engineers were needed, the chances for the embryonic engineer improved and within a few years he might have a pretty good freight run. Pulling freights was where the engineer learned how to work an engine and handle trains, on the long upward climb to the coveted passenger run.

This key to the arch of train service, the engineer, not only had to know the steam locomotive from trucks to stack, but to be successful in his work had to have a practical and comprehensive mind, alive to his own duty and alert to that of others as well. The braggart, explosive, and spectacular type of man did not last long. In addition to the necessity for complete mechanical knowledge and understanding of his engine, the engineer also had to have such things as regulations, rules, and signals at his fingertips. A prudent man, weighted with heavy responsibilities, the good engineer was wedded to his work.

Long familiarity with the performance of steam

(Courtesy Richard J. Cook)

The "young buck" at left is the author's father on his first trip "on his own" firing a road engine. He was seventeen when this old faded photograph was made at Frederick Hall in 1883 and as proud of the old C&O consolidation engine No. 267 as his engineer, Bob Cavedo (shown at right). The run was over the 97-mile Piedmont Division between Richmond and Charlottesville, Virginia, and whether the time between terminals was 6 or 24 hours, the pay was the same—one dollar and a quarter.

The good engineer trusted inspection and care of his charge to no man. (Courtesy Norfolk & Western Railway)

No engineer ever knew what lay ahead on his run. Leaning from the cab-window of *Old 55*, L. F. (Lon) Alley was about to pull out of Alderson, West Virginia, with his C&O eastbound train No. 14 on the afternoon of Friday, March 26, 1891. *Old 55* had just started to "whisper good" when rounding a curve at the approach to Second Creek Tunnel at 2:23 P.M., she plowed into the rear section of a local freight which had broken in two. Miraculously there were no fatalities, although Alley and his fireman, Lewis Withrow, were both injured. Both trains caught fire almost immediately after the crash.

Lon was a brother of George Alley, killed in the wreck made famous in the song, "The Wreck On The C & O." Singularly, Lewis Withrow (not Jack Dixon as the song states) was George Alley's fireman on engine No. 134 when she carried her train No. 4 (Fast Flying Vestibule) into a landslide three miles east of Hinton at 5:40 A.M., October 23, 1890, but jumped just before the impact, without serious injury. A short time after the wreck, Withrow had become the regular fireman for George's brother, Lon Alley.

Like many other passenger engineers, Lon Alley was proud of his calling, as evidenced by his shaving mug. (Both pictures made available through the courtesy of Lon Alley's grandson, William L. Alley, Jr.)

375

"Captain of the Train" (Courtesy Santa Fe Railway)

locomotives enabled engineers almost instantly to detect when something went wrong. Just as the leader detects a false note coming from a symphony orchestra, the trained ear of the engineer distinguished some strange sound coming from the tumult of hammering and clashing steel that was a part of the engine's movement. That same familiarity enabled him to know with uncanny accuracy the approximate speed he was making—day or night and in any kind of weather.

THE CAPTAIN OF THE TRAIN

The route to "Captain of the Train" was also long and in places fraught with danger. Here, a youngster might start as a yard brakeman, and in the old days when cars were coupled and uncoupled with link and pin, many were minus some fingers when their promotion to freight conductor came. Gravitating to road service these fellows learned train operation, and when opportunity presented itself passed the required examination for conductors. Like the engineer, the conductor learned railroading in freight service, as he awaited the passenger run when he would don his brass-buttoned uniform, which in the old days included the long-tailed cutaway coat.

Whereas the intimate mechanical knowledge and the working of the engine was not a requirement of the conductor, his natural makeup was similar to that of the engineer. In charge of the train, the captain also had great responsibilities and the constant and great demands upon him called for a man of tact, patience, and forbearance in the management of his train. The necessity for these prime requisites multiplied perhaps tenfold when he got into passenger service, for it was here that he had to represent the entire railroad in his close contact with the public, in addition to his other exacting duties.

Because Train Service is what it is, not everyone can appreciate the vast and varied responsibilities that rest upon the conductor and engineer. The effect of the responsibilities sober these men. Once they get their appointments, men who might have been more or less indifferent to responsibility earlier, come to assume and strive to make themselves meet it fully. There is little triviality and superficiality in the natures of these men who are successful; the other kind weed themselves out along the way and turn to other pursuits.

No other department of a railroad afforded greater opportunity for advancement than Train Service. Not all men were endowed with the insight to recognize and the ability to seize the opportunity to elevate themselves in position; some didn't want to, finding a sufficiency for their desires in Train Service. Some did, however, and many able general managers and presidents of railroads first entered railroad service as a fireman or brakeman. When those fellows arrived at the top they made their indelible marks in railroad history, for these were the railroaders who literally knew the business from the ground up.

KNIGHTS OF THE ROAD

Following the close of the Civil War many disheartened and dislocated men became restless. They didn't know where they wanted to go, only having the urge to travel. Broke financially, and some in spirit, the wanderers were lured to the rails as a means of transportation, and these tramps presented quite a problem to the railroads from about 1870.

Since the majority of tramps rode freights, the ideal station for beginning the trip was the yard, and night the preferred time of departure. Cautiously keeping an eye peeled against observance by some railroad employee, the traveller would spot a train ready to move in the desired direction and secrete himself in it. An empty boxcar was preferable, if a door happened to be open, and unless he was the first passenger to crawl in he generally found company. If the night was chilly or stomachs empty (as they usually were), fires were sometimes built on the floor and supper cooked as the train rolled; not infrequently the car would catch on fire. Some preferred the top of the car, weather permitting.

As the horde increased and became more of a problem to the host carrier, getting aboard in the yard undetected became more difficult for the non-fare-paying guests. To counteract this the tramp would select a spot alongside the track, some distance from the maze of tracks in the yard where the train was made up, and catch her on the fly as the train headed out on the mainline. The experienced ones had learned to make the selection of their boarding place, along the cinder stretch beside the rails, one that was clear of a switch lever or other obstruction that might trip them in the darkness.

Nailing (grabbing hold of the iron ladder at the ends of a freight car) a moving train at night re-

The all-important chore before starting a run: Captain and Engineer check train orders with each other. (Courtesy Richmond, Fredericksburg & Potomac)

All of the personnel who kept the steam trains rolling were not visible to the travelling public. Here we see an old-time machinist, who kept the engines moving from the roundhouse to the ready-track at the turn of this century. Later, a Design Engineer, Longan C. Phillips, now approaching fourscore and ten, explains the operation of Stephenson inside valve gear on a locomotive model he built about 1900.

378

The old title, Master of the Depot, was a fitting one. As traffic increased, the post of Station Master carried with it increasing burdens and responsibilities in addition to the prime ones of receiving and discharging trains. One-time conductor, Douglas S. "Captain" Brannan, Station Master at Broad Street Station, Richmond, gives alert attention to some activity at the busy station in 1947.

quires skill as well as nerve, and some of the more experienced acquired real art in getting aboard. The real artist would squat in the darkness until the glare from the headlight of the approaching locomotive had passed, then make his run alongside the moving train. When his sense of timing indicated, he would make his dive and grab for a rung of the ladder on the front end of the car. If his hold didn't break he was thrown violently against the side of the car, where he clung until equilibrium returned sufficiently for the climb up the ladder to the top. Sometimes the nail wasn't successful, and the force of impact knocked the 'bo into the drainage ditch beside the track. If he was lucky he got by with only some bruises and abrasions from the cinders in the bottom of the ditch. Some weren't so lucky and serious injury or death resulted. An experienced 'bo considered grabbing a ladder on the rear end of a car as an attempt at suicide; if he missed his hold the chances were that the impact would throw him under the wheels of the car following.

Those more fastidious and selective of accommodation scorned freight travel and rode passenger trains. The traveller with this yen would secrete himself on the rods or sometimes in an empty battery box beneath the car. Others showed preference for the front end of the baggage car, just behind the locomotive tender, where the door to the car was false or blind, and rode "Blind Baggage."

Whereas some of these uninvited passengers were just harmless tramps on the move, others were yeggs who broke into and pilfered cars and warehouses and otherwise created loss and damage to the railroads. In addition, shyster lawyers would seek out those travellers injured or alleged to have been on railroad property, and bring suits against the companies for injuries.

Although the figures will never be known, it has been estimated that during the nineties, upward of 60,000 wanderers were riding the rails. With the number increasing and decreasing with the rise and fall of the country's economic condition, it has been estimated that in times of depression as many as a million tramps were on the railroads at times. This horde continued riding the rails through the big depression of the 1930's, when it gradually subsided as the itinerant travellers took to "thumbing" rides in automobiles along the highways.

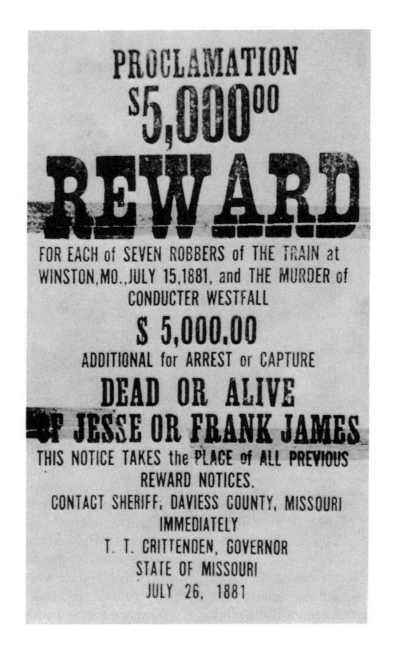

PROCLAMATION
$5,000⁰⁰
REWARD
FOR EACH of SEVEN ROBBERS of THE TRAIN at
WINSTON, MO., JULY 15,1881, and THE MURDER of
CONDUCTER WESTFALL
$ 5,000.00
ADDITIONAL for ARREST or CAPTURE
DEAD OR ALIVE
OF JESSE OR FRANK JAMES
THIS NOTICE TAKES the PLACE of ALL PREVIOUS
REWARD NOTICES.
CONTACT SHERIFF, DAVIESS COUNTY, MISSOURI
IMMEDIATELY
T. T. CRITTENDEN, GOVERNOR
STATE OF MISSOURI
JULY 26, 1881

ROAD AGENTS LURED TO THE RAILS

Gold has ever held its lure for man and he has sought it wherever it might be. To get it, the seeker has worked from the frozen vastness of the Arctic regions to the Transvaal of South Africa. Some sought and got the stuff from trains, the strong box in the express car being the chief attraction.

The first train robbery in history occurred just as May 5, 1865, was dawning. An Ohio & Mississippi train enroute from St. Louis was approaching North Bend, Ohio (14 miles west of Cincinatti), when the engine plowed into a pile of cross ties stacked on the rails. Little is known other than that some men "robbed the passengers as others looted the express safes and made off with a large amount of cash and bonds. They were thought to be guerillas and escaped across the river [Ohio] in skiffs."

But this was just the beginning of train robberies that would plague some railroads for a quarter of a century, and the second strike for easy gold was to follow close behind the first. This time the modus operandi employed by the gold seekers was different. Having been free of such occurrences, the messengers had not yet learned to keep the doors of the express cars locked, and of course were sitting ducks for what occurred. An eastbound Ohio & Mississippi passenger train had just pulled out of Seymour, Indiana, on October 6, 1866, when two masked men stepped through the rear door of the express car, pointed the business ends of their forty-fours at the messenger and took his keys. Hastily scooping up

380

$13,000 from the safe, they pulled the bellcord and as the train slowed down shoved an unopened safe through the side door and themselves followed it into the darkness. Nonplussed by what had occurred, the train moved on to the next station, where armed men were sent back to the scene of the robbery on a handcar; they found the safe unopened but the robbers gone.

Two of the Reno brothers, John and Simeon, and an accomplice, Frank Sparks, were later arrested for this job but released on bail for a postponed trial that never took place. Known as the Reno gang, the brothers and several other shady characters lived near Seymour, where the Ohio & Mississippi and Jeffersonville, Madison & Indianapolis railroads crossed, and it was these two roads that received the preferred attention of the first organized gang of train robbers.

Nearly a year passed before there was another robbery and ironically the same eastbound train was robbed in the same manner and at the same place on September 28, 1867; however, the two holdup men, Hammond and Collins, so far as is known, were not members of the Reno gang. But the Renos knew the robbery would be pulled and as the two robbers looked over their loot the Renos stepped from a patch of woods and hijacked them.

Leaving the railroads unmolested for a few months, the gang turned to bank robberies in Missouri and Iowa, where a number of them were captured and jailed at Council Bluffs, but they made a jail break on April 1, 1868, and returned to their home stamping ground.

On the night of May 22nd, a northbound JM&I passenger train had stopped at Marshfield, twenty miles south of Seymour. While the engine was taking on water the express car was boarded by several armed men as two others cut it loose from the rest of the train, then rushed ahead and, after forcing the engineer and fireman from the cab, pulled the throttle open and headed into the night with the express car. After a terrific beating, the fatally injured express messenger was thrown from the car as the short train sped through the night. Just before dawn, the express car (looted of nearly $100,000) was found a mile from Seymour.

While Pinkerton men were making arrangements for the arrest of members of the suspected Reno gang for this robbery, another following the same pattern was attempted on a westbound O&M train at Brownstown. However, the express company had now taken steps to thwart the robbers, and when the car was stopped some eight miles down the line, armed guards inside successfully drove the looters off—all but one, Val Elliot, a former O&M brakeman, who had been wounded during the fray. Within a day or two Pinkerton had picked up two other members of the gang, and the three had been lodged in jail in Cincinatti.

At this time, parts of America were not overpopulated nor were its people overcivilized or overregulated. Corruption had sometimes delayed and at other times defeated justice, and to counteract this trend Vigilantes had come on the scene. These "committees" were composed of determined men whose methods of administering justice may not have been in accordance with accepted legal procedure but nevertheless were prompt and very effective. A few days after the attempted robbery, the bandits were being moved by rail from Cincinatti, when a party of determined men boarded the train a few miles east of Brownstown. Perhaps fearing that justice might again be cheated, the Vigilantes took the three prisoners from their captors, escorted them to a nearby tree, and strung them up.

The rest of the Reno gang met similar justice, when a large posse of Vigilantes visited the jail at New Albany, Indiana, at 2:00 A.M. in late November 1868. Overpowering the sheriff and his deputies, the Vigilantes yanked the prisoners from their cells and within a few minutes left them dangling from the noose-end of ropes suspended from beams in the jail corridor.

JESSE JAMES

After the dispatch of the first known organized gang of train robbers there was a respite for the railroads of about two years before lightning again struck in 1870—in Kentucky, Nevada, and Tennessee. In 1871, staid old New England was set agog when an express messenger was shot and his safe robbed on the Boston & Albany. But these crimes, and those that had gone before, were just the preliminaries for what was to come. Jesse James and his brother Frank, along with the Younger brothers and a few others, were soon to come on the stage; not only as rail bandits but, as time went on, as the subject of dime novels.

From 1866 through the spring of 1873, horse

stealing and many bold bank robberies in Kentucky and Missouri had been charged up to Jesse and his gang, but as yet they had been credited with no train robberies. Just before 8:30 P.M. on July 21, 1873, engineer John Rafferty was pulling a heavy grade with an eastbound Rock Island passenger train about four miles west of Adair, Iowa, when he approached a sharp curve. Coming into the curve his headlight picked up a section of rail being pulled out of line by a rope. In a vain effort to stop, Rafferty pulled his reverse bar back and opened the throttle, but the locomotive hit the open section and turned on its side, killing both the engineer and fireman.

Firing their six-shooters as they rushed from the bushes, some of the bandits boarded the cars, forcing passengers to make contribution of their valuables into an empty meal sack; two others held their guns on the express messenger, but the safe gave up only about $3000; the $75,000 shipment in gold, scheduled to be moved on this train, had been put on a later one. Foiled, the outlaws ran for their horses and vanished into the night as quickly as they had come. The sheriff's posse followed the gang to St. Clair County, Missouri, where the trail was lost.

Taking time out for a stagecoach robbery in Arkansas, the gang did not strike at the rails again until January 31, 1874. At 3:30 in the afternoon, the gang tied up the station agent and several loungers at Gads Hill, Missouri, set the semaphore at "Stop," and waited. Shortly thereafter the whistle of a southbound Iron Mountain train from St. Louis cut through the air, and as it came to a stop the gang followed the same pattern, accepting contributions from the terrified passengers and rifling the express safe, as they had done six months earlier in Iowa. This time the chase by the sheriff's posse ended at a large cave near Stanton, Missouri, from which the outlaws escaped by means of an underground river, leaving their horses in the cave.

Perhaps to throw the Pinkertons off the trail, Jesse and his pals next cut a swath through Arkansas and Texas, giving their attention to stagecoaches. The respite for the railroads ended on December 13, 1875, when the gang suddenly appeared at Muncie, Kansas, tied up the station agent and others present, and again set the semaphore at "Stop." As the Kansas Pacific train came to a halt, passengers were relieved of their valuables and the donation of the express messenger, as he faced the robbers' guns, was between thirty and fifty thousand in gold.

Waiting until the night of July 8, 1876, for the next assault on railroads, the outlaws followed the now well known procedure and scooped $17,000 from the express safe on a Missouri Pacific train at Rocky Cut, Missouri. After hiding out a few weeks the gang attempted a bank robbery at Northfield, Minnesota. A few of the gang were killed and wounded in the ensuing gun-battle and others were later captured, but Jesse and Frank made a clean getaway.

When the attacks ceased for a period of three years, the railroads perhaps thought that the uncatchable James boys had met their deaths, or else reformed, but such was not the case. Following the previous pattern, the gang robbed a Chicago & Alton train at Glendale, Missouri, shortly after 7 P.M., October 8, 1879. Nearly two years was to elapse before the next rail strike; this time it was on the Rock Island at Winston, Missouri, on July 15, 1881, when in addition to looting the safe of $10,000 the gang wantonly shot and killed the conductor.

Within less than sixty days the Chicago & Alton was struck again. On the night of September 7, 1881, rocks were piled on the track at Blue Cut, Missouri, and as a westbound train approached it was flagged down by a lantern with a piece of red flannel around its globe. The express safe contained no money, and only jewelry and cash of the passengers and crew were dropped in the ever-present meal sack. Jesse may have had a premonition that time was running out on him and that this was his last train robbery, for when he held the sack for the brakeman's deposit and the brakie told him he had already contributed fifty cents—all he had—Jesse gave the man a dollar, saying, "This is principal and interest on your money." The outlaws even shook hands with the engineer and fireman and as the train pulled away headed for their horses, tied in a clump of bushes a half mile away.

The sand in the hour glass was fast running out for Jesse James, who had lived a charmed life of outlawry since 1866. Many rewards had been posted for his capture, dead or alive, and, as often happens, one of his own gang, Bob Ford, emptied a 44 Smith & Wesson into the famed outlaw as he stood unarmed on a chair at his home, dusting a picture.

Although the death of Jesse James broke the epidemic of train robberies it did not stop them. These robberies occurred from time to time, principally in the middle and far west, for years to come;

as late as 1905 there were seven. The last known attempt was made against the Southern Pacific in 1923, when three hoodlums stopped a train at Siskiyou Pass, Oregon, shot and killed the engineer and a brakeman, threw a slug of dynamite into the express car, which killed the messenger, and retreated without a dime. Happily, these punks, who had perhaps been inspired by too many western movies, were quickly captured, tried, and placed in the Oregon Penitentiary.

Railroading, particularly in the days of steam, was a natural for the production of ballads. As to be expected, most of the ballads centered around the brave engineer who "kept his hand on the throttle" as his engine left the rails or plowed into some obstruction, causing his death. The words were simple and carried the story, and the sad voice of the balladeer frequently brought tears to the eyes of his listeners. Without question, the two most famous are those which tell the stories of the last runs of Casey Jones and Joseph A. Broady, who pulled Old 97.

There were hobo songs and the chants of the gandy dancers as they tamped ballast around the ties. Ballads were even composed about ghost trains; perhaps the best known, "The Phantom Drag," tells the story of a hobo riding a fast train through space, with Casey Jones at the throttle of an engine numbered 97, as it runs its race with the changeless pace of time.

And speaking of ghosts in connection with railroading, many old lines have their ghost stories. The Atlantic Coast Line perhaps has one of the most unique—and more, the Coast Line says their ghost still exists.

In 1889, the presidential train carrying President Grover Cleveland was moving over the Wilmington, Manchester & Augusta (now the Atlantic Coast Line) Railroad when it stopped near Maco (14 miles west of Wilmington, North Carolina) for the little wood-burning engine to take on fuel and water. As the weather was balmy, the President left his coach to take a walk along the tracks. Seeing the train brakeman with two signal lanterns, one green and one white, Mr. Cleveland asked the purposes of the two lanterns. Before the train started rolling again, the President had the full story of "Joe Baldwin's Ghost Light," and also learned that the two lanterns were used so that engineers would not be deceived by the waving of Joe Baldwin's ghost light.

A late employee of the ACL, named Jones, was there when the presidential train stopped and, although a small boy at the time, remembered being lifted by his father that he might shake the President's hand. He also remembered the Baldwin light. "One night I was in a group of boys who were walking along the track," Jones recalled, "when we saw the light. It seemed to be weaving along, directly over the tracks at a height of about five feet. Then the light described an arc and landed in a swamp beside the track."

The legend of Joe Baldwin's ghost light started in 1867 when a train came uncoupled near Farmer's Turnout (now Maco). Link and pin coupling was then in use and as Conductor Baldwin tried to recouple the cars he was killed (with his lantern in his hand). Shortly after the fatal accident, the mysterious light appeared for the first time—and scores of witnesses say it still appears. The popular explanation is that Conductor Baldwin, decapitated in the accident, takes nocturnal walks in search of his head. Many say they have been close enough to the light to see the guards around the lantern. In 1873, a second light appeared and the two, shining with the brightness of a 25-watt electric light bulb, would seem to meet each other.

It took an earthquake to temporarily halt Joe Baldwin's nightly search for his head, for shortly after the 'quake in 1886, the two lights disappeared. Soon afterward, however, the lights reappeared, weaving silently along the tracks near Hood's Creek. Folks knew then that Joe was again searching for his head and they speculated that the other light was Joe's head in search of his body.

The ghost light story gained sufficient interest to bring a Washington, D.C., investigator to Maco to explain the mysterious occurrences scientifically. But Joe was too fast for him. A detachment from Fort Bragg, N.C., encamped at Maco briefly in an attempt to solve the mystery. They didn't.

An ACL operations official, veteran of forty years of railroading, actually saw the light from the cab of a locomotive and knew of instances where trains stopped because of it. On one occasion, the engineer with whom he was riding applied his brakes to stop for the light when it suddenly disappeared.

An old Negro stated that when he was a youngster, working with the section gang in the area and living in a shanty near the tracks, the light suddenly appeared in front of a freight train. The engineer

(Photo by F. L. Worcester)

384

set his brakes and as the engine slowed down both he and the fireman jumped; the fireman suffered injuries which made it necessary for another member of the train to fire the engine to the terminal.

Some explain the phenomenon as automobile lights reflected from a nearby highway, but there were no automobiles at the time the light first appeared. The highway has been rerouted several times, with no effect on the appearance of the light.

Neither weather nor seasons have any connection with the light's appearance or visibility. Sometimes it vanishes for a month at a time, only to reappear several nights in rapid succession. It seems to be a matter of Joe's discretion.

Recently some thoughtless youngsters have been parking their cars across the Maco tracks to view the light. ACL officials say that unless the practice stops, Joe is going to have company.

10
Into the Yonder She Returns

In the short span of one lifetime, steam railroads had completely revolutionized America—and in many different ways. Whereas through the first quarter of the nineteenth century man had been compelled to use water transportation, the horse, or his own means of locomotion, long before the beginning of the last quarter of the same century he could travel by rail within almost any section of the land, and from the Atlantic to the Pacifiic.

Literally, American railroads had colonized the vast middle and western part of America, and at the same time brought to the more populated East a quick and reliable means of transportation for both man and his merchandise. Whereas it is true that many of the little pioneer roads, particularly those along the Atlantic seaboard, were originally laid out to operate between cities or towns, many others just started and headed into and across open country, hoping that the growing population would follow the high iron to new frontiers and opportunities.

The hopes of these farsighted entrepreneurs generally resulted in fruition as new towns, some to grow into mammoth cities, sprung up along the rights-of-way. From the standpoint of the settlers who had come from across the seas, America was then young and its vast reaches underpopulated. For the most part the great mineral wealth and natural resources had not yet been discovered.

American railroads not only moved the populace then living in our land, to new fields to conquer, but many of them maintained offices in Europe, where they spread the word about the great opportunities existing here. Many of our railroads, particularly those operating in the middle and far west, had ob-

tained from the government great grants of land along their roads. Land was plentiful then and cheap, and in spite of the fact that some justifiable criticism might be leveled against some of the land deals, it was this cheap land that enabled the railroads to accomplish what they did in colonizing.

But to most railroads, passenger traffic was responsible for only a small part of the service rendered, and incidentally of the revenues received. As America grew, both in population and industry, so did the railroads—finding their real niche as haulers of freight. Without them, America could never have become the richest nation on earth.

To be sure, the railroads had their share of ups and downs, just as is common in all pursuits. Many were forced into bankruptcy and receivership, but nearly always to rise again, stronger than before. The railroads of America act as a barometer to all other commerce and industry of our land. When they are on the upswing of the pendulum, with traffic heavy, so are all other endeavors; and when the downswing comes to the rails it takes all other commercial pursuits with it in the descendancy.

Although it takes an army of men to run a railroad, its very heart has always been the locomotive; and since Horatio Allen first opened the throttle on the little Stourbridge Lion on August 8, 1829, for well over a hundred years steam gave life to practically all motive power on American railroads.

For about seventy of those years the iron horse had no competition. And then the electric locomotive made its appearance around 1900, to be used in terminal work in New York City by the New Haven, New York Central and Pennsylvania

Her job well done, the scoop turned down, the iron horse heads back into the yonder from which she came.

railroads. Although a good type of motive power, installation costs prohibited its general adoption. Of the seven mainline roads using this type of locomotive in 1948, only 3 per cent of their total mileage was electrified, and 6 per cent of their locomotives operated electrically.

Following close upon the advent of the electric locomotive, another competitor of the steam locomotive put in its appearance. This was a gasoline powered rail car with an electric transmission. Although in itself this was a poor competitor, and from its advent, about 1905, to 1936, less than a thousand were put into service, it was the "handwriting on the wall" that would eventually spell out doom for the iron horse.

The Electro Motive Corporation had built approximately 500 gasoline powered rail cars between 1920 and 1930 when it merged with General Motors Corporation and substituted a diesel for the gasoline engine. In 1933, one of the first lightweight high-speed diesel engines suitable for railroad service was exhibited at the Chicago World's Fair; the next year, improved models of this engine were pulling the Chicago, Burlington & Quincy Zephyrs between Chicago and Minneapolis.

This was something new, something that seemed to have many advantages over the true and tried steam locomotive. Many things had combined to put a squeeze on the railroads—maybe this was the way out. As the bugs were shooed out and improvements came about rapidly in this new diesel-electric motive power, things began to happen.

Although it may seem that this severe change in motive power on railroads had taken place quickly, such was not the case. Both American Locomotive Company and Baldwin Locomotive Works had come into the picture with diesel-electric power about 1924, when they built some switching units. The steam locomotive builders had realized about 1935 that the iron horse had just about reached its pinnacle in advancement, and recognizing the advantages of diesel-electric power, they really had but one choice—accept and change over to meet the new demand or hope with a forlorn hope. American Locomotive Company built their last steam locomotive, a 2-8-4, for the New York Central in 1948; the following year, Baldwin built and delivered to the Chesapeake & Ohio the last locomotive for mainline service outshopped in the United States.

The disappearance from the rails of these alive, busy steam monsters didn't happen overnight, but rather as expressed in the lines of a beautiful poem from the pen of Mattie Powell Trice: "Our friends are like leaves, slowly drifting away,/Not all gone at once, but a few day by day."

Even in the early 1940's more and more diesels could be seen heading trains throughout the land. And by 1950 the roar of heavy internal combustion engines and a raucous blast from an air horn had replaced in considerable measure the bark of cadenced exhausts and the melodius tones of the chime whistle which were part and parcel of the much alive and busy iron horse. When one got close to this new successor of the steam locomotive his olfactory senses were insulted with the stench of burnt gases; the pleasant odor of warm oil, coal smoke, and steam, blended in its own indescribable formula, had vanished. Animation and grace? There was none.

With few exceptions, by 1960 the steam locomotive had disappeared from the mainlines of America, and those that had been spared from the execution torch rested inanimate in museums, where coming generations may look upon the final development of what Richard Trevithick started that Monday morning in February so long ago.

Those of us who grew up with and knew it, loved the faithful old iron horse that played such a large part in building America. For over a hundred years her familiar, sometimes lonely whistle calls had echoed from the flat lands along the Atlantic coast, across the plains and through the canyons to the Pacific, and from the regions along the Canadian Border to the Gulf of Mexico. They were like friendly voices reaching from the mountain tops to the valleys below, telling listeners of express, freight, mail, and people—rushing and roaring through the darkness of a stormy night or the heat of a noonday sun. That long, lingering, and lonesome wail is forever still and will not return. We miss it, for when steam left the rails of America, the romance of the high iron went with it.

Bibliography

Alexander, E. P. *Iron Horses, American Locomotives 1829–1900.* New York: 1941.

Allen, Horatio. *The Railroad Era, First Five Years of Its Development.* New York: 1884.

Botkin, B. A. and Harlow, Alvin F. *A Treasury of Railroad Folklore.* New York: 1953.

Bradley, Glen D. *The Story of the Santa Fe.* Boston: 1920.

Breihan, Carl W. *The Complete and Authentic Life of Jesse James.* New York: 1953.

Brown, William H. *The History of the First Locomotives in America.* New York: 1874.

Bruce, Alfred W. *The Steam Locomotive in America.* New York: 1952.

Carter, Charles Frederick. *When Railroads Were New.* New York: 1909.

Casey, Robert J. *The Lackawanna Story.* New York: 1951.

Douglas, W. A. S. *Pioneer Railroad.* New York: 1948.

Corliss, Carlton J. *Main Line of Mid-America.* New York: 1950.

Daggett, Stuart. *Chapters in the History of the Southern Pacific.* New York: 1922.

Davis, John P. *The Union Pacific Railway.* Chicago: 1894.

Dodge, Maj. Gen. Grenville M. *How We Built the Union Pacific Railway.* Washington, D.C.: Government Printing Office, 1910.

Galloway, John Debo. *The First Transcontinental Railroad.* New York: 1950.

Griswold, Wesley S. *A Work of Giants.* New York: 1962.

Harlow, Alvin F. *Old Waybills.* New York: 1934.

Herr, Kincaid A. *Louisville & Nashville Railroad 1850–1963.* Louisville: 1964.

Holbrook, Stewart H. *The Story of American Railroads.* New York: 1947.

Hungerford, Edward. *Men and Iron: The Story of New York Central.* New York: 1932.

————. *Men of Erie.* New York: 1946.

————. *The History of the Baltimore & Ohio Railroad.* New York: 1927.

Imboden, Brig. Gen. John D. "Jackson at Harper's Ferry in 1861," *Battles and Leaders of the Civil War.* New York: 1884.

Johnston, Angus James II. *Virginia Railroads in the Civil War.* Chapel Hill: 1961.

Kaempffert, Waldemar. *Modern Wonder Workers.* New York: 1924.

Kromer, Tom. *Waiting for Nothing.* New York: 1935.

London, Jack. *The Road.* New York: 1907.

Love, Robertus. *The Rise and Fall of Jesse James.* New York: 1926.

Marshall, James. *Santa Fe, the Railroad That Built an Empire.* New York: 1945.

Moody, Ralph. *The Old Trails West.* New York: 1963.

Mordecai, John B. *A Brief History of the Richmond, Fredericksburg and Potomac.* Richmond: 1940.

Morse, Frank P. *Cavalcade of Rails.* New York: 1940.

Mott, Edward Harold. *Between the Ocean and The Lakes: The Story of Erie.* New York: 1901.

Reck, Franklin M. *The Romance of American Transportation.* New York: 1962.

Rolt, L. T. C. *The Railway Revolution.* New York: 1960.

Shaw, Frederic. *Casey Jones' Locker.* San Francisco: 1959.

Starr, John W. Jr. *One Hundred Years of Ameri-*

can Railroading. New York: 1928.

Stevens, Frank Walker. *The Beginnings of The New York Central Railroad: A History.* New York: 1926.

Tanner, H. S. *A Description of the Canals and Rail Roads of the United States.* New York: 1840.

Taylor, Frank J. & Wilson, Neill C. *Southern Pacific.* New York: 1952.

Index